Your Towns and Cities in

Sheffield's Great War and Beyond

On the front cover is one of several paintings by Edward Skinner (1865-1924) of Cammell Laird's Sheffield works during 1917 and 1918. Some of these paintings were used on postcards sold at the time in aid of the Red Cross.

Author's royalties from this book will be paid by the publisher direct to the Royal British Legion for use in the Sheffield area.

Your Towns and Cities in the Great War

Sheffield's Great War and Beyond

Peter Warr

Pen & Sword
MILITARY

First published in Great Britain in 2015 by
PEN & SWORD MILITARY
an imprint of
Pen and Sword Books Ltd
47 Church Street
Barnsley
South Yorkshire S70 2AS

ISBN 978 1 47382 786 8

A CIP record for this book is available from the British Library

Printed and bound in England
by CPI Group (UK) Ltd, Croydon, CR0 4YY

Typeset in Times New Roman by Chic Graphics

Pen & Sword Books Ltd incorporates the imprints of
Pen & Sword Archaeology, Atlas, Aviation, Battleground, Discovery, Family History, History, Maritime, Military, Naval, Politics, Railways, Select, Social History, Transport, True Crime, Claymore Press, Frontline Books, Leo Cooper, Praetorian Press, Remember When, Seaforth Publishing and Wharncliffe.

For a complete list of Pen and Sword titles please contact
Pen and Sword Books Limited
47 Church Street, Barnsley, South Yorkshire, S70 2AS, England
E-mail: enquiries@pen-and-sword.co.uk
Website: www.pen-and-sword.co.uk

Contents

Preface and Acknowledgements

The catastrophe of the First World War has given rise to many publications. Almost all of these look at military or political issues or describe what happened to individual servicemen or (occasionally) servicewomen. Much less has been written about the lives of civilians at home.

This book takes the second approach, focusing on changes, problems and achievements in one of Britain's largest cities. Like the separate *Sheffield in the Great War* it covers the full period, but the two books emphasize different aspects and this one also extends into post-war years. It draws together material from many wartime publications and letters, and brings the city to life in more than a hundred photographs and drawings.

As well as illustrating the activities of individual people, the presentation is distinctive in setting local events into a national framework. Britain's laws, priorities and social standards changed in many ways during the war, and to understand developments in Sheffield we should be aware of the national story. For more specialist readers, Notes at the end of the book provide additional detail, and two Indexes make it easy to find people, topics and places.

Sheffield's Great War and Beyond opens with an account of the city's early experiences – recruiting thousands of troops, coping with an influx of refugees, living with restrictions, air-raids and absent menfolk, making voluntary contributions by the thousand, and forming and operating around twenty military hospitals. Chapters Two to Four provide a unique review of Sheffield's role in the production of armaments and equipment, with many previously-unreported details of work in individual companies. Readers are introduced to the crucial role of the newly-formed Ministry of Munitions, the city's 'national factories' and 'controlled establishments', and the ways in which women were gradually allowed to take over jobs that were, previously, only for men.

Two of Sheffield's principal organizations – the university and the Cutlers' Company – are described in Chapter Five, again presenting material that is now almost entirely unknown. For instance, the city had its own aeroplane – 'Sheffield'. Where did that come from and what happened to it? Chapter Six covers the stresses and problems of the later war years, looking at military conscription, conscientious objectors, prisoners-of-war in the city, food shortages and eventually rationing. The local impact of the world-wide influenza epidemic is explored, and events in Sheffield on Armistice Day are given particular attention. In legal terms, the war did not formally end until the middle of 1919 and many celebrations and commemorations were delayed until then. The book's final chapter reviews the follow-up – remembrance in different ways, widespread grief and disability, substantial unemployment and poverty, and the occurrence of riots in the city. Two appendices bring together largely unknown facts about Sheffield factories and the city's businessmen who worked for government departments.

Considerable effort has been devoted to learning from personal diaries, family collections, archival material and hard-to-find newspaper items. Hundreds of hours have been spent studying the city's newspapers, council minutes and other documents, and in this work I have received considerable help from the staff of Sheffield's Local Studies Library and Archives. I am extremely grateful to them

In addition, I would like particularly to thank three people whose assistance to both books in this set has been enormous. Dean Hill has been an extremely generous provider of information and guidance across a wide range of the book's topics. His in-depth knowledge was always available (see also www.sheffieldsoldier.co.uk, with website management by Stuart Reeves), and he resolved many of my uncertainties about the details of military life. Second, I have been greatly helped by Clara Morgan, Curator of Social History at Museums Sheffield, who kindly provided information, followed up my many queries, and made available items from the museum's collection. Third, Dave Manvell offered to work on the digital restoration of unclear images, and his work on many illustrations has been greatly appreciated.

In addition to those invaluable sources of support, many other people kindly responded to requests for information on websites or at meetings and I have been hugely impressed by their generosity and helpfulness.

Both books have gained considerably from these many individuals' willingness to assist in this venture, and I thank them once again for their kindness: Don Alexander, David Baldwin, Christine Ball, Colin Barnsley, Peter Bayliss, Christine Bell, Pauline Bell, Keith Burnett, Eric Chambers, Nigel Clark, Paul Clarke, Michael Collins, Miles Connell, Chris Corker, Yvonne Cresswell, Dawn Crofts, Peter Davies, Michael Deal, Alison Duce, Malcolm Dungworth, Sylvia Dunkley, Mike Dyson, Dan Eaton, John Eaton, Jonathan England, David Flather, Richard Ford, Thelma Griffiths, John Grove, Judith Hanson, Stephen Hardcastle, Angela Harpham, Ken Hawley, Doug Hindmarch, Chris Hobbs, Derek Holdsworth, Christopher Jonas, Roy Koerner, Erik Lonnedahl, Annette Manvell, Anthony Marshall, Peter Mason, Roy Millington, Barbara Moffatt, John Moore, Dorothy Moss, Gerald Newton, Pat Oldham, Panikos Panayi, Robert Proctor, Jane Salt, David Sandilands, Elaine and Peter Scott, Mark Sheridan, Anthea Stephenson, Christine Stirling, Mark Tiddy, Ian Trowell, Geoffrey Tweedale, Joan Unwin, Brian Ward, Stephen Woollen, and members of Sheffield History Forum (http://www.sheffield history.co.uk/forums). Preparation of this book has extended over several years, and I fear that a few helpers may have been omitted from that list. I hope not, but sincerely apologize for my error if that is the case.

Across both books, Sheffield Libraries and Archives kindly permitted reproduction of images from Picture Sheffield: s09387, s10739 (thanks also to H D Sports), y00132, y00146, y00235 and y00251. Other organizations that have generously provided material and granted permissions include Kelham Island Museum, the National Trust, Manx National Museum, Museums Sheffield, the Peace Pledge Union, Sheffield Hallam University, Sheffield Local Studies Library, and Sheffield Newspapers. Thanks very much to all of them.

Thanks of a more general kind are due to the charitable organizations that have worked to assist the military and civilian victims of the Great War and subsequent conflicts. With that in mind, my royalties from this book will be paid by the publishers direct to the Royal British Legion for use in the Sheffield area.

Peter Warr
Sheffield, December 2014

CHAPTER 1

War on Sheffield's Home Front

The First World War was a period of appalling carnage and suffering. It has very properly been recalled in terms of life and death in military conflict. But this book is different; it describes events back home. Between 1914 and 1918, Sheffield – the nation's sixth largest city – saw changes and felt distress on an immense scale[1]. (Notes for more specialist readers are provided at the end of the book.)

Approximately 52,000 men left the city to fight (considerably more than half of the eligible male age group), and at least 6,000 of these (11½ percent) died[2]. Nationally, around 750,000 soldiers, sailors and airmen lost their lives[3], with an overall death rate of almost 12 percent[4]. Women also died serving their country. The Imperial War Museum estimates that 700 were killed, mainly when providing medical assistance in a war-zone. In addition to deaths during the war, 2,000,000 British men were injured. For those who became disabled, remedial operations and equipment or aids for daily living were primitive by modern standards, and hundreds of thousands of injured still-young men returned to shattered lives and family relationships that were often difficult and always less than they might have been.

Many military deaths and medical problems arose from illnesses rather than from shells, bullets or bombs[5]. For example, around 75,000 British troops were admitted to hospitals in France suffering from frostbite during very cold winters, or trench-foot from waterlogged trenches. Several types of fever were transmitted by lice that became established in clothes and blankets. In addition, dysentery was caused by impure drinking water, sometimes taken from pools in shell craters, and bites from the many trench rats could infect a soldier's kidneys or heart with potentially fatal results. As in many other conflicts, war-induced sickness added greatly to the death and mutilation that resulted from direct injury in battle.

The conflict also had a huge mental cost. Emotional illnesses became officially recognized as the war proceeded, and from 1915 seriously disturbed behaviours and experiences were increasingly described as 'shell-shock'. Patients could exhibit some partial combination of facial tics, nightmares, lost memories, inability to talk or walk, a jerky gait or shuffle, stomach cramps, sweating, unrelenting anxiety, uncontrollable shaking, diarrhoea, a fear of noises, repeated recollections of particularly awful events, paralysis, grotesque body movements, or extended periods of silence. Different individuals exhibited different combinations of symptoms (never all of them), and these appeared to be linked to a person's battlefield activity[6]. Emotional problems affected the mental health of many thousands of men for years after the war. It seems certain that a large number of soldiers who escaped with their physical health more-or-less intact later suffered periods of depression, anxiety, panic attacks or horrible flashbacks[7]. And, of course, that would also be the fate of many who, in addition, were physically disabled.

The autumn of 1914

At 11 pm on 4 August 1914, Britain declared war on Germany[8]. Police barriers were set up on twenty-six main roads into Sheffield[9], and power stations, reservoirs and other public utilities in the city were placed under guard. A large number of Sheffielders took the precaution of buying stocks of food, and a temporary surge in demand soon created shortages and pushed up prices. At the same time there was some relief that a decision had been taken. It was widely expected that the war would be successful and short, perhaps over by Christmas.

In the next few days several Acts of Parliament gave the government considerable power over daily life and work. It took control of all the (privately owned) railway companies, and for the first time on 5 August issued one-pound and ten-shilling (£0.50) notes. People were asked to exchange their gold sovereigns and half-sovereigns for these notes, boosting the Bank of England's reserves of gold. Almost all national and local newspapers expressed patriotic enthusiasm for the government's decision, urging readers to support the national effort, and most recent opponents of Britain's involvement in the war (such as the Labour party

MOBILIZATION.

All ex-Territorial Soldiers who are willing to rejoin the Colours should report themselves either personally or in writing to their former Corps without delay.

HORATIO MENDS,
Brigadier General.
SECRETARY,
West Riding of York County Association.

York, 4th August, 1914.

Sheffield newspapers published this recruiting request as soon as war was declared.

Your King and Country need you.

A Call to Arms.

An addition of 100,000 men to His Majesty's Regular Army is immediately necessary in the present grave emergency.

Lord Kitchener is confident that this appeal will be at once responded to by all those who have the safety of our Empire at heart.

Terms of Service.

General service for a period of 3 years or until the war is concluded.

Age of enlistment between 19 and 30.

How to Join.

Full information can be obtained at any post office in the kingdom; or

At any military depot.

God Save the King!

By 20 August 1914, recruiting advertisements in the city's newspapers were providing more details.

and the women's suffragette movement) now accepted the requirement to fight. The food-buying panic subsided after a few days.

The country urgently needed more men to expand its entirely voluntary army. The government appointed as Secretary of State for War the distinguished soldier Field Marshal Lord Kitchener (1850-1916), who immediately ordered a massive increase in troops. Sheffield's newspapers contained striking requests from Lord Kitchener for men to join the army, and widely displayed posters urged 'every patriotic young man' to 'answer the call'. Prominent in each case were the phrases 'Your King and Country Needs You' and 'God Save the King'. The British monarchy was still a powerful unifying symbol.

Anti-German feeling was encouraged by newspaper and magazine repetition of German 'atrocities', 'barbarism', 'brutality', 'outrages' and 'savagery' in the 'murder of civilians' in Belgium. Recruiting speeches in local factories raised enthusiasm among entire work-groups, and prominent citizens and churchmen added their encouragement. Friends and families urged men to enlist, and volunteers came forward in large numbers.

This striking image of Lord Kitchener was used in many different recruiting posters.

FOR KING & COUNTRY.

MEN URGENTLY NEEDED

FOR

HIS MAJESTY'S ARMY.

Men can join for duration of War, and will be discharged directly War is over.

Recruiting Offices:

10, St. George's Terrace, Brookhill.
429, Attercliffe Road.
534, Brightside Lane.

GOD SAVE THE KING.

These recruiting details were made available in Sheffield's newspapers on 27 August 1914.

The city's established units – the Hallamshire Rifles, Royal Field Artillery and others – mounted their own separate campaigns, and in addition an entirely new unit was formed, which became the Twelfth York and Lancaster (Service) Battalion – the Sheffield City Battalion known informally as Sheffield Pals. The War Office had very soon become overburdened with other demands and required that the City Council, local territorial units and the university together form the new battalion and provide the necessary finance, clothes and training until it could be taken over.

No uniforms were available and initial training for most men was carried out in civilian clothes. Members of the battalion continued to live in their own homes while a new hutted camp was built at Redmires on the western edge of the city. This became available in December, and Sheffield Pals stayed there until May 1915. After further training and service in Egypt they were sent to the Western Front, where they suffered dreadfully in the Battle of the Somme, which opened on 1 July 1916.

In practice, unemployment in the city did not increase as expected. Within a month many Sheffield companies were receiving orders to meet

No uniform or equipment was available at first for the hastily formed Pals, here on drill practice at Bramall Lane.

the needs of war – not only for armaments and steel but also for cutlery, razors and a wide range of supporting items. Retailers in the city sought to turn a difficult situation to their advantage, promoting many articles in terms of their special value in wartime. Department store John Walsh advertised its stock of 'Regulation Army Blankets – suitable for use in army camps', and John Atkinson's offered to mail its blankets to military recipients: 'if you want to help our soldiers, purchase a blanket'. Pharmacists Boots, with branches in High Street and West Street, claimed that 'when its feet give out the Army must give in'. They offered to send to the troops some of the company's foot comfort ointment on behalf of every purchaser. Cole Brothers took advantage of the great increase in nursing requirements by advertising nurses' uniforms and hospital beds.

As Christmas 1914 approached, the local newspapers gave prominence to suggestions about clothes and other presents to be sent to soldiers and sailors. Cigarettes were extremely popular at the time (at least for men), and retailers and other organizations were enthusiastic in requesting cash

City centre stores found opportunities in the new situation for patriotic business.

donations from the public and promising to send packages to the troops. Newspapers' other requests were aimed specifically at 'our lady readers', asking for 'soldiers' comforts', such as socks, mittens, gloves, scarves, cardigans and other clothes. These were to be sent to a paper's 'Lady Editor' for onward transmission. Before long, cakes, jam, eggs, vegetables and other food items were also sought for wounded soldiers in local hospitals. Newspapers in the city published details of items donated by each named individual (nearly all women and a few children), and groups of women (often linked to a church) came together – in both the early stages of the war and later – to make extra clothes.

Newspapers every day reported events on the Western Front, at this stage retaining optimism about 'British dash and daring' and German demoralization, and claiming by October 1914 that 'German surrender [was] possible' in 'only a question of days'. However, articles about the fate of local men soon became common, with headlines like 'Local officer killed', 'Sheffield doctor's son wounded', or 'University man killed'. By November 1914, the *Sheffield Daily Telegraph* and the *Sheffield Daily Independent* regularly published long lists under the heading 'Casualties from the front line' or 'Roll of honour'. On some days these extended over eight complete columns. Within each group, men who had been killed in action, who were casualties, or who were still missing were identified by name – not all from Sheffield although those were often picked out for special mention.

Almost all of the country's churches supported military activity in the face of Germany's aggression, and special prayer sessions were held regularly throughout the city. At least forty Sheffield clergymen volunteered for service as military chaplains before the end of 1914, and many churches set up working parties to provide clothes and comforts for the troops or to raise funds to help families in distress. On the first Sunday of 1915, a Day of National Intercession was held in all churches, based on prayers 'for the Nation and Empire'.

Thousands of homeless Belgians

The pains of war were in these ways thrust on the people of Sheffield. A different and completely unexpected development came in the sudden arrival of Belgian refugees. Starting in late August, tens of thousands of civilians and wounded soldiers left Belgium to escape from the advancing German Army. Some of these moved into neighbouring, neutral Holland, but Britain also offered assistance and within a few months more than

250,000 refugees had arrived in the country – with around 3,000 coming to Sheffield[10].

Linked to St Vincent's (Catholic) Church in Solly Street, a District War Refugees Committee and a Belgian Refugee Fund were established. By 7 September 1914, they had obtained use of Shirle Hill House in Nether Edge to provide refugee accommodation in a receiving base, and across the next few weeks, individuals, groups and churches of all denominations made available around 100 other properties to house Belgian families[11]. In each case, volunteer groups were formed to provide clothes, furniture, utensils and coal for heating, to collect subscriptions from well-wishers, and to organize concerts and other fundraising activities. The City Council supplied free electricity to the Shirle Hill base for a period, and many tradesmen decorated or undertook necessary modifications to houses without charge.

The first group of around fifty Belgian refugees arrived in Sheffield by train on 21 September 1914, and many other train-loads arrived over the next few months. Local newspapers published many accounts of refugees' experiences as they escaped from the invaders, often by walking for days with very little food and sometimes carrying young children. In some cases, family members had become separated without knowledge of

Belgian refugees were initially housed in Shirle Hill in Nether Edge. Considerable help was provided by nuns and others from St Vincent's Catholic Church.

the whereabouts of each other before accidentally coming together again – occasionally only after arrival in Sheffield. The refugees adapted to life in a foreign city as well as they could, receiving financial support from the Belgian government sometimes supplemented by a local church or the War Refugees Committee. Money was collected through boxes in the city's trams, and donations were also widely sought of cash, food, clothing, bedding and furniture. Throughout the city, church groups, schools and others organized social events, concerts and similar activities to raise funds.

Belgian children attended schools in the city, sometimes receiving financial assistance, and a small number of Belgian teachers worked in Sheffield schools. A Belgian newspaper was created, the city's libraries obtained some books in French, and Sheffield University provided English lessons with the help of around fifty volunteer teachers. For at least a period, refugees could travel without charge on the city's trams and were given free admittance to Heeley slipper baths once a week.

Belgian men of military age were required to return home and enlist for the duration of the war. Others found work in the city, and the city's Refugee Committee reported in 1917 that 'employment has been found for every refugee who is capable of working'. However, some families suffered considerable financial hardship, especially those without a male wage-earner, and throughout the war the city's newspapers continued to plead for gifts of clothes and for material that could be made into clothes.

Over the years, the refugees to varying degrees became part of the community, and many, especially the children, made friends with local people. At the end of the war, most returned home despite their country's devastation. More than 1,400 left in two trains on 28 January 1919 and others returned later. Members of the Belgian War Refugees' Committee and hosts from the city were at the station to say goodbye on that day, and the *Sheffield Daily Independent* of 29 January reported that 'at least twenty Belgians took with them Sheffield girls as wives, whilst conversely a number of Belgian girls remain behind having married Sheffield men'.

Little now remains of the city's contribution to 3,000 foreigners in distress. An almost unknown memorial is sited next to the disused Catholic chapel in City Road Cemetery. This was unveiled on 21 July 1921, 'in memory of the soldiers of the Belgian army and of the refugees who died in Sheffield during the Great War 1914-1919. May they rest in peace.'

This memorial to Belgians who died in the city was erected in City Road Cemetery in July 1921.

1915 and 1916: Regulations and restrictions

The demands of war soon led Britain into what became a broad and lasting shift in national thinking. For many years it had been taken for granted that the country would best flourish in a climate of private personal initiative and voluntary endeavour. Free choice by individuals was considered better than being organized by a government. But the war brought change, as efficiency was increasingly sought through state organization and restrictions on individual freedom – in censorship, price regulation, rent control, military conscription, industrial development and many smaller constraints. A Liquor Control Board determined pubs' hours of opening, the maximum strength of beer and the operation of breweries. A National Registration Act required all households to provide information about every adult member. Personal Registration Cards were issued and had to be carried at all times, and any change of address had to be reported to a Local Registration Authority, in Sheffield's case located in the Town Hall. Some foreigners in the country were imprisoned, and a huge range of components and raw materials could be bought and sold only by the government. As described later in the book, control boards of many kinds were created at local as well as national levels, and later in the war a national Food Controller introduced several types of rationing. This slide to state control occurred also in the production of munitions, which came under expanding government control from mid-1915, and in the enlistment of servicemen. Initial persuasion was eventually felt to have reached its limit, and coercion and decision-making by the state took over.

However, in some areas the shift to government control occurred with dramatic suddenness. On 8 August 1914, a wide-ranging Act of Parliament was passed with the soothing title 'Defence of the Realm Act'. Abbreviated as DORA, this Act and its Amendments and follow-up Regulations came to cover a huge variety of activities. The initial emphasis was (in the Act's words) on 'securing the public safety and the defence of the realm', but its restrictions gained force in many areas of life. By the end of the war there were more than 400 pages of Consolidated Regulations. Some of these are illustrated in Display Box 1.1.

The cost of living rose steadily, with food on average costing almost two-thirds more by the end of 1916. The government imposed controls on many food prices, but these had to be changed frequently to keep up with the market. House rents kept climbing in response to the arrival in the city of more munition workers, the loss of housing to factory extensions, and the almost complete absence of domestic building. Successive national budgets raised direct and indirect taxes. However, wage rates also increased steadily and more hours at work became possible. Unemployment was rare. The First World War was, for many, a time of financial prosperity.

Display Box 1.1
THE MANY FACES OF DORA – THE DEFENCE OF THE REALM ACT

This Act of Parliament of August 1914 and its later additions gave the government powers over many aspects of daily life. DORA regulations were backed by the threat of a trial in a court of law or, in some cases, in a military court. The Act or one of its subsequent Regulations made it illegal, for instance, to:

- talk about military matters in public
- spread false or damaging reports
- loiter near railway lines or bridges
- collect or publish information that might be of use to an enemy
- purchase binoculars
- provide liquor to a soldier on duty
- spread rumours that might cause alarm
- enter an enemy country without authorization.

Government officials, military authorities and police forces were empowered to:

- take possession of land or buildings and of power and water supplies
- erect and destroy buildings as needed
- enter and search any premises considered to be suspicious
- seize any material
- control the content of newspapers
- determine the opening hours of public houses
- arrest suspected individuals without a warrant
- take any other action considered necessary for the Act's purposes.

In addition to these general controls, other Acts made detailed interventions in specific areas of personal and commercial life.

Bank holidays were cancelled in 1916 to allow factory work to continue, and in the summer of that year daylight working time was for the first time extended by moving all clocks forward one hour. The number of passengers on the city's trams surged, especially to and from the east-end factories. The demand for electricity and gas became so great that the city's supplies were sometimes restricted or interrupted without warning.

Factories lost key workers to the army or navy and often had to turn away new business. Hundreds of men left their City Council jobs, and staff shortages developed in civilian medical services as well as in companies of all kinds.

News from the Front

For Sheffield families wanting to learn about their loved ones overseas, information was very limited. In the absence of radio and television, newspapers were almost the only source of information and their content was often distorted – both by the government and by newspaper editors themselves.

The government's press bureau acted as the principal channel of information from all official departments to the public. The bureau introduced a process of censorship to prevent the publication of information considered to be 'injurious to the naval and military operations of the British Empire' or 'likely to cause needless alarm and distress among the civil population'. This meant that newspapers in Sheffield and elsewhere were able to report only certain aspects of the war. Editors complained frequently, especially in the war's early stages, about the limited information supplied to them. But they also exercised their own discretion, seeking to avoid the greatest excesses of the battlefield. The tone of reports was usually optimistic as far as the facts would allow.

However, the city's papers also reported military life and death by publishing letters received by families or friends. (These had always been censored, usually by a junior officer in the writer's unit, before being accepted for posting.) Soldiers' letters were often cheerful, but they could be very explicit about the horrors of their situation. For example, Sheffield readers were told:

> We lost ten out of twenty-one in a troop. It was awful. I saw Mickie hit in the back with high-explosive shrapnel. [...] There I was amongst ten of them, all wounded, screaming for help. God! I will never forget it. (November 1914)
>
> It was death every inch of the way – a terrible sight. As we raced forward towards the guns our men simply fell as they were hit, and lay there in long lines as straight as if on parade. The Germans had six machine guns on that hill alone. (May 1915)

Letter-writers' names and addresses were published, so readers were sometimes able to identify with soldiers they knew. More generally, casualties were listed several times a week in published Rolls of Honour, often extending across several columns of a newspaper page. Following the tremendous number of casualties after mid-1916 (in the Somme and other battles), these published lists were reduced in size and prominence.

The war had killed more than 2,000 Sheffield men by the end of 1916. Official communications about a death were mailed on standard War Office forms completed for men identified either as dead or missing. For officers, telegrams were sent. Weeks could elapse before a family received official confirmation of a death, but the Red Cross worked to obtain and send earlier information after particularly fierce battles. Some next-of-kin received both an official notification of death and a letter from a friend, junior officer or chaplain.

Conscription and military tribunals

Britain's long reliance on a volunteer army had been made possible by maintaining only a small number of soldiers. However, as the conflict came to need more and more men, voluntary recruiting became inadequate. In late 1915, the government made one more effort to recruit volunteers, and from January 1916 a sharp change in policy was announced. In that month a first Military Service Act ordered compulsory enlistment of unmarried men between 18 and 41, and a second Act in May 1916 extended conscription to married men also[12]. Individuals no longer had a free choice. Instead, decisions about a man's fate were taken by officials of the state.

Families under threat of losing a wage-earner (although a dependants' allowance was paid) sought ways for him to avoid call-up, and recently-established military tribunals acquired considerable power. These examined claims for exemption on the grounds of occupational or personal need or because of conscientious objection. Sheffield's military tribunal is illustrated in Chapter Six.

Air-raid warnings and a Zeppelin attack

Prior to the First World War, Sheffielders could not envisage being attacked from the sky. However, German airships were soon threatening the country, and raids from the air had become a worrying possibility. Originally developed by Count von Zeppelin in the 1890s, airships now became increasingly effective in night-time attacks on Britain. In December 1914, an Anti-Aircraft Corps was formed in the city. Initially, two guns were provided for separate stations at Wincobank, and additional

This Zeppelin bombed Sheffield on 25 September 1916, but missed the munition works.

stations were later placed in Manor Lane and at High Storrs in Ecclesall. Each had a petrol-engine-powered searchlight 200 yards away.

Around half-a-dozen air-raid warnings were sounded during the second half of 1915, in the form of a buzzer in the city centre and in more than twenty other locations, but Zeppelins did not reach Sheffield in that period. In the following year, warnings became more common (some reports suggest twenty-three) and people became used to taking cover in cellars or similar places, sometimes feeling safer in fields, woods or parks. In the evening of 25 September 1916, a fleet of seven German airships set out to bomb inland towns including Sheffield. Alarms were sounded, and just before midnight a single airship was heard. It flew over the city as if seeking its target, and then headed in the direction of the east-end munition works. In practice, its bombs all fell away from factories, instead landing on or near houses, a pub and a chapel across Burngreave, Grimesthorpe and Darnall. The bombs killed twenty-eight people and around nineteen more were injured. Some eighty houses were seriously damaged and more than 100 others also needed repairs.

By 1917, the design and manufacture of aeroplanes had been greatly improved and, although Zeppelin attacks on Britain (but not Sheffield) did continue, bombing by plane became more likely, especially in London. As a result of the 1916 airship raid, Sheffield's defences were strengthened by additional searchlights and guns on local hills, but German aeroplanes

Some damage from the Zeppelin raid on Sheffield in September 1916.

were unable to reach Sheffield and the city experienced no more raids from the air until the Second World War.

Hospitals throughout the city

In addition to around 750,000 lost lives, a huge number of other servicemen required medical attention. Initial care was provided near the front line, but more serious and long-term problems demanded a move to hospital and for that purpose almost 2,500,000 soldiers were returned to this country. It is important to note that around half of these were formally defined as sick rather than wounded. Although press reports and everyday conversations referred (and still refer) to wounded soldiers or casualties in the city and elsewhere, implying that they had been damaged by the enemy, many military patients, although ill because of war service, had not themselves been injured by German weapons.

Whatever the cause of their ill-health, hospitalization in Britain was often required and more buildings and staff became essential. Sheffield became home to two large institutions – the Third Northern General Hospital[13] and the Wharncliffe War Hospital. In a very short period of time, these two Sheffield hospitals were able to provide more than 6,000 military beds.

Although many patients were seriously ill, requiring intensive and possibly long-term treatment, a large number had reached the convalescent stage. These were placed in convalescent units and might be allowed to spend their days outside their hospital. Invalid soldiers thus became a common sight around Sheffield. They received free travel on the city's trams, and seats were provided in convenient locations in many streets. Away from their hospital the men wore a 'going-out' uniform of light-blue cloth with white lapels and a red tie. Across all years of the war, Sheffield's military hospitals received in excess of 70,000 men. They were transported from the railway station by ambulance or car, in many cases by volunteer drivers from the city who together contributed many hundreds of hours to this work.

The Third Northern General Hospital This had been established by the Royal Army Medical Corps as a territorial unit in 1913. Soon after war was declared the corps, with headquarters in Gell Street, requisitioned the Teachers' Training College located in Ecclesall Road and Collegiate Crescent. The college's three principal and other buildings were refurbished and equipped with operating theatres, an X-Ray unit and other facilities, and on 3 September 1914 the first patients arrived from the Western Front.

Initial medical staff came mainly from hospitals in the city, and supervising matrons were drawn at different times from the Royal Hospital or Royal Infirmary. Local clergymen served as visiting chaplains in addition to a resident army chaplain. Staff from the Royal Army Medical Corps numbered around 200, and several dozen support workers were employed for cooking, cleaning, maintenance and similar jobs.

As in other parts of the country, qualified nurses in Sheffield's military hospitals were assisted by volunteers from a Voluntary Aid Detachment. Detachments were part of the nation's territorial force and could undertake a wide range of nursing and non-nursing activities within and outside Britain. Women (the majority) served mainly as nursing auxiliaries, undertaking less technical but necessary tasks in support of qualified staff. By mid-1915, around eighty VAD assistants worked in Sheffield hospitals, and that number is thought to have doubled in later war years.

Voluntary Aid Detachments were made up of volunteers to assist military hospitals in this country and abroad.

Principal buildings of the Third Northern General Hospital were in Ecclesall Road and Collegiate Crescent. They were referred to as the hospital's 'Base'.

Display Box 1.2
UNITS OF THE THIRD NORTHERN GENERAL HOSPITAL

This large military hospital had many units around the city and nearby, centred on a 'Base' in Ecclesall Road. Details changed slightly from year to year, but enlargement meant that around 4,600 beds had become available in all sections by 1918. (Bramall Lane Hospital – last in the list below – started work in that year.) Principal locations and sizes of units in 1918 are listed in the sequence of their opening:

Primary units (2,602 beds in total)
Ecclesall Road Base, 438 beds
Royal Infirmary, 87 beds
Royal Hospital, 80 beds
Winter Street Hospital, 134 beds
Firvale Hospital, 462 beds
Carterknowle School, 115 beds
Lydgate Lane School, 130 beds
Ranmoor School, 110 beds
Greystones School, 150 beds
Shiregreen School, 145 beds
Firshill School, 150 beds
Western Road School, 70 beds
Ecclesall Infirmary, 200 beds
Endcliffe Hall, 130 beds
Oakbrook Officers' Hospital, 51 beds
Bramall Lane Cricket Pavilion, 150 beds

Auxiliary and convalescent hospitals
In addition to the hospitals listed above, around thirty other institutions provided about 2,000 beds for less serious cases. One was the Woofindin Convalescent Home in Whiteley Wood, and outside the city were (for example) St John's Hospital at Dore (in Derbyshire until 1934), Longshaw Lodge at Grindleford, Aston Hall in Derby, Loversall Hall in Doncaster, and the Devonshire Hospital in Buxton.

This recreation hut in grounds of the base hospital was financed by donations from people in the city.

As the war's medical needs continued to expand during 1915 and 1916, the base hospital in Ecclesall Road built new wards and other buildings in its large grounds, and more widely the Third Northern General Hospital came to include around fifty units in the city and neighbourhood. More serious cases were treated in the Ecclesall Road base, the Royal Hospital and the Royal Infirmary, and other patients were placed in auxiliary and convalescent hospitals elsewhere.

For example, seven of the city's schools became hospitals in 1915. Lydgate School Hospital in Crosspool opened in October 1915 with a sister-in-charge, five nurses, two VAD helpers and many volunteers. The large majority of the first year's patients in Lydgate Hospital suffered from dysentery and other intestinal complaints, with a smaller number being treated for gunshot or shrapnel wounds, shell-shock and other results of enemy action. Unfortunately, patient records for this and other Sheffield hospitals are no longer available, so it is not possible to determine the overall mix of problems treated in the city.

Of course, pupils had to be moved from these seven schools into nearby buildings. For example, Lydgate children were transferred into Wesley Hall and Crookes Baptist Church. Throughout the war, children and teachers from a transferred school cared particularly for 'their' hospitalized

This version of the Third Northern General Hospital's standard greetings card was from the auxiliary unit at Endcliffe Hall.

soldiers, visiting them, presenting concerts, and providing gifts at Christmas and other times. More generally, children and parents across the city collected eggs, fruit, vegetables and other items, and worked throughout the war to help soldiers in their neighbourhood hospital.

Among the other units shown in Display Box 1.2, Firvale and Ecclesall Hospitals were located in Sheffield's two workhouse infirmaries, each run by one of the city's two boards of guardians. Overall during the war, Sheffield Guardians' Firvale Hospital treated as many as 10,000 wounded and sick soldiers and carried out around 1,000 operations. Endcliffe Hall in Ranmoor (headquarters of the territorial Hallamshires since January 1914) was converted to provide eight military wards, including one of thirty-two beds in the Hall's ball-room. Next door to Endcliffe Hall was (and is) Oakbrook, which in the spring of 1917 became a hospital for around fifty officers. It had been offered rent-free to the War Office, and furniture and equipment were funded through a special appeal by the lord mayor to local firms and individual businessmen.

Many convalescent units of the Third Northern Hospital were outside Sheffield, but one was located in Dore, then part of Derbyshire. This was

St John's Hospital, improvised in October 1914 in the Church Institute on Abbeydale Road South. Created to help wounded Belgian soldiers arriving in the city, it was at first staffed entirely by volunteers: Red Cross[14] nurses, cooks, cleaners and other helpers. Furniture, food and money were provided by local people both at the outset and through subsequent fundraising events. St John's Hospital subsequently became a convalescent unit within the Third Northern General Hospital and cared also for British and empire troops. In at least the early days a local general practitioner doctor visited regularly and was on call as needed.

Just outside the city was Longshaw Lodge convalescent hospital. This was made available to the Third Northern General Hospital in early 1915 by the Duke of Rutland (it was his shooting lodge), and came to accommodate around sixty men, including many (referred to as 'colonials') from dominions of the empire. In addition to a small number of Royal Army Medical Corps (RAMC) soldiers, staff included two nursing sisters and three VAD nursing assistants, supported by a laundress and other workers. Running costs at Longshaw were greater than the War Office allowance, and (as in other cases) Sheffield's lord mayor appealed for donations from the public. In addition to that fund, many gifts of money, food and other items were received directly from individuals and groups throughout the war.

A volunteer-funded outing from Longshaw Hospital in one of Sheffield Corporation Tramways' new motor-buses.

Wharncliffe War Hospital The city's second military hospital was created from South Yorkshire Mental Asylum at Wadsley. That was taken over by the Royal Army Medical Corps at the beginning of April 1915[15]. Inmates were transferred to other institutions or sent home, and the asylum was renamed as Wharncliffe War Hospital. Up to its closure in August 1920, the hospital treated almost 40,000 serving and medically-discharged soldiers. It had around 1,750 beds, and was newly fitted with its own X-Ray machine and three operating theatres. The commanding officer, Lieutenant-Colonel William Vincent, was previously and subsequently director of the asylum and, in addition to RAMC staff and several chaplains, previous asylum employees were appointed as assistants.

Wharncliffe War Hospital had previously been the South Yorkshire Asylum at Wadsley. It later (in 1948) became Middlewood Hospital.

The overwhelming majority of military patients in Sheffield were treated in the newly created hospitals listed above, but a few were placed in the existing sixty-five-bed hospital within the long-established Hillsborough Barracks. As in other cases, the city worked to make life better for the barrack's patients, donating furniture, extra food and other items and arranging visits to social and entertainment events. Another medical unit making a significant military contribution was the charity-based Edgar

The privately funded Edgar Allen Institute provided physiotherapy for injured soldiers as well as for patients from the city.

Allen Institute in Gell Street. Each year this provided out-patient physiotherapy treatment ('founded on the Swedish system of physical exercises') for around 1,000 soldiers from the city's military hospitals.

The city's voluntary work

Looking back on the war, the 1919 *Sheffield Yearbook* noted that people in the city 'have never wearied in well-doing'. Voluntary help and unpaid civil defence work were central to many lives. For example, ladies' working parties were set up all over the city to assist the local military hospitals. Dozens of groups provided an unceasing supply of clothes, food and other items, sometimes sent directly to a particular hospital but often co-ordinated through the Soldiers' Personal Comforts Depot. This started work in September 1914 in Leopold Street and supplied a colossal number of meals and other items to troops in the city's hospitals – food for more than 500,000 breakfasts and 500,000 teas in the peak year of 1916. Pork pies, sausages, eggs, cakes, ham, bacon, oranges and apples were channelled through the depot in enormous quantity, as were cigarettes, clothing, chairs and other items. In addition to the provision of meals in bulk, groups of volunteer ladies were permitted to pass through hospital wards offering fruit, cakes and other delicacies to individual patients. The depot's huge number of deliveries and visits required detailed continuous planning and considerable personal commitment.

Volunteers from the city's Personal Comforts Depot supplied a huge number of meals to local military hospitals.

The depot's nonstop work also included gathering supplies and money from individuals and companies across the city. Public interest was maintained by regular articles in Sheffield's newspapers, providing also the opportunity to seek additional contributions. For instance, in January 1915 an article urgently requested 'eggs, vegetables, sausages, cakes and dried fruits', and later in the year requests were made for hot-water bottles, books, slippers, sacks to hold vegetables, and zinc baths for storing eggs. Deliveries and some collections from donors were initially made by a single van provided by an Ecclesfield family, but in 1915 a second vehicle was also donated by well-wishers. In addition, the depot co-ordinated a range of other activities. For example, its Arts and Crafts Committee helped military patients develop skills in practical handiwork.

A large number of other Sheffield ladies set up their own schemes to provide materials. For example, in August 1914 the Mistress Cutler formed an Army and Navy Aid Committee to collect, make and distribute mufflers, mittens and other garments. A work-room was established in the Cutlers' Hall and, by the end of 1915, as many as 85,000 items of many kinds had been distributed, with around a quarter of those going to hospitals in the city. In addition to items made in the Cutlers' Hall itself, individuals and groups from all over Sheffield (including more than sixty churches) brought in tens of thousands of garments for onward transmission. In 1917, the committee became part of a nationwide organization and was renamed the Sheffield Voluntary Aid Association – also known as the Sheffield Voluntary Association. It delivered more than 200,000 items during the war.

The city's newspapers vied with each other to persuade readers to send in items for onward transmission to serving troops, war hospitals or British prisoners-of-war. 'Smokes' were given great prominence, with papers offering different-priced packages of cigarettes both for individuals and as bulk purchases. Advertisements in the *Sheffield Daily Independent* asked for money 'in sending cigarettes, tobacco and other comforts to the Sons of Britannia whose glories will be sung right through the coming ages' (in April 1916) and cried 'SOS' – 'Send out Smokes' (in January 1916).

Sheffielders were also keen to assist in the supply of vehicles. At least two dozen ambulances for the battle zone or for transporting injured soldiers around the city were financed and provided by individuals or groups. Other gifts from the city included an entire hundred-bed hospital for British soldiers and officers in France (in December 1914 and onwards, by Sir Robert and Lady Hadfield) and several 'motor field kitchens' for the Front (from Sheffield motorist groups and others). A YMCA-operated

This social institute at Redmires camp was funded by two Sheffield people and administered by the YMCA.

social institute for the Sheffield City Battalion and subsequent troops at Redmires Camp was financed by Mr and Mrs Meggitt-Johnson, and the Master Cutler co-ordinated money-raising for a 'Sheffield' recreation hut at Ripon military camp. The funding of Sheffield's own aeroplane will be described in Chapter Five. On a smaller scale, books and magazines were collected through local libraries for onward transmission to serving soldiers, and it became usual at Christmas for churches to send presents to troops serving from their parish.

Convalescent military patients were sometimes invited to 'smoker sing-songs' or were offered activities elsewhere in the city or nearby. For instance, in August 1916 the Original Thursday (angling) Club entertained soldiers to lunch and three hours fishing at Brigg, and in September of that year patients from Longshaw Lodge Hospital were taken on a tour of the offices and printing facilities of the *Sheffield Daily Telegraph*, followed by tea in the newspaper's canteen. In October 1916, the Ladies 'B' Team of Hillsborough Park Bowling Club (pictured in large hats and long dresses) competed against men from local hospitals. Other groups of ladies devoted many hours and much effort to helping hospitalized men acquire skills in handiwork, with products sometimes sold to aid hospital finances.

A large number of other outings were arranged by local well-wishers and motoring groups. On 18 August 1916, the *Sheffield Daily Telegraph* described how around sixty patients from military hospitals: 'were conveyed by motors to the green at the Stag Inn, Psalter Lane. Games of clock golf, target bowls and doubles were indulged in with evident delight, prizes being given to winners in each event.' Many other contributions were made by local churches and groups formed to assist a particular hospital.

Volunteers also staffed an Invalid Soldiers' Rest Room in premises (previously the Black Rock Hotel) in Castle Street[16], and a separate Sailors' and Soldiers' Rest Room and Buffet for troops in transit was operated by unpaid helpers on a platform of the Midland Station. Volunteers also assisted in the Sheffield Soldiers' Home founded in 1907 opposite the barracks in Langsett Road, and worked in YMCA canteens for local munitions workers and at Redmires Camp. A volunteer-operated Hospital Supply Depot was established by Sheffield University to prepare and deliver bandages and other medical requirements.

Cash was acquired in many ways. Schools and firms had regular collections and events to raise cash, artistes and orchestras from local theatres performed unpaid in fundraising matinees, and boxes to receive donations were provided in the city's trams and picture houses. Local boy scouts carried out paid tasks and donated their earnings to the Ambulance Fund, and the Girls' Friendly Society in Dore raised money through a Patriotic Social Evening and other events. Flag days were held almost weekly to raise funds for a wide variety of organizations, and many companies operated weekly optional deductions from wages for local and national appeals. Around 500 War Savings Associations were formed in the city to provide income (through loans) to the government, and Sheffield's Central Savings Committee sponsored a large number of motivational lectures and local campaigns. For example, during 1917 and 1918, the committee contributed to the National Welfare and Economy Campaign and it mounted a Tank Week, a Cruiser Week, a War Weapons Week, a Gun Week and a Feed the Guns campaign. Each of those provided substantially more than a million pounds in loans to the government[17].

A different kind of unpaid contribution was made by members of the Sheffield Volunteer Defence Corps. This had been established as part of a national trend in the autumn of 1914. Membership was open to men who were not eligible for military service because of their age, health limitations or employment on government work, and call-up would only happen if an invasion of the country was imminent. The Sheffield Corps was largely self-financing (for example, its band played at local

For a week in December 1917, Sheffielders could lend money to the government by purchasing War Bonds from a 'tank bank' in Fitzalan Square.

fundraising events), and members were required to pay a monthly subscription[18].

By the end of 1915, the Sheffield Volunteer Corps had around 1,800 volunteer members in two battalions who met for training and drill practice several times a week, including Sundays. Initially they wore an armband rather than a uniform. Parades were held in the city's parks and football grounds, and different sections received training for motorcycle, motor-vehicle, ambulance, signalling and other types of work. A camp was held annually, in later years jointly with a regular unit. Members assisted with crowd control during public events and at night they guarded important sites and communication lines, also manning the barriers on main roads into the city. Some training exercises at the time involved imaginary attacks on Sheffield by German troops. They were also called into action whenever air-raids were threatened, visiting homes and ensuring that darkness was maintained. The corps' ambulance section was required at those times to stand ready for action.

Also busy were volunteer special police constables. The number of 'specials' increased substantially in this period, as regular Sheffield policemen joined the armed services and the city's population grew through an influx of munition workers. They accompanied regular policemen on routine patrols and other activities to maintain public order, and were granted the same powers as those policemen. Whenever an air-raid was threatened, they had to report for duty at the central police station.

Voluntary service also occurred on the football field. For example, under the headline 'Daughters of Vulcan Play Football', the *Sheffield Daily Independent* at the end of December 1916 described a charity match between two teams of lady footballers drawn from Vickers' South and East Projectile shops. Around 10,000 spectators paid their entrance fee in aid of sick and wounded soldiers in the city's hospitals, and the tone of the *Independent*'s report would cause problems today. 'The matronly goalie [...] was a formidable obstacle [...] of magnificent physique.' 'The floundering and slipping about was done with a subtle grace which mere man could never hope to emulate.' The winning goal came after 'little Fattie' passed the backs who 'made sure their hair was all right'. Feminism was still years away.

CHAPTER 2

Arming the Troops 1: Government, employers and trade unions

The people of Britain had long been accustomed to considerable personal liberty within the law (referred to as a *laissez faire* outlook), but the government's control of daily life increased steadily throughout the war. Within munition-producing companies, employers were forced to abandon cherished customs and workers had to accept restrictions that would have been unacceptable in earlier times.

Obtaining materials and men

In terms of the nation's established strategy, Britain had prepared well for war. The large navy was modern and powerful and an intentionally small army was ready as planned. However, there was a problem that is obvious in retrospect – the plan was, as later officially admitted, 'grotesquely inadequate'[19].

Although the original expeditionary force of around 150,000 men soon reached continental Europe and joined battle with German troops, it rapidly became clear that many more were needed. Initial recruiting went extremely well, and the extra troops required weapons, ammunition, equipment and clothes. The government placed contracts around the country and before long manufacturers in Sheffield and elsewhere were receiving more orders than they could cope with. Production backlogs became common and by the end of 1914 a number of politicians had become concerned about a possible German victory because of Britain's less-than-adequate supply of weapons and ammunition.

Before the war, the country had obtained its armaments from three government-owned factories – the Royal Arsenal at Woolwich, the Royal Gunpowder Factory at Waltham Abbey, and the Royal Small Arms Factory at Enfield – together with a small number of private companies appointed by the government as official suppliers. The latter included John Brown and Company, Cammell Lairds, Firths, Hadfields, and Vickers in Sheffield, and others elsewhere such as Armstrong Whitworth in Newcastle, the Coventry Ordnance Works and the Birmingham Small Arms Company. These firms were well-equipped and effective, but they were soon unable to meet ever-growing requirements from the Admiralty and the War Office[20].

At first the government's focus was mainly on the Admiralty, seeking to increase naval power through more ships, guns and projectiles. However, within a few months it was clear that a shortage of weapons and ammunition in the army also required urgent action[21]. In May 1915, supply problems hit the headlines in what became known as the 'shell crisis' or the 'shell scandal'. The war correspondent of *The Times* newspaper learned from a high-ranking officer on the Western Front that recent British attacks had failed because troops lacked high-explosive shells to dislodge the enemy. His article in *The Times* proclaimed 'the want of an unlimited supply of high explosives was a fatal bar to our success'. It caused uproar. The complaints were echoed and elaborated as the government's 'tragic blunder' by the widely-read *Daily Mail*[22], and considerable public anger contributed to the downfall of an already-troubled Liberal government.

In its place came a coalition of Conservative and Liberal MPs, with a small number of Labour (trade union supporting) members. Discussions had recently been initiated between politicians and trade union officials about possible wartime adjustments to industrial working practices, and a general recognition that action was needed quickly led to the creation of an entirely new government department – the Ministry of Munitions. Announced to the press on 26 May 1915, and officially established on 9 June, this was charged with 'organizing the munitions of war', taking over many aspects of work from the Admiralty and the War Office[23]. The first minister of munitions was Liberal David Lloyd George, previously the chancellor of the exchequer, and his four-man advisory team included Winston Churchill and Dr Christopher Addison MP. Dr Addison had lectured in anatomy in Sheffield Medical School between 1897 and 1901,

Charles Ellis from John Brown and Company served as deputy director of the Ministry of Munitions. Other Sheffield men also worked for the ministry. See Appendix Two.

also holding a commission in the volunteer Hallamshire Rifles[24]. The new ministry (Armament Buildings, Whitehall, London) departed from traditional civil service procedure by including among its top executives around a hundred company directors and managers with direct experience of materials production and supply. David Lloyd George explicitly sought senior colleagues who had 'push and go'. Among Sheffield appointments was Charles Ellis from John Brown and Company, who was placed in a central position as deputy director of the ministry.

The shell crisis had focused narrowly on the army's lack of artillery ammunition, but the need was more general. In addition to being short of equipment, workers and factories, the country also required huge amounts of raw material. Much had previously been imported and was no longer available in sufficient quantity. For example, in 1914 about a third of the ore converted by British manufacturers into pig-iron came from abroad, and special efforts were now needed to maintain supplies, especially since Germany was competing for ore in the same international markets as Britain. Among the steps taken, Albert Senior of Sheffield's George Senior and Company[25] was, in July 1915, sent on a purchasing tour of Sweden, which led to a valuable increase in supplies. Substantial ore imports were also obtained from Spain and the United States, both of which were neutral in the war until the latter joined the Allies in 1917[26]. From that year Sheffield University successfully developed procedures to use British-sourced alternatives to high-grade imported ore, reducing the need for some imports.

Steps were also taken to provide optical and other glass for military use, almost all of which Britain had previously obtained from Germany. Sheffield University expanded its research in that area and a department of glass technology was created in 1915 to work closely with industry to meet the deficiency. Also threatened by the war were supplies of tungsten powder, which were essential in making alloy steels and also largely imported from Germany. At the end of 1914 a number of Sheffield steelmakers came together to form High Speed Alloys Ltd, a company that established a powder-processing plant in Widnes and arranged its own tungsten supply from Burma.

As well as dealing with shortages, the government had to improve the movement of materials into and between companies and find ways to restrain price rises. In these and other respects detailed intervention by officials became the norm. The country's railways had been taken over as soon as the war started and the entire coal-mining industry gradually became controlled by the government. Owners of private companies in the two industries retained possession of their companies, but they now had to work within government regulations and priorities. Acids, fuel oils and other essential materials, including sacking for sandbags, were soon exclusively channelled through the government at centrally-determined prices. Official purchasing mechanisms and/or maximum prices were introduced for a wide range of metals, forgings, armament components and part-completed products. Allocations of many essential materials were fixed for each manufacturer by the government either centrally[27] or by the establishment of decision-making committees representing key producers. For example, deliveries to and from specialized steel producers were co-ordinated by two groups set up in Sheffield – the High-Speed Tool Steel Committee in February 1916 and the Aircraft Steel Committee in July 1917[28].

In the spring of 1915, many of these developments lay in the future, but the shell crisis, continuing arguments within government, and rumblings in the press were together creating a sense that something must be done to bring greater order and effectiveness to the country's munitions management. In June, a speech in Manchester by the new minister of munitions, David Lloyd George, sketched the scene:

> It is a war of munitions. We are fighting against the best organized community in the world, the best either for war or peace, and we have been employing too much the haphazard, leisurely, go-as-you-please methods, which, believe me, would not have enabled us to maintain our place as a nation even in peace very much longer.

Increased central control seemed to be essential, but finding the best way forward was complex and controversial. One insider later described this initial period as 'a gigantic improvisation', a series of 'experiments, often hazardous, and not always based on a considered plan'[29]. From now on the government steadily increased its regulation of industry[30]. Many of the country's working practices were transformed and a powerful network of new factories was constructed.

Britain's national factories

Through the Ministry of Munitions, the government created and directed around 215 of its own national factories[31]. These included expanded armament producers at Woolwich, Waltham Abbey and Enfield, but largely came from a new programme spread across the country. By creating specialized factories, high production levels were envisaged from relatively unskilled workers focusing on a narrow range of operations.

Thomas Firth and Sons built and operated this national projectile factory on a greenfield site at Templeborough.

Initial planning began in April 1915, and the first decision to create a government shell factory (in Leeds) was taken in May. Overall progress was remarkably rapid. The Leeds factory started production in September 1915 and many others followed, including four in Sheffield (see Display Box 2.1 and Chapter Four). Construction and equipment were almost entirely financed by the government, but everyday management was typically in the hands of a manufacturer from the area. These companies acted as managing agents for the Ministry of Munitions and received a fee for their work[32]. They had to follow government rules for staffing, purchasing, accounting and other functions, and their output was taken by the government at fixed prices. Although managing companies did not own the factory, they worked for profits that depended on their effectiveness in keeping costs low. In some cases, national factories were operated directly by a local board of management rather than a single

Display Box 2.1
THE GOVERNMENT'S NATIONAL FACTORIES

From September 1915, the government financed more than 200 new factories to produce armaments and materials. Many were newly constructed, but others were in extended or refurbished works. All these national factories were owned by the government, but most were managed by a local company in accordance with detailed requirements from the Ministry of Munitions. Those in Sheffield are mentioned below and described more fully in Chapter Four. Government influence also extended to many privately owned establishments after they had become designated as controlled.

National Projectile Factories produced medium and heavier types of unfilled shell: Fifteen new factories of this kind were built, including two in Sheffield, managed by Firths and by Hadfields, and one in Nottingham, managed by Sheffield-based Cammell Laird.

National Shell Factories made smaller varieties of unfilled shell: Forty-eight factories, including two in Barnsley and one in Rotherham.

National Ordnance Factories repaired artillery weapons: Four factories were created, including one in Sheffield (Hadfields) and one in Nottingham (Sheffield's Cammell Lairds), both of which had previously operated as National Projectile Factories.

National Filling Factories packed empty shells with explosives or chemicals: Twenty-seven factories, recognized to be particularly dangerous working environments; none were in Sheffield.

National Explosives Factories produced TNT and other explosives or components of explosives: Thirty-one factories were opened around the country; none in Sheffield.

National Cartridge Factories manufactured small arms ammunition: Six factories, none in Sheffield.

National Aircraft Production Factories made aeroplanes and some balloons: Eight factories, none in Sheffield.

Other National Factories repaired equipment and manufactured their own kind of product – gauges, boxes, optical instruments, anti-gas apparatus, specialized ammunition, etc: Approximately seventy-five factories, including two small ones in Sheffield in 1918.

In addition, the country's established ordnance suppliers were expanded. The Royal Arsenal at Woolwich (established around 1695), the Royal Gunpowder Factory at Waltham Abbey (from 1787), the Royal Small Arms Factory at Enfield (from 1804), and the recently established Royal Aircraft Factory at Farnborough (from 1905, renamed in 1911).

company and a few, usually small or established only late in the war, were administered by the Ministry of Munitions through a regional office. In some cases an engineer from the ministry was based in the factory to monitor and assist technical progress.

Initial production from the national factories was necessarily limited as new workforces and new equipment were installed and tested, but gradually the increased resources and standardized procedures began to yield clear benefits. The ministry improved its procedures for centralized buying of raw materials, usually selling those to factories at prices below free-market levels. Economies were also created by imposing the same accounting systems in all government-owned factories and requiring each one to submit detailed costings for comparison with each other and with national benchmarks. Improvements to a factory were demanded when cost or other indicators were unsatisfactory. New methods of scrap utilization were introduced nationally, as were modern procedures for what we now call human resource management. Research investigations were initiated to improve knowledge of steel and other materials, and findings and recommendations were disseminated widely throughout industry.

Controlled establishments

The national factories were invaluable with each one producing its own kind of product. But they necessarily took several months to become operational and the country's need was immediate and extended to many other items. What about already established companies – ones that had never before produced munitions? Could their experience and equipment be directed instead to war work?

Changes came at two levels – from companies themselves and from government initiatives. In the first case, industrialists in many parts of the country had, by the spring of 1915, started to consider how they could help the war effort. No doubt some were also seeking to profit from government contracts. Local organizations and Chambers of Commerce were developing ways to bring together resources, for example, by co-operation between companies or through a local co-ordinating committee[33]. At the end of March 1915, the first group of firms, in Leicester, reached agreement with the government to start munitions work. Sheffield soon followed.

Secondly, the government was itself developing plans for some central regulation and increasing the effectiveness of company operation. Engineering and other trade unions had traditionally required that skilled work be undertaken only by a restricted range of craftsmen, and had insisted that many changes to a company's working procedure could not go ahead without union approval. Other union-imposed conditions set limits, for instance, to the maximum hours that may be worked and the number of apprentices that were permissible. However, by the spring of 1915, many national union officials had come to accept the government's argument that in this time of urgent military need increased flexibility was essential.

A two-day meeting in Sheffield's Victoria Hotel between engineering employers and unions led to signature on 5 March 1915 of the nationwide Shells and Fuses Agreement. This allowed men from a variety of trades to undertake some previously-prohibited skilled jobs, and agreed that 'operations on which skilled men are at present employed, but which, by reason of their character, can be performed by semi-skilled or female labour, may be done by such labour during the war period'. And in the so-called Treasury Agreement of 17 March 1915 between the government and officials from several unions, it was accepted that, for the duration of the war only, some jobs or parts of jobs could be undertaken by a wider range of workers than usual. Unions also pledged to recommend to their members that 'during the war period there shall in no case be any stoppage of work upon munitions and equipment of war or any other work required for a satisfactory completion of the war'. In practice, shop stewards and union members in the factories did not always accept the deals agreed by their faraway national officials.

Against that background the government introduced legally-backed changes to industrial practice. Drafts of a Munitions of War Act had been discussed with principal trade unions before it was presented to and passed by parliament, including by union-linked Labour MPs, and became law on 2 July 1915. The Act required sacrifices from both employees and employers in companies engaged in munitions work[34]. The original focus was on armaments themselves, but it soon became clear that companies making other articles required for use in war – uniforms, eating utensils, etc – also needed inclusion. The government took powers, through the Ministry of Munitions, to declare any firm engaged on munition-related work to be a controlled establishment, in which certain rights of workers were removed and owners' profits and freedom were limited for the duration of the war. The number of these controlled firms increased steadily in the following months.

The 1915 Munitions of War Act also made it illegal for workers to strike, and trade union restrictive practices and rules were to be suspended[35]. As a parallel restraint, controlled employers were forbidden to 'lock out' workers in a dispute (i.e. refuse to continue their employment at those times), and companies breaking the new law became subject to large fines. In part to prevent companies poaching workers from another firm through higher wages, employers were prohibited from increasing wage rates without approval from the ministry. To additionally discourage the turnover of munition workers, individuals could not be re-employed anywhere within six weeks of leaving a controlled establishment unless their previous employer had provided a leaving certificate approving the resignation[36].

Some companies (in this case W. T. Flather of Sheffield) indicated on letterheads and other documents their status as a government-controlled establishment.

Owners of controlled companies were required to provide to the Ministry of Munitions regular details of employees, equipment and jobs undertaken, and a new tax was imposed on any excess profits – more than 20 percent above pre-war net levels. Contracts with the ministry were at prices determined from information obtained from other controlled organizations and from the government's own factories. The ministry was given power to issue legally-enforceable rules for the general ordering of work, which included timekeeping, absences, the maintenance of discipline, and the attainment of reasonable output. Disputes about applying these rules were to be settled by newly established munition tribunals. Around sixty relatively informal courts were speedily established around the country, each comprising an independent adjudicator advised by one member each from an employers' and a workmen's panel.

Proceedings of the Sheffield Munition Tribunal were reported in the local press and ranged widely across behaviours falling within the Act. Employers brought complaints against individual workers, for example for drunkenness, disobeying orders or absence from a job, and employees found guilty were usually required to pay a fine. Workers themselves were able to appeal to the tribunal for a leaving certificate that their employer had refused to grant them. Examples are in Chapter Four.

The 1915 Munitions of War Act also empowered the ministry to issue badges that could be worn by individuals in munition factories and shipyards who were shown to be 'On War Service'. The badges were intended to protect civilian workers from insults about possible cowardice or lack of patriotism; see the next section.

It was explicitly stated that the Act would be in force only during the life of the Ministry of Munitions (i.e. for the duration of the conflict), and that unions' and employers' rights would be restored without change at the war's end. No overall list of controlled establishments has survived,

Unofficial 'On War Service' badges included this one from Cammell Lairds, which was worn by William Ray, who lived in Cartmell Road in Woodseats.

Steelmakers Edgar Allen issued this 'On War Service' badge to its workers early in 1915.

The badge of Howell and Company made it clear that workers were 'On His Majesty's Service'.

This is an early version of the war service badge issued by John Brown and Company.

J. H. Andrew and Company indicated that its people were employed on government work.

and, partly because of variations in the definition of 'munition' work, historians have differed in their estimated total. Nationally the number of controlled establishments certainly exceeded 5,000 and may have reached 6,000. Sheffield had around 350 (estimates vary between reports, up to a maximum of 450).

War service badges

Although the general idea of a badge to show that a civilian is employed on war service seems straightforward, changes in the demands of war and the needs of industry led to shifts and confusion across the years. War service badges were introduced initially to help munition companies dissuade their employees from offering themselves for military service rather than continuing with factory work[37]. But after the introduction of compulsory conscription in early 1916, the issue or withdrawal of a badge and its accompanying certificate came to have a different meaning. It was then backed by legal force, and the state's decision to award or withdraw a badge had major implications for life and possible death or injury in battle.

In the war's opening period of enthusiasm for men to volunteer as soldiers, those who instead continued to work in factories and other jobs could become objects of criticism or scorn – widely referred to as shirkers[38]. Some munitions companies soon created their own badges for employees to wear, and at this initial stage any such arrangements were merely informal between an employer and employee. By early 1915, the government approved some firms' self-designed badges, but the

Display Box 2.2
'ON WAR SERVICE' BADGES FOR MUNITION WORKERS

Frequent changes in policy may be summarized in four overlapping stages:

Stage One: Some companies issue their own badge (autumn 1914)
In the initial period of mass volunteering, munition production suffered greatly as factories lost many key workers to the armed services. Some employers sought to retain workers of military age by issuing company-specific badges for an employee to show that he too was serving his country.

Stage Two: Initial government issue (spring and summer 1915)
In this period the Admiralty (for the navy) and the War Office (for the army) still worked largely separately from each other. From the end of 1914, the Admiralty issued its own authorized badge to provide visible protection for workers defined as indispensable in its own dockyards and privately owned naval suppliers. After some reluctance, in March 1915 the War Office introduced a similar badge for its own suppliers to the army. In both cases, distribution of badges was through an employing company.

Stage Three: De-badging and a single government badge (from August 1915)
The new Ministry of Munitions (established in June 1915) took over many responsibilities from the Admiralty and War Office, and introduced a single On War Service badge for all eligible men. Earlier versions and accompanying certificates were withdrawn, and new badges were issued only to individuals now freshly assessed as definitely working on munitions.

Stage Four: Conscription, more de-badging, and new exemptions (1916 onwards)
From January 1916, medically acceptable men of military age became required to join the services unless they held a certificate of exemption and its accompanying On War Service badge. As pressure grew for still more troops, increasing numbers of badges were withdrawn from unskilled and semi-skilled workers. Schedules of certified or protected occupations were repeatedly modified throughout 1917 and early 1918, forming the basis for issuing protection certificates. Those could be withdrawn at short notice so that men might be called-up if needed. As pressures for more troops became extreme during 1918, the national emphasis shifted away from individual decisions based on a man having a certain kind of job to conscription being required for a whole age group.

complexities and slowness of dealing with government departments encouraged other companies to simply proceed without official permission.

Changes from then on are simplified in Display Box 2.2. In practice, there was some overlap between the stages shown there, and it was never possible to avoid the inevitable ambiguities and contradictions in seeking to satisfy mutually incompatible needs. How should priority be determined between conflicting manpower demands by the army and industry? How should the issue or withdrawal of badges be adjusted from time to time to meet changing military needs? Should badging allocations be made at the level of entire firms, for certain departments only, or for individual workers? Who should decide eligibility – an employer, the government, or perhaps a trade union?[39] If the government allocates badges, should decisions be taken in London or by an official based in the locality? What about individuals working for only part of their time on munition work? Or those who transfer into a different job?

At the end of 1914, the Admiralty made available its own 'On War Service' badge to shipyards and factories that supplied the navy.

From March 1915, this badge was the standard War Office issue to men working on munitions.

At the beginning of September 1914, manufacturers Vickers asked the Admiralty for permission to issue its own badge, and other companies supplying the Admiralty soon followed that lead, often without formal approval. By late December 1914, the Admiralty thought it better to issue its own authorized badge to dockyards and suppliers. These were sent in bulk to admiralty contractors, and those issued a badge to men they considered to be 'absolutely indispensable'. The Admiralty badges (more than 400,000 were issued) had no numbers on them and thus could not be individually traced, but companies were required to maintain a list of holders.

The (separately-functioning) War Office was troubled by the expense and complexity of issuing and monitoring badges for its own suppliers and at this stage doubted their importance. However, pressure from politicians and the public was great and, from March 1915, numbered badges were provided in bulk to War Office contractors who themselves decided which of their employees should receive them. To reduce expenditure, the initial enamelled version was replaced by a brass version and within three months around 80,000 War Office badges had been issued[40].

Display Box 2.3 illustrates how uncontrolled the issue of badges had become, and soon after its formation in June 1915, the new Ministry of Munitions decided to issue a single type to replace both the Admiralty and War Office versions. The new badge was to be granted specifically to named and approved individuals rather than being issued to entire companies. In a huge nationwide administrative task, up to 500,000 previously issued badges had to be called in and assessments made of a

Display Box 2.3
BADGES FOR ALL?

By the summer of 1915, war service badges were obtainable through several channels. However, confusion was widespread. On 15 July, the *Sheffield Daily Telegraph* carried a letter signed by an unhappy 'Badger'. Here are some excerpts:

> Some months ago my employers presented me with an official war service badge to wear in the lapel of my coat. I was informed that the badge, which is of brass with a crown, surrounded by 'On War Service 1914' in blue enamel, was provided by the government for men of military age engaged in munition and kindred trades. (Incidentally, I was made to deposit 2s. 6d. with my employers, which is to be returned when I return the badge at the conclusion of my service.)
>
> Judge of my surprise when I saw the self-same badges advertised for sale by a Birmingham firm of button makers. I have also seen colorable [sic] imitations, the only difference being the counterfeit in one case bore the legend 'He is doing his duty' or some such twaddle, and in the other the crown was routed out and the initials of the firm, together with a number, substituted.
>
> In other cases, firms are issuing elaborate buttonhole badges of quite different design to the official badge.
>
> A druggist's assistant several years over military age showed me an official badge which he had obtained through a friend in one of the local armament works. Today I saw a gentleman between 50 and 60 years of age wearing one of the official badges [...]
>
> It is so easy to obtain a badge that the possession of one is no guarantee that the wearer is not a slacker, so I now leave mine at home.

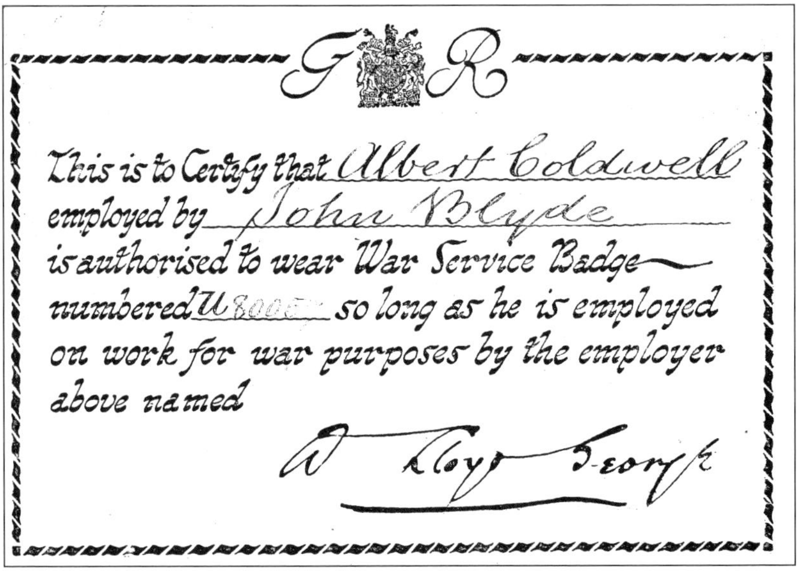
G R

This is to Certify that Albert Coldwell
employed by John Blyde
is authorised to wear War Service Badge
numbered U 800[illegible] so long as he is employed
on work for war purposes by the employer
above named

Standard war service badges were accompanied by a certificate signed by the Minister of Munitions, here for an employee of Sheffield's John Blyde and Company.

similar number of men in potentially appropriate jobs. This process was carried out in Sheffield by the city's Committee on Munitions of War (see Chapter Five), and more than 10,000 new badges and accompanying certificates were issued to local men after recommendations from the committee[41]. The nation was now in an era of de-badging and re-badging.

The aims and operation of war service badges were transformed by the introduction of compulsory call-up from January 1916. Exemptions from call-up were possible for workers on war-essential jobs, and only exempted men were entitled to hold a war service badge. Authorized possession of a badge and certificate thus became essential to avoid being sent to war. Several government departments and committees struggled at different times to define the criteria for badge allocation and to reduce contradictions between policies[42], and across the following months decisions about which types of worker were eligible for a certificate of exemption gradually became more systematic and centrally determined. Badging and de-badging became based on detailed nationwide schedules of protected occupations rather than on the needs of particular companies.

Decisions about whether or not a particular worker was in a protected job were now primarily made by an area's recruiting officer on the basis of national guidelines and lists of jobs[43]. By late-1916, fewer and fewer eligible men were left in industry to be called-up, and decisions about the conscription (and de-badging) of individual workers became more and more controversial. Although accompanied by numerous disputes and complaints, procedures for war service badges stabilized during 1917 and they then remained largely unchanged until November 1918[44].

This brooch for women munition workers was worn in Sheffield by Hannah Roberts. Her husband was in the navy, and she had to find care for her 4-year-old son during the working day.

Across the years, arguments about badging and de-badging had mainly concerned men of military age – those who initially had to choose whether to volunteer or not, or who were later liable for call-up. However, other men also sought war service badges to demonstrate their own contribution. For example, munition workers above military age and younger ones who had volunteered but been rejected as medically unfit wanted other people to know that they had not shirked their duty. In general, wearing a badge could increase public respect, and it could bring practical benefits in preferential treatment on a congested tram network and elsewhere.

Firth's National Projectile Factory at Templeborough used an 'NPF' version of the women's war service brooch.

Women munition workers also wanted a badge. Until late in the war, women could not volunteer for military service, and regulations for the issue of war service badges did not apply to them. In the early days of single-company badges, firms could issue their own version to female as well as male staff. During 1915, as company badges became replaced by standard-issue versions and the number of munition companies employing women increased, their recognition through a badge became widely demanded. The government was concerned about the high financial and administrative cost, but in May 1916 agreed to introduce a women's version. On the reverse this had a pin for attaching to clothes and was in effect a brooch rather than a badge. As well as workers directly making munitions, women employed as clerks, canteen assistants and similar jobs could receive a brooch, whose issue was left entirely to employers without close government supervision. Several thousand Sheffield women received this version of a war service badge.

Release from the colours and 'substitution'

War service badges were part of the attempt to retain munition workers in industry while simultaneously seeking to meet the needs of the army. The munition workforce was also boosted by the arrival of new volunteers[45]. In addition to these civilians, from the beginning of 1915 munition workers who had previously volunteered to join the services were asked to think again and return to their civilian job. Release from the colours in this way could result either from an employer's request or, less frequently, because a soldier had put himself forward to return.

An invitation was sent to almost 10,000 firms around the country to identify essential munition workers now in the army. Requests from applicant companies were assessed by local inspectors, and names of approved individuals were forwarded to the War Office for transmission to unit commanding officers. In addition, some previous munition workers now in army units were approached directly, and in both cases potential returnees were examined by military officers and sometimes by civilian assessors. If deemed appropriate, soldiers were encouraged to offer themselves for munition work within the reserve force. As reservists, they would be committed to active service if needed but otherwise were available for approved civilian jobs.

Employers in Sheffield were required to make their requests for release through the Sheffield Committee for Munitions of War, which checked each application and submitted recommendations to the government. Around 80 percent of the committee's recommendations were accepted, and more than 2,000 soldiers were released for return to the city's factories. By 8 August 1915, the *Sheffield Daily Telegraph* could report that 'a considerable body of ex-soldiers' have been 'fetched home from the army' and 'are now working at their former civilian jobs'.

Other release procedures also developed. From 1916, arrangements were made to retain in industry some conscripted workers who had not yet been sent to a unit. These men could be placed in the Army Reserve and then returned to their previous job or allocated to another munition company. Estimated numbers of men made available through these schemes vary widely between reports, but it is clear that nationally many thousands of enlisted men were provided for industry. For example, Francis Woollen of Sandford Grove Road in Sheffield joined the King's Own Yorkshire Light Infantry in December 1915. He was immediately placed in its reserve battalion and was able to remain in his job as a crane driver for William Jessop and Sons until he was called to active service in

September 1918. In February 1918, Henry Moore, a driller/plater with John Brown and Company, was instead required to undertake shipyard work in the North of Scotland Special Military Area at Scapa Flow. Jabez Woodruffe, a gardener from Greystones Road, was transferred in May 1917 from the Machine Gun Corps into a job at Cammell Laird's Cyclops Works.

Munition workers were also acquired from within the civilian workforce through schemes of 'substitution'. From early 1916, substitution officers were installed in local recruiting offices to identify potential substitute civilians who could replace workers in key jobs. A replaced employee would thus become available either for call-up or could undertake another nationally important job. It was planned that substitute workers should be drawn from non-essential jobs and would include men over military age, those medically unfit and some who had been invalided out of the army. Increasingly, as more and more men were called-up, women also became seen as possible substitutes.

By 1917, special efforts were being made to persuade people to offer themselves in that way. National service committees[46] were established throughout the country to campaign for volunteers to move into munition work and in February 1917, Neville Chamberlain, the briefly serving director-general of national service, addressed meetings in Sheffield and elsewhere to gather support for the scheme. Employers were required to provide regular lists of all their male workers of fighting age, and recruiting offices worked to identify and examine all male workers in companies within their area[47].

Sheffield's recruiting office established a committee charged with distinguishing between skilled, semi-skilled and unskilled men in the city and checking those against the government's current Schedule of Protected Occupations. Many protected workers defined by the committee as skilled or semi-skilled were granted certificates of exemption from call-up, but all others were viewed as replaceable by a substitute. Ex-soldiers were also sought. Arthur Woollen of Newman Road had enlisted in September 1914 but was invalided out in January 1916 and placed on the local list of possible substitutes. He then returned to his previous job at Meadowhall Iron Works, working as a moulder with John Crowley and Company. This firm also received several other ex-servicemen at different times within the national substitution scheme.

Although the number of workers was increased in these ways, the substitution process was slow and cumbersome as documents about each individual had to pass between up to eight offices in three different government departments. In addition, many replacements were less than successful in their new job. Perhaps unaccustomed to manual work or medically unfit in some respect, individuals introduced as substitutes into munition work were often criticized by managers and new colleagues alike as unable to make a full contribution.

In what became the final year of war, the need for more troops became desperate and manufacturing goals had to give way to military requirements. In early 1918, a 'clean cut' removed nearly all previous exemptions from men under 25, and a new Military Service Act in April 1918 set the general age limit for conscription as high as 50, with slight variation between occupations and military units. Most previous essential-job protection was cancelled and, in many cases, a company's entire male workforce of military age was medically examined[48]. In Sheffield's Corn Exchange it became common for sets of up to 100 men to be processed through a sequence of five examining doctors, and large numbers of medically acceptable workers were called-up irrespective of the importance of their job. An individual's medical category now became even more significant to him and his family since that determined whether or not he would be conscripted. Companies had to fill more and more vacant positions in some way, and dilution of the nation's workforce became widespread. That gradual shift and the expanding role of women will be examined in the next chapter.

CHAPTER 3

Arming the Troops 2: Dilution, women and concerns for health

As more and more workers moved into military service, Sheffield and the rest of Britain experienced a gradual dilution of its labour force – placing a wider range of people in jobs previously reserved for men who were defined as skilled. Time-served craftsmen and their unions had long dominated engineering and related industries, and these groups fought hard to protect their privileged position[49]. However, by 1915 national union officials accepted the country's need for more armaments and in the spring of that year joined with the government to find a way forward. The broad-ranging Munitions of War Act was passed by parliament on 2 July 1915, and in a national agreement of 19 September 1915 several unions agreed to 'assist in the reorganization of the skilled labour employed in government arsenals and controlled establishments, in order that semi-skilled or unskilled labour may be employed on a much more extensive scale'. That process later spread far beyond merely organizations that were owned or controlled by the government.

Through dilution, tradesmen became released for essential munitions work (or later for call-up) on the basis that all or part of their job could be assigned to less skilled workers. Initially, the focus was on wider employment of older or unfit men who were not eligible for military service or on boys below 18, but gradually the introduction of women became common across industry. In the Britain of 100 years ago, that was a very remarkable change.

Diluting the workforce: Women as well as men

From early 1915, steps were taken to identify women who were willing to accept wartime employment. In March of that year, advertisements were placed throughout the country asking volunteers to include their names on a Register of Women for War Service, which was to be maintained by the local labour exchange[50]. More than 1,000 Sheffield women signed up at that point but the majority failed to obtain work. They were widely considered to be unsuited for most jobs – certainly those requiring more than a minimum of skill and physical effort. However, as more and more men left for the army and navy, less skilled individuals of either sex gradually became drawn in as replacement workers. By 1917 and 1918, men and women from outside a trade could move into jobs or parts of jobs that required quite high levels of skill.

Dilution received strong encouragement from the new Ministry of Munitions (created in June 1915) and the government's Women's Employment Committee (formed in November 1915)[51]. Many of the new national factories were explicitly required to employ a substantial number of women, and other firms undertaking munition work were similarly encouraged, often by conditions laid down in government contracts. For example, from the start of 1917 new contracts for smaller types of shells

Several different posters encouraged women to become munition workers.

Another idealized poster urging women to move into munition work.

In 1918, Edward Skinner painted these workers in the city's Cammell Laird and Company.

Women making shells in Sheffield Simplex Motor Company.

included the requirement that 80 percent of operatives must be women. The ministry published a regular *Dilution of Labour Bulletin*, and circulars sent to all controlled establishments frequently urged that more women be employed[52].

Dilution officers were appointed in every area to identify workers who might be released by a company after replacement by a non-conscriptable man or by a woman. In some cases that could involve changing parts of the job, for example by installing lifting tackle or other equipment. Dilution could thus introduce changes in factories' own procedures as well as bringing in more women and a wider range of men. Dilution officers also liaised with local recruiting offices and the local employment exchange to place militarily ineligible men into jobs, and they worked to persuade companies in their area to provide training for a wider range of workers.

Those developments were supported by nationwide activities of the Ministry of Munitions' own training department, and in addition local authority technical schools were expanded to meet war needs and new programmes were offered by colleges and universities. For example, Sheffield Education Department used facilities provided by the university to increase its courses in clerical and commercial subjects and to introduce instruction in basic drawing-office work. Thousands of women in the city attended daytime or evening courses run by that department, which also provided brief introductory classes for (in the words of Council minutes) 'girls and women who have been at home with leisure time on their hands'. Sheffield University introduced training for women in metallurgical analysis and for men in shell turning and lathe work. Commercial providers were also active. De Bear Schools in Fitzalan Square advertised day and evening courses in 'high-speed shorthand, commercial English, business correspondence, touch typewriting, office routine and book-keeping'. They emphasized that 'progressive posts at excellent salaries are easily found for qualified students'.

Display Box 3.1 illustrates some of the very first (1915) changes in Sheffield, and by June 1916 the *Sheffield Daily Independent* had this to say:

> Twelve months ago it was a common remark that women would be of little use in the steel trade [...] This attitude of hostility to women, like scores of other prejudices and traditions, has been swept away under the pressure of war, and at the present time

Display Box 3.1
SHEFFIELD'S WOMEN WORKERS IN 1915

Under the headlines FEMALE LABOUR and DEMAND AND SUPPLY IN SHEFFIELD the *Sheffield Daily Telegraph* of 13 April 1915 illustrated the situation early in the war and displayed some prejudices of the time:

> The Sheffield register of women who are prepared to replace in suitable occupations men who are serving their country in the army or navy now contains over 1,000 names. Many women and girls have already been placed in situations. A considerable number of younger ones are tending light machinery in shops where small tools and metal parts are produced. Owing to these machines being largely automatic, and their output mostly repetitive, this work is easily learned by fairly intelligent girls, and the experiment is proving successful.
>
> The number of girl mechanics is therefore likely to increase. Several local firms have under consideration plans for utilising the services of women during the war in the place of men in various other directions, and some interesting developments may result therefrom.
>
> There is likely to be an unprecedented demand for women typists and clerks, as several of the armament firms and a number of ordinary steel works who have hitherto refused to employ females in their offices are being compelled by circumstances to put aside any prejudices they may have held on the subject. Some have already installed staffs of female clerks, and others are making arrangements to do so at an early date.

Five months later, on 10 August 1915, the *Telegraph* was able to report a strong increase in women working in jobs 'hitherto considered exclusively masculine'. By then the city's workforce included female munition workers, bank clerks, brick-makers, carriage cleaners, gardeners, letter-sorters, mail deliverers, porters, toolmakers and tram conductors; the number of female school-teachers had increased substantially. In the following months, women in Sheffield also found work as car drivers, crane operators, factory police, farm workers, materials inspectors, taxi drivers, tramcar ticket inspectors, and window cleaners. Times had changed very rapidly.

> women and girls [*i.e. females under eighteen*] are performing a thousand and one tasks which it was honestly believed formerly could only be done by men. The adaptability which many of these women have displayed, even to jobs requiring skill and judgment in a high degree, has proved a revelation to managers of works.

Women were also needed as farmworkers to produce food in a time of increasing shortage.

In that year the *Independent* itself, having lost many men to military service, took the unprecedented step of appointing women in some apprentice production roles. One of these, 19-year-old Alice Goodall of Aston Street, Park, was subsequently promoted to head proofreader at the Independent Press – a job that before then had been open only to a qualified male member of the Typographical Association.

Nationally between 1914 and 1918, the number of women workers in all occupations grew by more than half, with greatest increases during 1915 and 1916. A few industries, such as textiles and clothing, saw a reduction in female workers as their trade declined, and the number of domestic servants also went down. On the other hand, the metals industry and the civil service both came to employ more than three times as many women as before the war and the transport sector also took on large numbers[53]. Railway companies took on female cleaners and ticket inspectors and, by 1918, Sheffield Corporation Tramways employed around 1,000 women as conductors and cleaners. Other jobs newly available to women in Sheffield and elsewhere included window-cleaning and letter-sorting and delivering. Additionally, we should not forget the expansion of nursing roles, women's contribution as non-combatant troops[54], and the vast amount of voluntary work undertaken by women.

From mid-1915, across the country around 1,000 (usually middle-class) women became trained and employed as police constables. Some of those worked in the government's national factories and others served the public directly. Sheffield City Council agreed to appoint two female constables only at the end of 1917, and these patrolled parts of the city

Female tram conductors were appointed for the first time in the city. They eventually numbered more than 600.

Women were recruited in large numbers to deliver mail around the city.

Nineteen-year-old Edith Ashley (to the left) lived in Burton Road and worked for Cammell Laird.

considered likely to threaten women workers. Increasingly, they also acted as investigators and court witnesses in legal cases involving women or children. By 1927, the city had three women constables.

Turning to munition production itself, the national number of female munition employees came close to a million, and in particular the government-owned national factories became a major employer of women. By 1918, those had nearly 200,000 female workers, around 60 percent of their overall 350,000 total[55]. Factory work required suitable clothing and some firms provided overalls. In other cases, clothing had to be purchased and (for instance) John Walsh's department store in July 1918 advertised 'the most attractive' shades and styles of overalls, caps and gloves – 'what a woman wears when she goes a'munitioning'.

In all factories women undertook tasks that were repetitive and unskilled, as did many men. But there are also accounts of women

Three of the several thousand female munition workers at Thomas Firth and Sons posing in 1917.

Names are not available for most of the munition workers appearing in photographs, but in this case the picture is of Ada Roberts, who worked at Firth's.

These women held responsible positions as inspectors in Firth's national factory, but their supervisors were men.

Sheffield's wartime factories often employed young girls and boys. Adelaide Morrell (seated) had been born as recently as June 1903.

acquiring considerable job expertise and responsibility. Heavy manual work was restricted to men, and women were also excluded from certain other positions. For instance, in June 1918 the head of Sheffield Tramways explained that women were not taken on as drivers because 'the steep gradients in Sheffield required nerve and skill'. Other reports make it clear that women often experienced prejudice in their new occupation[56].

A 1916 description of Vickers' Holme Lane works indicated that 'the "lasses" workshop, which is about half the size of the works, is now in full swing [...] Not only have women and girls been brought in as shell cleaners, gaugers, checkers, etc., but in several cases they are working men's lathes [...] In our own shop, I have seen men have to give up their lathes and before doing so instruct a lass how to go on with the operation. Not very pleasant, but it has to be done, and one by one the men are disappearing [*i.e., after being called-up*], leaving a lass as successor'[57].

The introduction of dilution – both male and female – was not trouble-free. In addition to the inevitable unease about change and many false starts, established workers' objections led to frequent conflicts. One issue arose from the segmentation and division of skilled jobs so that less complex parts could be undertaken by unskilled workers. That change sometimes left skilled men with only the more difficult and variable activities, so that they were now paid on a timework rate rather than by the more lucrative piecework. In those circumstances, the novice worker might undertake easier sections of the job and could sometimes earn considerable piecework money[58]. Furthermore, skilled men might be required to provide instruction to the new workers and some objected to this imposition. More generally, many skilled men in the Amalgamated Society of Engineers and other craft unions felt threatened by a loss of traditional privileges. Some were tired from months of working long hours, and morale may sometimes have been affected by repeated claims in parts of the press that workers were under-performing because of idleness and drunkenness (see Display Box 3.2). From 1915, a surge of union demands led to some extremely damaging strikes.

The Munitions of War Act of July 1915 made strikes in controlled establishments illegal, and for senior trade union officials it was important to work only within the law. However, that was not always the case at company level, and locally elected shop stewards now became increasingly influential in Sheffield and other centres[59]. Some chose to take illegal strike action despite that being opposed by the leaders of their own union. Major stoppages occurred in the South Wales coalfield, Clydeside shipyards, Lancashire engineering works and in many individual firms around the country. Some disputes were mainly about wages, but in many cases male workers would not accept their company's decision to allocate women to previous male jobs or objected to the call-up of a particular colleague[60]. For the nation as a whole, the number of days lost through strikes, which had declined after August 1914, rose steadily from mid-1915 – and so did the number of dilutees.

Display Box 3.2
ALCOHOL AND MUNITION WORKERS

During the spring of 1915 sections of the press and certain politicians insisted that the country's ammunition shortage had arisen because workers' drunkenness led to poor attendance and timekeeping. Temperance societies and individual protesters joined in, writing letters to the press, organizing public meetings, and demanding that all sales of alcohol should be banned. The Shipbuilding Employers' Federation claimed that 80 percent of avoidable lost time in shipyards was due to drinking: 'the call of the public house stifles the call of duty.'

The campaign received encouragement from the chancellor of the exchequer's widely-publicized statement on 29 March 1915 that 'we are fighting Germany, Austria and drink, and as far as I can see the greatest of these deadly foes is drink'. On 5 April, newspapers in Sheffield and elsewhere published full-page advertisements asking readers to send to the chancellor an anti-alcohol letter together with the printed campaigning form provided. Those were submitted in huge numbers from all around the country.

Although some cases of workers' drink-related absenteeism or misbehaviour were reported in Sheffield in this period, the managing directors of John Brown and Thomas Firth and Sons wrote jointly to local newspapers that their workers' attendance and performance were 'most commendable'. 'There is no ground of complaint in this direction.' From the workers' standpoint, the president of the Vickers' River Don Works Approved Society seemed to recognize a problem by arguing that the 'greater proportion of slacking' was caused by bad housing. 'Let Mr Lloyd George [*then chancellor of the exchequer*] spend a seaside holiday in Scotland Street for a month – he'd need to take solace in the Green Pig.'

National persuasion to reduce alcohol consumption included a promise in April 1915 by King George V that no alcohol would be consumed in the royal household until the war was over. Lord Kitchener, the secretary of state for war, and other prominent individuals took the 'King's Pledge', but the House of Commons preferred to keep its bars open.

Working conditions and health

As the government struggled to provide a steady supply of armaments and equipment, an underlying set of issues gradually came to the fore – how to maintain the health and effectiveness of the workforce. The Ministry of Munitions combined with the Home Office, which administered the Factory Acts and associated legislation, to learn about and reduce the harmful effects of long working hours and poor working conditions.

These issues came under the spotlight after concern in the summer of 1915 about bad timekeeping in some munitions factories. Frequent absences or lateness for work were widely reported to be damaging the nation's output of shells, guns and ships. The ministry's first response in July 1915 was to require controlled establishments to post rules of work in prominent positions, demanding sobriety and good behaviour, obedience to legal requirements, and diligent attendance at the specified times[61]. Perhaps unsurprisingly, this simplistic approach had little impact and attention turned to possible causes of good or bad timekeeping.

Hours of work Soon after the war had started, and especially in periods of greatest military need, munition factories were required to continue production without pause for most or all of the week[62]. It seemed likely to some observers that problems could arise because workers were spending excessive amounts of time and effort at the workplace. Having to carry out manual work for long periods every day, or perhaps during the night, might contribute to poor levels of attendance and timekeeping and also to the build-up of fatigue and reduced performance.

In 1914, there were no legal limits for male workers' hours (and that remained the case), but women and young people under 18 were officially restricted to sixty hours a week in most industries and were excluded from Sunday or night work. Small changes occurred in the legal maxima for women and young people in 1915 and 1916, but the restrictions were widely ignored. Workers themselves regarded sixty or seventy hours a week as normal, and were sometimes at their job for longer than that. Systematic overtime was usual, and reports of eighty or more hours weekly in the factory were common[63]. In some munition factories women as well as men were present for twelve-hour shifts, in addition to coping with tram or other journeys before and after those times. A meal break was taken within a shift.

Soon after the Ministry of Munitions was formed in June 1915, it joined with the Home Office to establish a Health of Munitions Workers

Committee to examine these and similar issues[64]. Investigations and experiments in several national factories and controlled establishments, including William Hutton and Company in Sheffield, soon provided clear evidence that working more than sixty hours a week for long periods did not further increase output and in some cases actually reduced it. Working on Sundays in addition to a full week was found to be harmful in the same way.

However, the government's attempts to persuade industry to remain within a moderate limit, considered to be around sixty hours a week, were widely unsuccessful. Regulations about the hours and night work of women and young persons were often ignored, and trade unions objected strongly to any suggestions that would reduce workers' pay. Overtime work received up to 50 percent additional payment and Sunday might provide double pay. Within government itself opinions were divided, especially in periods when high output was particularly needed and additional hours seemed an obvious way to help. During the spring of 1916, the Ministry of Munitions collected and published evidence from controlled establishments (including 187 in Sheffield) showing that on average health and attendance both improved after the abolition of Sunday work. However, military needs continued to be extremely pressing, and working time in many munitions factories did not decline greatly before 1917. From May of that year Sunday work in controlled establishments was banned, with some exceptions, and from then on weekend and overtime work gradually become less common[65]. However, hours remained greatly above the levels we consider acceptable nowadays, and at no point were weekly limits prescribed for men.

Canteens The Ministry of Munitions also worked to improve other aspects of factory life. Many changes were driven by the need to integrate the growing number of women workers into settings that had previously been exclusively for men. In December 1915, a welfare section was established in the Ministry with B. Seebohm Rowntree as Director[66]. Over the next three years this campaigned actively for the establishment of factory canteens, the employment of medical staff within companies, and the availability of women's rest rooms. One female munitions worker wrote later about her experiences: 'There was sometimes not even a place to hang one's coat and nowhere to sit and eat one's sandwiches [...] In my last job we ate our midnight meal in the cloak room, and any injury was dealt with by the foreman. As I worked at night and my foreman was always on the day shift, it meant that if I got a steel chip in my eye during the night I would have to wait till the morning for him to remove it with his penknife'[67].

Early in the war employers rarely provided any facilities for meals. On dayshifts, some wives and children would wait outside a works for husbands and fathers to emerge in the 'dinner hour' and pick up food for eating inside. Otherwise, and on night shifts, a meal had to be taken in for eating in a workshop. A 1915 account of Vickers' Holme Lane works reports: 'there is no mess room and we have to fix up where we can [...] We sit on packing cases or planks propped up on chunks of machinery or in any odd corner we can find while eating, and that is the only time we do sit'[68]. However, before long it became usual to provide at least a separate room with cooking equipment, and in larger works canteens were introduced to prepare and serve hot meals[69].

By the middle of 1915, a national Munition Workers' Canteens Committee had been formed by Lady Lawrence and other women of high social standing. This offered assistance to munition firms (known to include Vickers in Sheffield) to establish and operate works canteens. Across the country facilities were introduced and managed by local voluntary groups such as the YMCA, the YWCA, the Salvation Army and nearby churches, and many received assistance from the Ministry of Munitions. For example, the ministry helped works and community canteens to obtain supplies of food in 1917 and 1918 after additional restrictions had been imposed.

Display Box 3.3 describes some new canteens for munition workers in Sheffield. Two were operated by the city's YMCA, receiving very public support from prominent citizens and national dignitaries. In July 1916, great excitement was caused by a brief inspection of each YMCA canteen by Princess Victoria of Schleswig-Holstein, accompanied by Countess Fitzwilliam and no less than four titled ladies, an admiral and one knight of the realm. British society was still very hierarchical[70].

Vickers' Swimming Club organized activities for the company's young male workers.

Display Box 3.3
SHEFFIELD'S MUNITION CANTEENS

The first canteen for munitions workers in Sheffield was opened in the middle of 1915 within Vickers, and others soon followed. In addition to individual companies, two canteens were operated by the YMCA, initially financed by the National YMCA Council and operated by local volunteers. For those, the Duke of Norfolk provided sites rent-free.

Arthur J. Ward of T. W. Ward Ltd was appointed chairman of a local organizing committee, and in initial charge of the city's two YMCA canteens were ladies of high social standing – the lady mayoress (Mrs O. C. Wilson) and Countess Fitzwilliam assisted by Mrs L. Burrows (wife of the Bishop of Sheffield). The first one opened on 20 October 1915 in Scott Road off Carlisle Street East. Staffed by a lady supervisor and up to twelve unpaid helpers, it was open from 5 am to 10 pm with pauses during the day. As well as buying sandwiches, pies, buns and other food and non-alcoholic drink, workers could bring their own meals to be reheated on a gas stove. The canteen was very successful, but by early 1918 several nearby companies had introduced their own canteens and the YMCA's Scott Road facility was no longer needed.

In the spring of 1916, a second YMCA canteen for munition workers was opened in Leeds Road, Tinsley. With heating from two central stoves and dining tables covered with brown linoleum, this served hot food such as sausage and potatoes and rice pudding 'at very reasonable prices'. However, the Leeds Road canteen was closed in late 1917 as the number of customers declined. At about the same time a separate canteen was opened specially for women workers in the parish rooms of St Anne's Church in Hoyle Street. Run by the Sheffield Advisory Committee on Women's War Employment, this provided meals and snacks, and (like the others) had a volunteer female staff.

The government could most readily influence its own establishments – the national factories. For example, the national projectile factory at Templeborough introduced a large women's canteen as well as a main canteen and a staff canteen. The Women's Canteen could serve around 2,000 meals in a single sitting. The privately owned controlled establishments were also pressed to improve meal facilities, and many received persuasive visits from ministry officials. Details about wartime canteens in specific private firms are scarce[71], but publications at the time make it clear that they were widely regarded as important in the city. Instead of a canteen, many Sheffield companies installed a basic mess room, providing facilities away from the workplace for the heating and consumption of brought-in food.

Welfare supervisors The ministry's welfare section was also influential in the appointment and training of female welfare supervisors to assist women and girls and, in some firms, young male workers[72]. Welfare supervisors, sometimes called lady superintendents, became obligatory in national factories with their high proportion of women, and they were pressed by the government on the larger controlled establishments. Women in this entirely new role were part of management and could be involved in female appointments, health, welfare and feeding arrangements, and perhaps in recreational activities. They might contribute to a wide range of non-technical management decisions about women in the factory, for instance after investigating a female worker's difficulties with a foreman or some background personal issues affecting her poor timekeeping[73].

This could be a difficult job, especially since neither the individual nor the company had previous experience of it. Welfare supervisors' middle-class backgrounds and manners in a class-based society may sometimes have been accompanied by an emphasis on moral guidance, and some

These workers at Firth's National Projectile Factory include welfare supervisor Beatrice Roberts, wearing a white blouse on the front row.

reports illustrate the suspicion with which they could be viewed. The ministry developed and sponsored training schemes for this new role and by 1918 around 1,000 welfare supervisors were in post nationally. Firth's National Projectile Factory at Templeborough employed four such ladies in addition to Mrs S. K. Davies, the chief welfare supervisor[74].

What happened to the Ministry of Munitions?

The end of the ministry occurred soon after the war, as had initially been proposed. After considerable work to terminate contracts, close down offices and so on, formal closure was on 31 March 1921. The ministry had achieved enormous increases in the production of armaments and other items and it substantially shifted the composition, expertise and behaviour of the nation's workforce. As a major centre of munitions manufacture, Sheffield was especially affected by these developments.

By the end of the war, Britain had produced almost 250,000,000 shells, some 3,500,000 rifles and 250,000 machine-guns, about 36,000 artillery guns and howitzers, 7,000,000 steel helmets, more than 40,000 aeroplane engines, millions and millions of rifle cartridges, and a huge number of other essential items. Of course, major credit must go to the more than 3,000,000 workers in the country's munition factories, but central co-ordination and direction from the Ministry of Munitions was essential.

As it took on a wide variety of additional tasks, the ministry spawned many new departments, requisitioned buildings across the country, and came to employ around 65,000 staff[75]. In addition, its own national factories directly employed around 350,000 people, more than half of whom were women. The ministry's ten area offices contained engineers, finance officers, labour specialists and transport officers, as well as a large (mainly female) clerical and administrative staff. Its inspection department, with offices in Sheffield and elsewhere, checked a factory's incoming raw materials and chemicals, monitored part-completed components and finished items, and assisted with new designs and manufacturing procedures[76]. By 1918, staff of its steel superintendent organized, with help from a committee of managers, the quantity of supplies to be made available to every principal firm in the city, and a priority advisory committee similarly allocated materials to local cutlers.

The Ministry of Munitions evolved in a sometimes confused manner, as government policies and military needs changed repeatedly. In the later words of a writer who was closely involved in many of the industrial developments, 'munitions policy was anything but coherent: it was a series of fits and starts, improvisations and expedients, out of which an organization gradually emerged.' The whole period was: 'a whirling succession of conferences and committees, understandings and misunderstandings, hurry and scurry in the midst of which the work somehow got done. "When in doubt, create a committee" was certainly the first precept of the time; and the second was "When a committee becomes troublesome, don't dissolve it, for that leads to further trouble. Gradually take away its functions, and let it die of inanition in its own time". The path of war on the home front was strewn with discarded committees painfully dying and not quite sure whether they were still alive'[77].

The phrase 'British muddling through' comes to mind. Alternatively, perhaps the process showed management flexibility of a high order.

CHAPTER 4

Arming the Troops 3: Sheffield gets to work

> If the battered shield of Prussian militarism lies rusted and rent on the ground, you will find on it the dent of Sheffield steel.

So proclaimed Prime Minister David Lloyd George on receiving the Freedom of Sheffield in October 1919. Furthermore:

> If anyone should ask you in this city what Sheffield did in the Great War, I will tell you your answer. Tell them to visit the battlefields of France and Flanders now; look at the torn wire and the shattered entrenchments of the enemy, and you will see what it is that Sheffield has done in the Great War. You not merely equipped the armies, but you equipped the navies of Britain with the guns of Sheffield. The armour of Sheffield is what helped the British Navy. It was with this the British Navy swept the seas and kept the seas. That is what enabled the Allies above all to win.[78]

As this implies, life in Sheffield during the war was dominated by a massive expansion of the city's armaments trade[79]. Tens of thousands of workers and their families found themselves part of a huge mobilization of effort and skill. Already at the end of 1914, the *Sheffield Daily Telegraph* saw it like this:

> With the exception of clothing for the men and saddlery for their horses, there seems scarcely a requirement of the war which Britain

> and her Allies are not looking to Sheffield to supply in some form or another [...] From a bayonet to an officer's sword, from a rifle barrel to the largest calibre gun, from the finished parts of a dashing scout boat to those of a super-Dreadnought, from an aeroplane dart to a shell weighing – never mind how much. Sheffield makes them all, besides many other things, from military workshops on wheels to camp kitchens, from thin bullet-proof hut steel to armour-plate many inches thick, from torpedo-net wire to net for big guns, from transport waggons to armoured motor-cars, from stretchers to ambulance carriages, and from hoop iron for military packages to horse-shoe iron. Sheffield makes the razor placed in the soldier's kit, the knife, fork and spoon he carries with him into the trenches, and the combination pocket-knife without which he would be at a complete loss, and also provides similar articles for the blue-jacket and marine. The Allied governments are coming here for entrenching tools. And the high-speed steel so essential in the production of much of the heavy war material is, of course, a well-known speciality of this district. For these things the nation has looked to Sheffield, and has not looked in vain.

Earlier chapters have described the nation's struggle to meet two incompatible needs – enough troops for the forces and enough workers for the factories. The country started the war with a small army whose munition requirements were modest and generally achievable. But, as troop numbers increased and the conflict turned into a battle between ever-more-powerful destructive machines, the demand for weapons and other items surged beyond anyone's anticipation. The city's factories and workers eventually met the challenge, but often with considerable difficulty[80].

Sheffield's war-related production came from five sorts of company – the established armament works, the government's new national factories, firms now making munitions, companies making other war-needed items, and firms supplying the other manufacturers with their equipment and materials. From 1915, many of these companies became designated as 'controlled establishments' (see Chapter Two), and estimates at the time, which varied between themselves, suggest that there were eventually around 350 controlled companies in the city.

Sheffield firms known to have received government orders in this period are listed in Appendix One at the end of the book, but no doubt others remain to be discovered. In addition to undertaking contracts with the British government, some companies also worked to meet orders from allied countries like France, India and Russia. Many needed to install new plant or machinery, including more than 100 new furnaces of different kinds, and the City Council granted planning permission for several thousand new buildings and factory extensions. Projectiles were not filled with explosive materials in any Sheffield factories. That particularly dangerous process was undertaken elsewhere in the country.

Sheffield's established armament firms

Munitions production in Britain had long been concentrated in a small number of ordnance factories controlled by the government[81], together with a few private companies. The latter included Armstrong Whitworth in Newcastle, the Coventry Ordnance Works, the Birmingham Small Arms Company, and several in Sheffield – John Brown and Company, Cammell Lairds, Thomas Firth and Sons, Hadfields, and Vickers. All of these became controlled establishments in the middle of 1915.

John Brown and Company was by now one of the world's largest producers of steel for armour plating and other uses. In addition to its Savile Street Atlas Works, it owned several collieries and iron mines and a substantial shipyard on Clydeside in Scotland. The company was thus able to construct entire battleships and other vessels with steels, and components it had itself produced. John Brown also owned part of Belfast's Harland and Wolff shipyard and had a controlling interest in Sheffield's Thomas Firth and Sons, it was a joint owner of the Coventry Ordnance Works, and in 1916 acquired a share of a steel works and collieries in Scotland for additional supplies to the Clydeside yards.

John Brown and Company worked intensely throughout the war[82]. More than balancing a reduced level of civilian work, large quantities of steel and armour plate were produced for military use in shipyards and companies around the country. The bulk of output was for the Admiralty, and a remarkable number of warships were assembled in the firm's Clydeside yard. Thirty-five destroyers and four battleships were produced, including the battleship *Hood*, which for many years was the world's largest military vessel and was eventually sunk in the Second World War. Forgings for these vessels were made in Sheffield in large numbers, and other products included engine crankshafts, armour plate, and components of guns and projectiles of many types. In addition, substantial deliveries were made to British and other countries' railway systems (crucial in wartime) of wheels, axles, springs, buffers and other products.

Bending armour plate at Cammell Laird's Cyclops Works in 1918.

Like other armament manufacturers during the war, John Brown and Company expanded its Sheffield works and installed new equipment and machinery. A rolling mill was opened in 1915, electric arc furnaces in 1916, new hammer shops in 1917, and additional forging and tempering shops in 1918. The composition of several important steels was improved, and production reached record levels. Published estimates suggest that the company had around 3,500 employees in Sheffield in 1916.

Also in the East End of the city were two plants owned by Cammell Laird and Company – Cyclops Works off Savile Street, and Grimesthorpe Works off Carlisle Street East. Additionally, the firm operated a steel works in Penistone and shipyards in Birkenhead, constructed a new national factory in Nottingham, and was (with John Brown) a part-owner of the Coventry Ordnance Works. For a souvenir brochure prepared for a royal visit in late 1918[83], its many products were described in the way set out in Display Box 4.1. These and other materials contributed to the company shipyards' wartime output of eight cruisers, sixteen flotilla leaders and eleven submarines.

As well as armaments, Cammell Laird before the war also produced a wide range of steel products for railway and other non-military uses. That side of the company's work declined after 1914, but overall the company's business flourished. Sales and the number of employees in Sheffield both

Display Box 4.1
CAMMELL LAIRD'S CYCLOPS AND GRIMESTHORPE WORKS IN 1918

The breadth of the company's activity is illustrated by these excerpts from a Cammell Laird souvenir brochure:

THE CYCLOPS STEEL AND IRON WORKS
These works, where the Registered Office of the Company is situate, cover an area of twelve acres. They are intersected by the Midland Railway Company's line, and have the advantage of their own private sidings.

A large part of the works is confined to the treatment and finishing of armour plates for ships, tanks, cars etc. The remainder is devoted to the manufacture of railway axles and other forgings, rolling spring and other steels, crucible tool steels and files and rasps.

THE GRIMESTHORPE STEEL AND ORDNANCE WORKS
These works [...] adjoin the Midland Railway's line and cover 26 acres. They embrace the manufacture of Siemens-Martin steel on the open hearth principle [...] The departments consist of:

STEEL FOUNDRY for manufacture of ship and general castings of the heaviest classes for marine and other engineering purposes, also mining castings.
FORGING PRESS SHOPS with presses ranging from 1200 to 4000 tons capacity for manufacture of the heaviest forgings for armour, guns and mountings, air vessels for torpedoes, marine shafting, turbine drums and other weighty forgings for general engineering purposes.
MACHINE SHOPS for roughing and finishing castings and forgings of the heaviest classes.
TYRE PLANTS for manufacture of locomotive, carriage and wagon tyres and angle rings for boiler purposes.
ARMOUR PLATE MILL for rolling armour.
SPRING SHOPS for manufacture of all classes of railway, gun recoil and other springs.
PROJECTILE DEPARTMENT for production of all types and calibres.
IRON FOUNDRY for manufacture of iron castings for the company's own works.

Heavy shell production at Cammell Laird's Grimesthorpe Works.

doubled between 1914 and 1918[84], and substantial extensions were made to plant and equipment. By 1918, Cammell Laird employed around 5,000 people in the city, around a third of whom were women. As part of the government's programme of national factories, the company drew on its Sheffield expertise to create and operate a government-owned projectile factory in Nottingham.

Another major employer in the city was Thomas Firth & Sons, with almost 3,000 workers in 1914. A producer of steel and steel products of many kinds, it was particularly noted for its armour-piercing shells, which had met rigorous penetration tests mounted by the British Admiralty and other countries. During the war, these and other shells were produced in huge numbers and the company also turned out a colossal number of forgings and other products[85].

Based in Tinsley, Firths installed new furnaces, presses, workshops and offices, and by 1918 its workforce had increased to around 8,000. Excluding its new national factory, the company employed 2,500 women in 1918 compared to a few hundred at the start of the war. Its military castings and forgings included many components for naval guns and mountings and discs for torpedoes. Engine parts and shafts were produced for well over 100 ships, and the company also made aeroplane cylinders and crankshafts as well as other components for British and French aircraft. At the same time it produced an enormous quantity of special steel for other manufacturers' use. The company's output of drills in 1918 was more than seven times that of 1914, and a wide range of other tools was produced – cutters, reamers, saws and war-needed items by the million.

In 1913, Firths' employee Harry Brearley had invented 'rustless steel', soon renamed 'stainless steel'. This was taken up by several other Sheffield companies and during the war the military value of its strength and resistance to corrosion became apparent. Stainless steel was particularly valuable in aeroplane engines, and from September 1917 its use in the cutlery trade was prohibited to allow full application to military use. Firths continued refining the production of stainless steel and turned out substantial quantities.

Overall, the sales of Thomas Firth and Sons, excluding the national projectile factory, increased around fourfold during the war. Great expansion also occurred in a fourth Sheffield armament manufacturer – Hadfields. Already in 1905 this company had described its steel foundry as 'the most extensive in the world', and its many products included armour plates and shells for the British and other navies. In addition to its original Hecla Works in Attercliffe, a second Hadfield site in Tinsley was known as the East Hecla Works.

Some of the many thousands of shells made at Hadfields.

During the war, Hadfields installed a new shell-making plant and expanded many of its processes and buildings[86]. As previously, the company produced armour-piercing projectiles and steel castings and forgings for a wide variety of military and non-military purposes, and it supplied steel in great quantity for processing by other manufacturers. Some of the company's steel was used for the army's steel helmet, which was introduced in the first part of 1916. The company also operated another of Sheffield's national factories, and by the end of the war its sales had increased fivefold. Hadfield's then employed more than 10,000 people, including about 1,000 women. A 1919 summary of wartime munitions output is shown in Display Box 4.2.

Display Box 4.2
HADFIELD'S 1919 LIST OF WARTIME PRODUCTS

Under the heading 'Supplied to the British Government During the War', Hadfields listed the following, apparently from the national factory it operated as well as the company's own works. In addition to this government work, steel and steel products were supplied to many different manufacturing companies, and in 1917 an order for armour-piercing shells was obtained from the American Navy:

Three and a half million projectiles, including armour-piercing shell, chiefly of large calibres 12-inch, 13.5-inch, 14-inch, 15-inch and 18-inch.
250 complete guns and howitzers up to 8-inch calibre.
700 guns up to 8-inch calibre relined.
3,500 gun tubes of large calibre.
3,400 trench howitzers, 6-inch calibre.
Also many thousands of gun parts, including breech bushes, cradle forgings, spring cases etc., etc.
7,000 tons of Hadfield's RESISTA steel for helmets and bodyguards, representing nearly 4,000,000 helmets.
Over 100,000 bullet-proof plates for tanks.
Tens of thousands of ERA (Trade Mark) manganese steel links, and RESISTA steel gear wheels and pinions.
4,000 tons of ERA (Trade Mark) steel for aeroplane requirements, including crankshafts, connecting rods, propeller bosses, bushes and other articles.

Like several other Sheffield companies, Hadfield's government work was for the Admiralty as well as the Ministry of Munitions. Administrative dealings with those distant bureaucracies were not always straightforward and payment was sometimes extremely late. Among the many complaints made by the company is a letter from its secretary to the accountant general of the British Navy in June 1918. The writer had: 'the honour to refer to [the company's] letter of the 24th May, and very much regret[s] we have not been favoured with a reply, nor yet have any of our outstanding claims been paid. We would again point out that the claims in question [...] have been duly certified as correct by the Naval Ordnance Officer [...] and as we have been in correspondence on this subject since the 12th December last [*i.e., six months ago*], without having been favoured with a single reply, we have now to request that the claims may receive immediate attention and be paid without delay.'

The city's largest armament firm was Vickers, with more than 10,000 Sheffield employees by 1916[87]. The company had moved beyond its Sheffield origins to become one of the nation's biggest employers with considerable international trade. By 1914, it operated a shipyard in Barrow and owned or part-owned several steel and engineering companies, as well as having subsidiaries or financial involvement in at least a dozen different countries. Vickers had for many years been successful as a producer of steel, ships and armour plate, and it had recently moved into the design and production of aeroplanes and of weapons for use in land warfare[88]. In

Posing for a photograph at the Admiralty's Inspection Laboratory in the university.

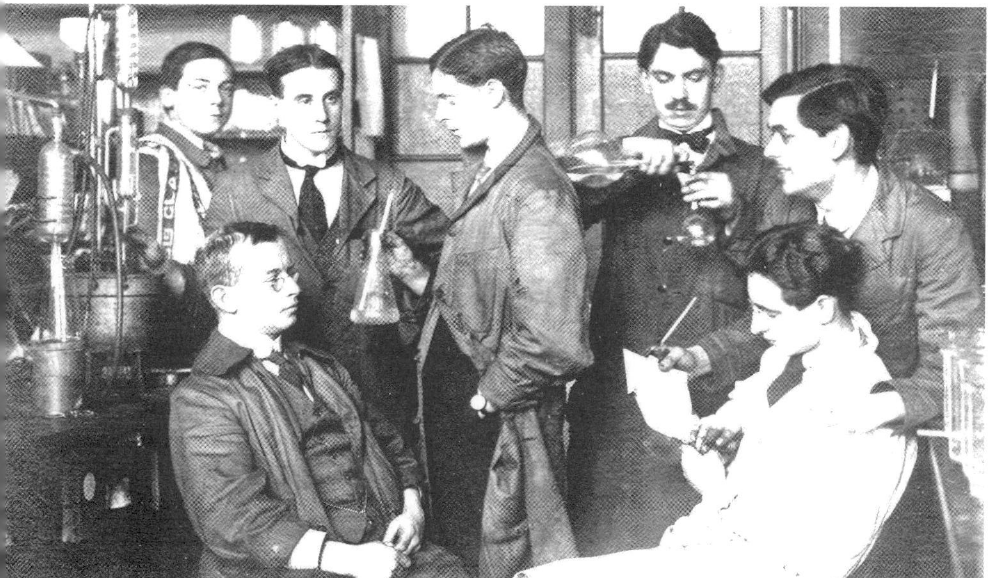

addition to increased contracts with the Admiralty, the firm was almost immediately asked by the War Office to produce a large number of artillery guns at great speed. By 1915, it had also introduced a new form of small gun required by conditions on the Western Front – the trench mortar – which was produced in large numbers.

Across the war as a whole, Vickers delivered from all its sites to the British government around seventy ships and fifty submarines, 2,500 artillery guns, 100,000 machine-guns and 5,500 aeroplanes. Its River Don Works in Brightside Lane and its Holme Lane (Hillsborough) factory produced hundreds of thousands of shrapnel and high-explosive shells. From the middle of 1915, women worked on the lighter shells, although supervision was (as usual) provided by men.

One of these supervisors was Septimus Bennett, who was promoted to chargehand a year after moving to Sheffield (see Display Box 4.3). His diary and letters for the period[89] describe the shell-finishing department of Vickers' Holme Lane works, where he became responsible on each shift for two boys and six women (some of whom were married – all referred to as 'girls'). The department primarily handled 18-pounder (mainly shrapnel) shells, but from time to time had to stop working because of machine breakdowns, non-arrival of rough shells from the company's Brightside works, lack of gas from the city's supplier, or union-management disputes in other departments. For most of the war, day-shift hours (with breaks for meals) were from 6 am to 5 pm, and the night-shift

Among the armaments produced by Vickers' River Don Works were these gun barrels made in 1917.

ran from 5 pm to 6 am. Alternate weeks were on days and nights, and Sunday working was usual in the earlier years.

In addition to their own work, the city's five established armament producers also helped other companies move into munitions work, for instance by providing advice about modifications to plant and processes. They carried out practical experiments to develop new materials and weapons, greatly improving several high-speed and alloy steels.

Display Box 4.3
SEPTIMUS BENNETT, ARTIST AND VICKERS SHELL WORKER

Septimus Bennett, who described himself as a 'ceramic craftsman', operated before the war from a pottery studio in Hanley, Staffordshire. His business suffered in the autumn of 1914, and he decided to contribute to the national effort by working on munitions in Sheffield. Aged 38, he left his family behind and arrived in the city at the end of May 1915. After a week's introductory training in lathe-work at the university, he obtained a shell-finishing job at Vickers' Holme Lane works in Hillsborough, lodging with a family in Malin Bridge.

Septimus (the name indicates that he was the family's seventh child) recorded in his diary many aspects of Sheffield life and work, and he often sent details to his brother Arnold for inclusion (without mentioning Septimus or Sheffield) in a newspaper or magazine article. In return, Arnold provided financial help to Septimus and his family throughout the war. Arnold Bennett was by then an internationally-celebrated author and his accounts of munition work in an unnamed factory received considerable public attention. His simultaneous attachment to the government's War Propaganda Bureau and subsequently the Ministry of Information was not made public.

As well as operating his own machine, Septimus was appointed a chargehand in June 1916 and described problems in organizing the work of his mainly female team. By 1918, the company's shell-production levels had declined considerably and many shell-workers were laid off. Septimus himself resigned a week after the armistice and returned to his family in Staffordshire. After the war, he found it difficult to regain his earlier pottery success and became increasingly unwell, dying at the age of 49 in 1926.

National factories in the city

However, the nation clearly needed armaments beyond those that could be made by the few established firms. From the middle of 1915, the Ministry of Munitions established more than 200 'national factories' around the country. Although owned by the government these were usually managed on a profit-making basis by local companies, and three of Sheffield's traditional armament firms took part in this programme. Firths and Hadfields constructed new factories in Sheffield, and Cammell Lairds took advantage of available space and workers 45 miles away in Nottingham. In addition, two small national factories operated in the city for a few months towards the end of the war.

In September 1915, Thomas Firth and Sons undertook to erect, equip and operate a national projectile factory on agricultural land rented from Earl Fitzwilliam in Templeborough. A forging shop to provide rough shells for machining in the new Templeborough works was erected about a mile away next to the company's current site in Tinsley. Although the forging shop was also built at government expense it was additionally used in Firths' other work, so its staffing and operations were undertaken by the company itself rather than as part of the national factory. The forge's workforce was entirely male.

Nearly 90 percent of Firth's national factory employees were women, and the factory had its own female police force.

The Templeborough works was erected very speedily, opening in January 1916 well ahead of any other national projectile factory[90]. Rough shells from the forge at Tinsley were delivered by steam wagons, and across the war more than 2,500,000 finished shells were made. Each had to pass through more than twenty stages and tests, with frequent assessments by government inspectors. On completion, a shell was varnished internally and painted externally. Separate processes created nose pieces from round bars of steel.

By 1918, Firth's national factory employed around 5,700 workers, of which as many as 87 percent were women – widely referred to as 'shell girls'. All had to be newly recruited and they received training for about a fortnight. Men were employed as supervisors and to set up and maintain machinery, and the works were patrolled by a section of women police. A regular factory magazine presented local news and humorous items, often extending to as many as fifty pages.

Bombshell *magazine was published by Firth's national factory. Some copies are held in the city's local studies library.*

The Templeborough factory had a blue-tinted glass roof and was centrally heated by steam. It provided several canteens and maintained a substantial welfare staff for female employees. Three eight-hour shifts (from 6.30 am) were worked, each including a half-hour meal-break. Otherwise employees remained on their feet throughout. Social events included parties at Christmas 1917 for around 4,000 employees, 1,200 children and 300 soldiers from local hospitals. The factory's choral society had around 100 members, and women's hockey and football teams played against other local groups. The *Templeborough Munition Song* opened like this:

We'll sing a song, a munition song,
A chant for the tired worker,
Who slaves away at the empire's call
With bitter scorn for the shirker![91]
England's at war – the world's at war –

To conquer the brutal Huns.
Rally each man in the hour of need,
And we – we feed the guns.
CHORUS:
Munitions! Munitions!
It's we who make munitions!
We'll carry on, we'll carry on
In spite of war's conditions!

In March 1916, a second national factory was opened in Sheffield, as usual financed from government funds. This was built by Hadfields for shell production next to their East Hecla works, on its own land now rented to the government. Its forging and machining shops gradually increased output to around 5,000 shells a week, mainly working on larger types of shell. However, during 1917, the factory's activities were gradually shifted from shell production to the repair of 60-pounder artillery guns. Soon those were constructed as well as repaired.

By the beginning of 1918, all shell-making in Hadfield's national factory had ceased (after an overall output of nearly 290,000), and it worked entirely on building guns and rifling the gun barrels sent from other factories. Within the Ministry of Munitions it was thus redesignated as a national ordnance factory. The factory employed around 2,500 when producing shells and around 1,300 when working on guns – all of whom were men.

The same shift from a national projectile factory to a national ordnance factory was made by Cammell Laird's works in Nottingham. This factory, mainly on land provided by Nottingham Corporation, also started production in March 1916[92]. It produced medium-calibre shells for the British Army and also some for Italy, totalling around 900,000 before its role was changed. As part of a general reorganization in the spring of 1917, the Nottingham works began instead to repair and later also to make 18-pounder guns. By mid-1918 it had ceased all shell production. The company's Nottingham workforce in early 1917 (when producing shells) was almost 6,000, of which about half were women.

As well as the two large national factories, Sheffield later in the war housed two smaller units in the government's programme. These both dealt with small arms ammunition and were controlled directly by the Ministry of Munitions. One was a manufacturing warehouse at 50 Porter Street, which originally made cupronickel ingots and brass discs[93]. It is not clear from published accounts when this was opened, but from early 1918 it ceased manufacture and served as a store and offices for a second unit, perhaps in addition handling cupronickel produced by local companies. This second small national factory was owned by Kent, Smith and Company in Bacon Lane, Attercliffe, making rifle bullets out of specially treated strip-metal by an experimental electrical process[94]. The ministry took it over in the middle of 1918, from when the Porter Street premises were again used on cupronickel work, but very few details of either unit are available.

Other government suppliers

As well as opening national factories, the government set about identifying companies whose manufacturing equipment and expertise in other kinds of work might instead be used to make munitions. Central to the establishment of links between the government and those varied companies were forty-one local munitions committees that were established throughout the country.

In Sheffield, the city's Committee on Munitions of War was set up in June 1915 with Herbert Hughes, president of Sheffield Chamber of Commerce, as its chairman, and members drawn from a number of medium-sized companies. Activities of the committee will be reviewed in the next chapter. In the present context, it was important for making and managing contact with firms in the city that might for the first time undertake munition work. The committee drew up a list of local firms available for this kind of work, negotiated contracts with the Ministry of Munitions, and worked to assist companies in switching and then maintaining their production. In some cases advice was also arranged from one of the city's established armament companies[95].

Within a few months government contracts were placed through the Munitions Committee with almost 100 Sheffield companies, and these were usually followed by repeat orders. For instance, several city firms received orders to make fuses, steel helmets, shells or shell components (see the list in Appendix One), in many cases needing to modify their equipment or even construct an entirely new factory. The Ministry of Munitions gradually developed its own links with local companies without needing the Sheffield Committee on Munitions of War as an intermediary, and many later ministry contracts were placed directly with firms themselves.

Some munition work required accuracy to a 100th or a 1,000th of an inch, and component dimensions had to be frequently checked during manufacture and inspection. For example, in making the body of a shell up to thirty measurement gauges had to be applied, and for shell fuses of complex design that figure could sometimes reach 150. Many gauges merely indicated (and still do) the limits within which a component must fit, and others were/are more sophisticated, adjustable instruments. Greatly expanded production of munitions naturally created a huge additional demand for gauges, and the Sheffield Committee on Munitions of War organized the manufacture of more than 20,000 in the war years. All gauges required certification as accurate before they could be used on munitions, and the university's Department of Applied Science was a major provider of inspection services. That department was also among the city's shell producers, with a special role as a training centre.

In addition to firms moving into munitions production for the first time, others received orders for military work of a kind already familiar to them but now to be carried out on an increased scale. For example, both J. A.

Wartime items produced in the city by Sanderson Brothers and Newbould.

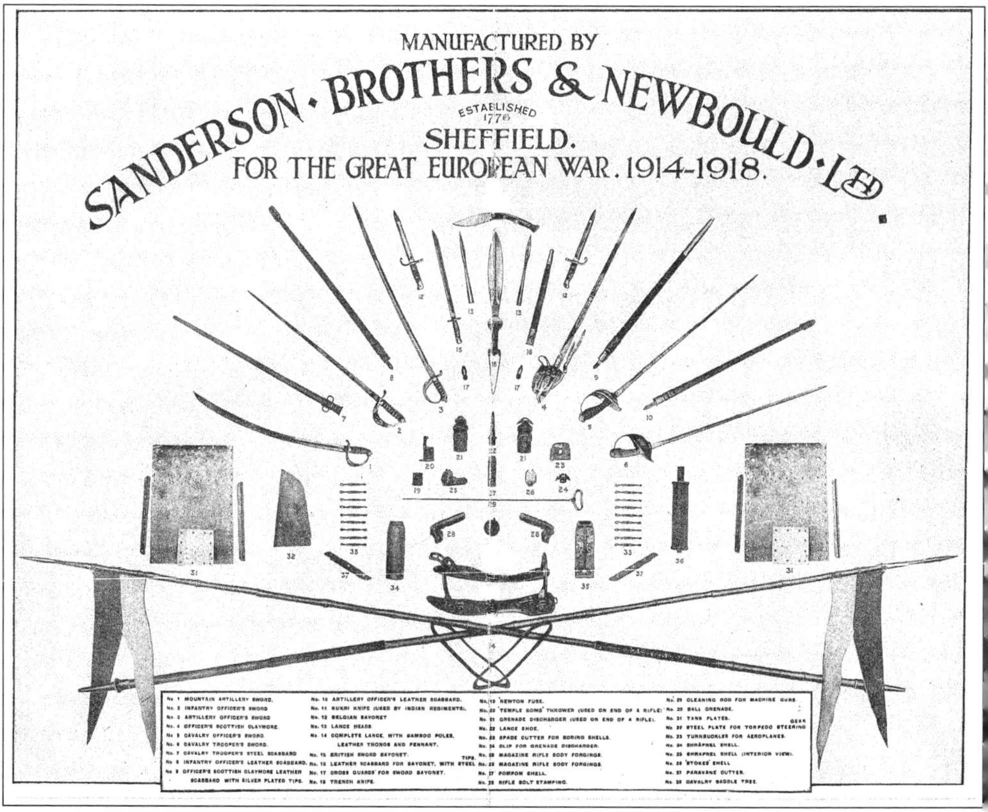

Chapman and Company and Sanderson Brothers and Newbould turned out a large number of bayonets. High-speed steel created by Jonas and Colver was soon in demand for aircraft engines, and James Neill and Company responded to the need for those engines' magnetos by taking over adjacent premises in Napier Street for the production of magnet steel. J. H. Andrew and Company already produced cast steel for shells and rifle barrels, and now greatly expanded its output. So too did Ambrose Shardlow and Company, whose crankshafts were urgently required for aircraft and tank engines. The company also started to make micrometers in place of imports that were no longer available.

Marsh Brothers increased production of twist drills to 30,000 a week. Wire-drawers J. Stead and Company expanded their range to produce springs for artillery guns, and Walker and Hall added to their cutlery activities by producing copper driving bands for shells. The 1918 Directors' Report of steel processors W. T. Flather indicated that, in addition to a general expansion of testing and inspection work: 'the Company have been able to give entire satisfaction to the many requirements of the Government, notably for air-craft, Admiralty, submarine and motor coaster, boat and balloon equipment. Large numbers of forgings have been made for gearing for aeroplane guns and tension rings for gun and howitzer mountings. The supplies of UBAS[96] steel for the production of gauges have been very large, and the results obtained [...] have been most gratifying.'

The subsequently-written history of Samuel Osborn and Company[97] paints this picture of wartime activity:

> Practically the whole output was used directly or indirectly for war purposes, although this was not obvious as the standard lines – tool steels, twist drills, milling cutters, springs, files, steel sheets and steel castings – were manufactured as usual.
>
> At the beginning of the war the company held War Office and Admiralty contracts for tool steels and their requirements doubled immediately, and after the National Shell Factories opened the demand was terrific. The number of workpeople was increased. The drill-making plant was extended, and for the first time women were employed in making drills. A very large quantity of shell steel was rolled and thousands of springs for motor vehicles were made. Tools for the making of shells, cartridge-making tools, special cutters, alloy steels for aeroplane parts, and tons of steel for balls and ball-

> bearings for aeroplanes and tanks were among the direct contributions to the war effort.
>
> Files were supplied to many Government departments and factories as well as to engineering firms employed directly in the making of guns, rifles, tanks and other implements of war. But it was in the steel foundry and sheet mills where the output could be most directly related to war work.
>
> In the foundry such castings as cylinders for shell-making plants, wheels and axles for the light army railways in France, castings for sea-mines, depth-charge throwers, boom defences of our naval bases, and for the paravanes[98], were supplied in large quantities. Possibly the most important contribution was the castings supplied for the first experimental land ships, or tanks as they were afterwards called, and others of later design. Aerial bomb cases up to a quarter of a ton were made in thousands.
>
> In addition to turning many thousands of shells, Regent Works was mostly employed on making steel squares from which protective helmets were made, body armour, eye masks, and bullet-proof armour for aeroplanes, guns and tanks, and plates for flame projectors. Considerable alterations were made to the plant and buildings.

The 'steel squares' referred to above were one part of Sheffield's considerable contribution to survival in the trenches. Before the First World War, soldiers in action had worn cloth or leather caps, which had been adequate in open warfare but soon proved useless against shells and shrapnel in the trenches. The Invention Department of the War Office was asked to improve on a recent French design, and during 1915 John L. Brodie developed and patented a stronger version, which was easily manufactured from a single sheet of metal.

Millions of these 'tin hats' for soldiers were made in Sheffield following their introduction in late 1915.

James Dixon and Sons of Cornish Place delivered around 1,000,000 steel helmets to the army.

In the course of initial trials and modifications, Hadfields' 12 percent manganese steel was found to provide greatest protection, and 'Type B' helmets were first delivered at the end of October 1915. Supplies gradually built up and by the Battle of the Somme (July 1916 onwards) Brodie 'tin hats' were in widespread use. Small design changes were made in 1917, and in total more than 7,000,000 helmets were produced during the war. Of these, in excess of 1,000,000 (slightly modified) were made from 1917 for the American Army.

Steel sheets, usually cut into circles or squares, were produced by Hadfields and other Sheffield firms – Edgar Allen and Company, Bury and Company, Thomas Firth and Sons, Samuel Osborn and Company, and Vickers – and also by two non-Sheffield companies. These were pressed and fitted with a liner and chin-strap by other companies including, in Sheffield, James Dixon and Sons[99], Harrison Brothers and Howson, William Hutton and Sons, Maxfield and Sons, John Round and Sons, and W. and E. Viener. A modified version of the Brodie helmet continued in service through the Second World War.

Sheffield's helmet-producers also worked on other military projects. For example, James Dixon and Sons, previously specializing in silver and

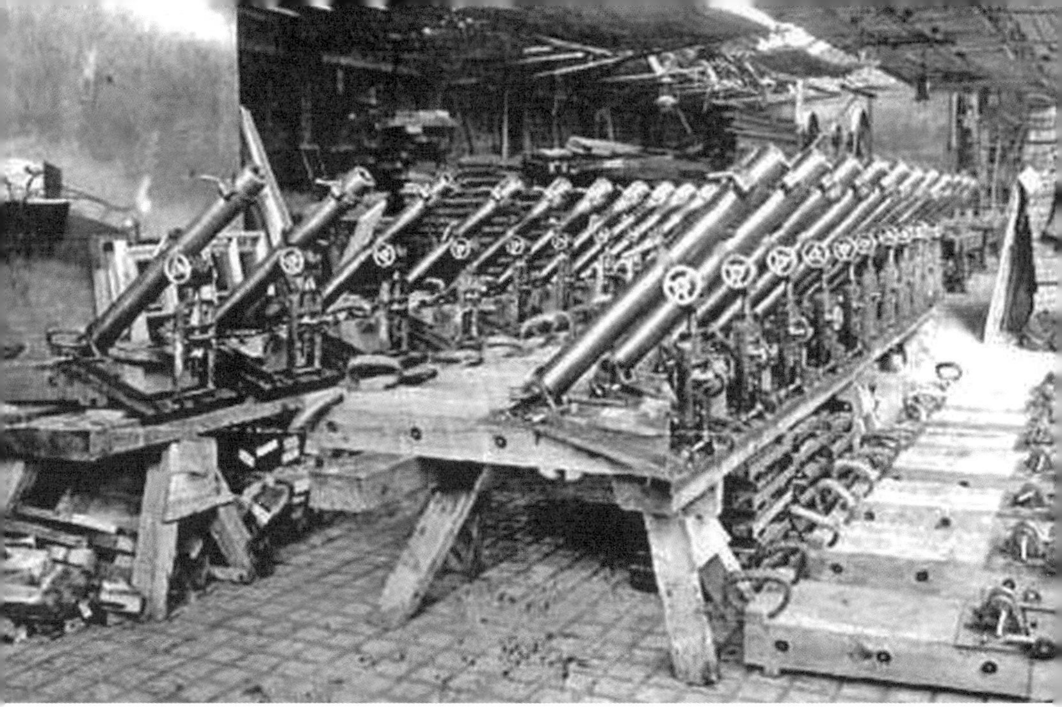

Norfolk Street-based engineers Hattersley and Davidson produced mortar guns for the first time.

electroplated goods, adapted their Cornish Place works to make, in addition to a million steel helmets, '100,000 pairs of piston rings for aeroplane engines, 250,000 liquid gas shells, and many thousands of parts for mines and depth charges, besides many tons of cupronickel' (*Sheffield Daily Independent*, 7 July 1919). Other firms also took on work that was completely new to them. Tool manufacturers Hattersley and Davidson produced mortar guns for the army and the Sheffield Simplex Motor Works developed an armoured vehicle from its 30 horse-power car, which was sold to the Belgian and Russian armies. Simplex's British contributions are included in Appendix One[100].

A surprising entrant to the munition industry was department store John Atkinson. A book published soon after the war indicates that in 1915:

> [T]he firm [...] had available a large area of works that had been vacated by cutlery workers and those engaged in allied trades, together with large stables and yard accommodation. Old grinding hulls were of no use, nor were the engine houses etc. They were swept away [...] and in their places were erected shops for drop stamping [...] There was an extensive stamping plant, with annealing shops, machine departments, die-cutting shops etc., space having been provided by the conversion of the stables and the covering in of the yards.

> From 1915 to 1918 the firm was responsible for making many hundreds of thousands of stamped parts for all descriptions of guns, shells, and tanks [...] Stamping and drop-forging produced such things as gun pivots, air vessel ends, crank-cases for aero-engines, discs, breech rings, breech screws, shell components, bolts and nuts, parts for lorries, brackets, levers, swivels, and things the name of which had never been uttered on the Moor[101].

Many government contractors were under considerable pressure to meet urgent orders, and employees worked long hours often for months on end. Buildings were extended, new machinery was put in place, and works were modified to handle the substantial orders. Financial assistance was sometimes made available through government loans, grants or allowances against tax. For example, Arthur Lee and Sons was helped by the Ministry of Munitions to build a new factory at Meadowhall for special steel and wire for aeroplanes. Funds were provided to assist Oates, Turner and Company to install a rolling mill for producing brass strips, which were then cut and made into shrapnel discs for shells. And government-financed factory extensions more than doubled the output of Sanderson Brothers

Armoured cars with this design were sold to Russia by the Simplex Motor Company, here shown with owner Lord Fitzwilliam's son.

and Newbould. Samuel Fox and Company at Stocksbridge was permitted by the ministry to write off around £750,000 of capital expenditure incurred on new equipment, building and extensions – mills, furnaces, machines of several kinds, store buildings, sheds, cranes, sewers, cars and locomotives, as well as a canteen, cottages, houses and a 'garden village'[102].

Another notable development was an increasing interest in the chemical and physical characteristics of different steels. Encouraged by the university's Department of Applied Science, several of the larger Sheffield producers undertook research programmes that fed through into improved materials used in the war and subsequently. Sheffield's East End merged into Rotherham's factory region and firms beyond the Sheffield boundary, like the Park Gate Iron and Steel Company and Steel, Peech and Tozer, also produced steels and munitions in enormous quantity[103].

Several firms installed electric furnaces, and the larger furnace-users came together in September 1915 to create a new company – the Electrode Company of Sheffield – to 'manufacture, buy, sell, and otherwise deal in' electrodes in order to make sure that those continued to be available for their furnaces[104]. All these developments led to a rapid increase in demand for electricity and gas to power the city's factories, and supplies built up to unprecedented levels – both around five times as much as before the war. Electricity came from the corporation's own generators, now enlarged with loans from the Treasury, and gas was provided by a private supplier. That firm suffered from a national government order to remove toluol and

Thomas Firth and Sons operated a fleet of steam-driven lorries.

benzole from its product for use instead in the manufacture of high explosive. One result was lower-quality gas, and 'there were many occasions, particularly towards the end of the week, when the pressures required to maintain high temperatures were insufficient, resulting in the loss of munitions either through spoilage or idle furnaces and equipment'[105].

Government work was thus spread widely around the city's factories, far beyond the five established armament producers. In addition to recurrent problems of labour shortage and poor supply of materials, particularly troublesome was transportation within a works and around the city. Horses were still essential to many companies, and even when motor vehicles were available petrol was rationed from 1916 and in very short supply[106]. Thomas Firth and Sons operated steam-driven lorries, and Thomas W. Ward and at least one other company experimented with using an elephant from a local circus, reputedly capable of towing weights previously requiring three horses.

T. W. Ward used circus elephant Lizzie to deliver scrap metal around the city.

For a period, boiler manufacturers Thomas Oxley used camels as well as an elephant.

Sheffield's equipment makers for the troops

Weapons and ammunition were obviously central to the country's war needs, but many supporting items were also crucial. Steel helmets and more than 3,000,000 table knives, forks and spoons for the troops were ordered from Sheffield firms. For a period, 80 percent of the city's cutlery output was said to be for military use. Several companies made trench knives, digging tools, attachments for bayonets, ammunition boxes, surgical instruments and similar equipment. Tin openers, cooks' knives, pocket knives, surgical scissors, water bottles, metal mirrors[107], axes, spades and saws were in great demand. The rapid initial expansion of the army gave rise to a great shortage of razors, and the War Office requested more than 2,000,000 of the open cut-throat variety. Sheffield firms and other suppliers received orders but could not meet the enormous demand, and the Cutlers' Company mounted a multi-national campaign to collect and refurbish used razors for military use; see Chapter Five.

For trench warfare on the Western Front the army needed tools as well as weapons.

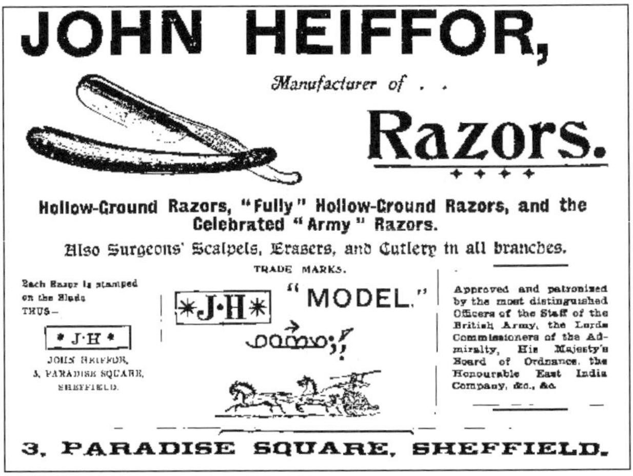

Millions of cut-throat razors were needed and many came from Sheffield. This advertisement is from 1911.

One very busy Sheffield company was Joseph Pickering and Sons in Burton Road. Linked to several decades' manufacture of polishing paste for the metal industry, the firm had also developed Blanco, a paste for cleaning web, leather and other items of uniform. To accompany the original white paste, Khaki Blanco was introduced for military use during the 1890s and became essential throughout the British Army and much of the empire. Blanco was always an individual purchase at the expense of a soldier, rather than being ordered by the military authorities, and the huge increase in troop numbers naturally resulted in a great deal more work for Pickerings. Many tiny firms were also busy as part of the city's expanded munition industry. For example, Sheffield's Henry Pickin provided his one horse and cart for transporting shells and other items between factories and to and from railway stations.

Blanco to clean soldiers' webbing (here in 1918) was made by Joseph Pickering of Burton Road.

Producers of equipment for munition factories

The fifth category of firm provided plant, equipment and materials necessary for other companies to produce the items illustrated above. A large number of Sheffield firms contributed to the war by supplying the factories that made munitions.

For example, George P. Wincott and Company made gas and coal-fired furnaces, which were suitable for shell and other work, and a range of electric furnaces was available from T. R. Watson and Company. Gregory Reddish and Company of Deepcar advertised their silica bricks, fire bricks, ganister and fire clay for furnaces. James Rolley prepared grindstones in their Howard Street works, and Newton Chambers and Company, in addition to supplying items directly to the government (see Appendix One), advertised locally their expertise in structural design and construction and in the production of girders, roofs and bridges. George Longden and Son were building contractors to Firth's national projectile factory at Templeborough and also undertook construction work for other munition firms. Both Thomas Turton and Company and Needham, Veall and Tyzack made grinding and other machines for use in Sheffield and around the country, and many types of general engineering equipment

SHELL FURNACES

(CONTINUOUS, GAS, SEMI GAS, & COAL FIRED).

We have built Furnaces each heating

35 60-POUNDER SHELLS PER HOUR

and other sizes in proportion.

Furnaces built for all sizes up to 15 in. dia.

SEND FOR PARTICULARS TO:—

G. P. WINCOTT, LTD. 180, ATTERCLIFFE RD., SHEFFIELD.

G. P. Wincott made furnaces for other companies in Sheffield and elsewhere. This local advertisement appeared in 1915.

ELECTRIC FURNACES

(GREAVES-ETCHELLS TYPE)

for High Speed, Alloy & Carbon Steels, Steel Castings, &c.

T. H. WATSON & Co. (Sheffield), Ltd., Lancaster St., Sheffield.

Electric furnaces were also manufactured in the city. This advertisement was published in Sheffield newspapers during December 1916.

JAMES ROLLEY,

GRINDSTONE MERCHANT.

BEST YORKSHIRE AND DERBYSHIRE STONES.

For Files, Edge Tools, Shears, Anvil, Hammers, Gun Barrels, Saws, Sickles, Blades, Vice, Spindles, Stove Grates and Machinery Grinding.

Mounted Grindstones. Scythestones. Razor and other Hones kept in Stock.

Contractor to His Majesty's Government, Woolwich and Enfield.

80, HOWARD STREET,

Depot: POND STREET STATION. **SHEFFIELD.**

Tel. Address—" WHETSTONE, SHEFFIELD." Telephone—2270.

Many metal products depended on the availability of grinding wheels, here advertised in 1917.

were provided by the Yorkshire Engine Company at Meadow Hall Works.

Of particular importance were the local firms of Thomas W. Ward and Davy Brothers. The first of those, with about a dozen controlled establishments around the country, brought together and processed scrap metal from equipment of all kinds. The company made available up to 1,000 tons of scrap each day for steelworks in Sheffield and elsewhere. Davy Brothers worked with twenty engineering sub-contractors to produce presses for forging, shell-banding and other purposes, often of great size and complexity. For example, the firm received orders to completely equip with presses and hydraulic power plant the large majority of national shell factories. Overall, it supplied presses capable of a total production of a million shells a week. Across its range of products, Davy Brothers manufactured for armament companies in this country and abroad nearly 650 presses of all kinds, around eighty hydraulic accumulators, 250 hydraulic pumps, nearly fifty steam hammers, 220 boilers and several other large pieces of equipment. In addition, the company produced around 20,000 bulletproof trench shields and more than 40,000 bulletproof plates for the hulls of tanks. In terms of workforce, the company lost 113 of its 700 men to the army and instead increased its female number from ten to 139.

Davy Brothers' subsequent summary of the firm's work[108] illustrates both its own contribution and early post-war thinking about the outcome:

> We have, during the entire period of the War, run practically the whole of our machinery continuously night and day, including meal hours, and, in urgent cases, including Sundays. The work

Davy Brothers provided presses, pumps, hammers and boilers to munition and other manufacturers around the country.

One of many shell-piercing presses made by Davy's in Sheffield.

accomplished, we feel, reflects credit both on our Staff and workpeople, and that they have thereby played a useful part in the accomplishment of the Great Victory[109] in the cause of justice and freedom over the threatened domination of Germany and the Central European Powers.

Munition huts and munition tribunals

As well as many changes and difficulties within Sheffield companies, the city had to cope with new and unexpected issues of a more general kind. Suddenly, accommodation was required for an influx of workers arriving for munition work – estimated in 1916 to number around 10,000. These included Australians and Canadians[110], volunteers from all over Britain, and people placed in local factories by government schemes. Sheffield was before the war already short of houses, and house-building had now almost stopped. Furthermore, wartime demolition of properties to extend East End works had made the accommodation situation worse. For example, an extension of Vickers' West Gun Shop in 1916 destroyed twenty-six established houses.

Among the city's several thousand additional workers were more than 500 from Australia.

By the spring of 1915, Sheffield Council had become extremely concerned about living conditions in the city. The lord mayor appealed for householders to provide temporary accommodation for incoming munition workers, and many hundreds of these found lodgings in a private house or hostel. Long negotiations between the council and government departments eventually led to agreement that additional residential properties, both permanent and temporary, could be built and partially financed from national funds.

For permanent houses, the Council's High Wincobank estate was to be extended with money borrowed from the government, and in addition some temporary hutted accommodation would be built entirely with government money. Rapidly erected huts for temporary workers were already familiar in the area, for example from the recent construction of moorland reservoirs by the Derwent Valley Water Board, and during 1916 the city set about providing streets of wooden huts in the area of Petre Street in Grimesthorpe and in Brightside's Tyler Street.

Overall, Sheffield's hut settlements contained more than 500 family houses and also enough hostel accommodation for more than 5,000 single men. (The cited number varies between published accounts.) A 1917 report is in Display Box 4.4. Initial furniture, bedding and household requirements were paid for by the Ministry of Munitions, and the ministry received a proportion of the rents paid. Although mainly for men and families from this country, the huts also accommodated some overseas workers including a small number of Belgian refugees engaged on munition work[111]. Canteens were provided for each settlement (in Tinsley run by the Brightside and Carbrook Co-operative Society), and at least

Responses to a housing shortage included temporary munition huts in the city's east end, which became home to nearly 5,000 people.

three communal halls were financed by the ministry for recreational and religious use. After munition workers left at the end of the war, several of the multi-occupancy hostels were modified to create separate family units, and some of the huts continued in use until the 1930s. The last occupants moved out in July 1939[112].

Display Box 4.4
SHEFFIELD'S MUNITION HUTS

Under the heading TOWNS OF HUTS, the 1917 *Sheffield Yearbook* contained this report:

> The housing of large numbers of munitions workers has been solved jointly by the Government and the City Council. Three new towns of huts and hostels have been erected at Wincobank, Tinsley and off Petre Street, near the works and yet on high ground above them [...] At Petre Street there are huts for 1,000 workers. They give shelter to 130 families, and the balance is made up of hostels for the single men. The family man has a five-roomed house at his disposal for 6s. 6d. [£0.33]. The boarding is thin, and when there are children in clogs next door the quietness is broken. But there are solid advantages, such as the bath and heater fitted in the scullery, where cold water is laid on, and an economical stove with oven in the front room. There are three bedrooms, and gas fittings are included in the rent. The women who occupy the huts are not insensible to the charm of living on the ground floor with no stairs to climb.
>
> The four blocks of hostels vary slightly in type, but in each the principle is the same. There is a cubicle for the lodger, and a common dining room is outside the block, and run by a local co-operative society at prices which defy competition. The lodger may either pay an inclusive 18s. 6d. [£0.93], which gives him his tiny bedroom (with its fittings) and full board, or else pay 3s. 9d. [£0.19] for the cubicle and buy his own food [...]
>
> One of the most interesting features of the scheme is a large recreation room to seat 400 people, with billiard tables and a stage. It is managed by a committee, including Church of England, Free Church, and Roman Catholic members [...] Each will have the use of the hall every third Sunday.
>
> The three colonies provide accommodation altogether for about 4,600 munition workers, with a total new population of nearly 7,000 persons.

A second set of issues for the city's employers and workers was a legal one. The 1915 Munitions of War Act placed a number of constraints on the operation of controlled establishments. For example, it was made compulsory for workers to follow company rules and they could not move immediately to another employer without getting a leaving certificate from their current firm. Without such a certificate, other companies were forbidden to employ a person for the next six weeks.

The Act proposed that complaints about applications of the new law should be examined by specially created munition tribunals, and a Sheffield munition tribunal met for the first time on 2 September 1915. It became exceptionally busy for the remainder of the war, dealing with more than 5,000 cases in each of the next two years. Courts were held between two and five times a week at different periods, initially in the labour exchange but also in the city's court house. All local tribunals comprised an independent, legally qualified chairman, who was the sole decision-maker, and two advising 'assessors' – one each from a panel of employers or workers[113]. The tribunal chairman in Sheffield was local solicitor and politician Sir William Clegg[114].

Munition tribunal sittings were regularly reported in the city's newspapers. Almost all cases were either a worker's appeal for a leaving certificate believed to have been unfairly withheld or complaints by an employer that a particular worker was at fault in some way. Employers were reluctant to dismiss troublesome workers at this time, as they would usually be unable to appoint another suitable person; labour was scarce and applicants from another employer had to hold a leaving certificate. Workers charged by their company and deemed by the tribunal to be guilty were usually fined between ten shillings (£0.50) and forty shillings (£2.00), which could be deducted from future wages, and applications for a leaving certificate (many hundred overall) were frequently refused.

A high proportion of Sheffield's large and medium controlled establishments brought some members of their workforce before the tribunal. On average, more than 400 cases were examined each month. These concerned, for instance, a worker losing time through absence or lateness, breaching works rules, idling, sleeping in the factory, card-playing[115], gambling, or leaving the works without permission. Employers also accused some men of abusive language, refusing to obey orders, not working diligently, assaulting other workers, or being drunk in the factory. However, Sir William Clegg emphasized on several occasions that, although many cases were brought before the tribunal, these represented only a small proportion of the city's otherwise excellent workers.

The tribunal's first case illustrated many that were to follow. The *Sheffield Daily Telegraph* of 3 September 1915 reported: 'complainants were Messrs Davy Brothers Ltd., of Sheffield, and the offending workman was George Edward Lamb, a machine hand, of 75 Handley Street, Sheffield. The complaint against him was that he lost time, was absent without leave, was drunk in the works, that he was asleep on one occasion when he should have been working, and that he spoiled some work.' After presentation of evidence, the defendant admitted the offences and was fined twenty shillings, to be deducted from his wages in weekly instalments of 2s. 6d. (£0.125). Later cases before the tribunal are illustrated in the following newspaper excerpts:

> John Edward Woodhouse, bricklayer's labourer, 22 Norroy Street, was summoned by Messrs Thomas Firth and Sons Ltd. for losing 176½ hours during the past seven weeks. Defendant said illness was the cause; he had been asked to work all night in heavy rain, the next day in front of a red hot furnace, and the following night in the rain again. It was more than anybody could stand. The Chairman: That is all very well, but [...] I see that you can work all day on Sunday when you are getting double pay. You will be fined 30 shillings.

In many similar cases employers reported that workers were regularly absent on weekdays but instead turned up on Sundays for which they received higher, sometimes double, pay.

> Percy Machin, general smith, 411 Attercliffe Road, and Albert Cutts, his striker, 29 Whiteley Lane, Ecclesfield, employed at Messrs Howells Ltd. applied for leaving certificates. The evidence showed that they were ordered to do certain work on the anvil instead of by a stamp, which was appointed for such heavy work [...] Machin said he had offered to remain behind all night and to do the work on the anvil [...] The Chairman: discipline in the works must be maintained, and the application will be refused.
>
> Bernard Graham, a turner living at 31 Birdwell Road, Grimesthorpe, and employed at Messrs Seebohm and Dieckstahl Ltd. [...] said he wanted to leave his present job at any cost. He admitted that he had lost time wholesale in order to get his discharge [...] He gave in a week's notice, and at the end of the time the firm

> refused him a leaving certificate [...] In refusing the certificate, Sir William Clegg said: 'You have been deliberately losing time at this very important juncture, and when you are engaged on very important work. You ought to be ashamed of yourself.'

The legal requirement that employees should always receive a certificate to confirm their employer's permission to leave was very unpopular with workers, whose freedom of action had been taken away and who often felt they had strong reasons to move to another job. After a succession of complaints had been described in the press and heard by munition tribunals all over the country, trade union objections were taken up by Labour and other members of parliament, and the requirement for leaving certificates was abolished in October 1917.

Krupp: A German armourer with British connections

As British companies worked hard to produce sufficient munitions and equipment, factories in Germany were, of course, doing the same. The German armament firm most feared and hated in Britain was Friedrich Krupp AG. of Essen. For a century this enormous company had won huge orders for armour plate, artillery weapons and projectiles in countries across the world.

Krupp had developed close links with Germany's ruling class and with the kaiser himself and, as war approached, many British observers saw the company's relentless advance as a central part of Germany's increasing aggressiveness. In his 1914 book *The War that Will End War*, H. G. Wells had no doubt: 'Beside the Kaiser stands the firm of Krupp, a second head to the State; on the very steps of the throne is the armament trust, that organised scoundrelism which has, in its relentless propaganda for profit, mined all the security of civilisation, brought up and dominated a press, ruled a national literature, and corrupted universities' (page 12). 'We are fighting to end Kaiserism and Kruppism for ever and ever.' (page 84.)

As the First World War unfolded, Krupp further expanded its factories, workforce and influence. The initial 82,000 employees had grown to more than 150,000 by 1918. Around forty new workshops were built and production surged far beyond already-high levels. For a period in 1916, some 9,000,000 shells and 3,000 artillery weapons were delivered each month. It is not surprising that Krupp was viewed from Britain as a major threat[116].

Despite the company's undoubted influence on German policy-making, it had long held an ambiguous position – trading with potential enemies as well as working closely with its own government. In effect, by persuading other countries to acquire ever-better weapons Krupp created the conditions that persuaded its own government to buy still more of its products. Around 1910, about half the company's sales were to other governments – in around fifty different countries. For example, in the years leading to war Krupp received substantial orders from Russia despite some people's fears (later realized) that those Krupp-produced weapons would be used against the home country[117].

Collaboration between nations in the development of armaments was surprisingly widespread in the pre-war period. A number of writers indicate that some of the armour plate in British ships was made under licence from Krupp, and several reports suggest that Vickers' high-carbon steel was used in some of Krupp's projectiles (perhaps later against Britain). Competing firms in different countries regularly shared armament information and worked jointly to increase their munitions output and profits. Some post-1900 examples of Anglo-German collaboration are in Display Box 4.5.

One of these pre-war agreements had unpleasant wartime consequences for Sheffield. Around 1895, Krupp's engineers perfected a time fuse for shells that was more effective than earlier models, and (consistent with their usual practice) they patented it internationally and sought to license it to other companies who would pay them a fee for each one made. In 1896, an agreement was signed with Vickers in Britain. Krupp would provide the fuse's detailed specification and Vickers would pay 1s 3d [£0.06] for each one fitted to a shell and would stamp on that shell the symbol *KPz* (Krupp Patentzünder; Krupp Patent Fuse). The agreement was renewed in 1904, and from then on the years of initial and renewed agreement were indicated on each Vickers' shell as *KPz 96/04*[118].

This fuse agreement worked smoothly in peacetime, but clearly presented political and moral problems for the two companies when their countries were at war with each other. In effect, Germany was making money from Britain's killing of German troops, and German fuses were contributing to the possible defeat of that country. Furthermore, in Britain itself trade of all kinds with Germany had been banned during the war and transactions in weaponry were illegal in the extreme.

The private deal became public outrage when repeated questions in parliament from April 1915 onwards asked about the suggestion that Krupp was being paid a royalty of 'a shilling a shell'. The government accepted that a licensing agreement with Vickers had been in force but

Display Box 4.5
COUNTRIES WORK TOGETHER TO SELL WEAPONS

In the years of peace before 1914, munition producers from Germany, France, Britain and other countries co-operated in many ways. Links and patent-pooling between German firms and Sheffield armament manufacturers were surprisingly close. For example:

1. Harvey United Steel Company, 1900-1911
To exploit the international potential of an American process to make exceptionally hard armour plate, this cartel was set up in 1894. It brought together German, British, American and French companies, including from Sheffield producers John Brown, Cammell Laird and Vickers. Information was pooled, and profits from outside the participating countries were shared between the syndicate members.
2. Steel Manufacturers' Nickel Syndicate Ltd., 1901-1914
This cartel handled the supply and purchase of nickel steel, which was used in ordnance and projectiles. Originally a British grouping including Cammell Laird and Vickers, the syndicate was soon joined by Krupp and several Austrian and other German companies, all working collaboratively.
3. Deutsche Waffen und Munitionsfabriken, 1901-1914
This arrangement between German armaments producer Deutsche Waffen and Britain's Vickers helped the two companies to sell automatic and semi-automatic smaller guns. The German company's approval was required for joint sales of guns in Germany and in a specified set of other countries, with profits equally divided between the companies.
4. Shared information and licences
Although individual firms retained their own technological secrets, much information-sharing also took place. In many cases, one company paid another for a licence to produce its patented product and obtain access to essential design and production information. Between-country overlap continued during the war years as British judicial permission to use specific German equipment was granted to several Sheffield companies.

claimed that the fuse patent had expired in July 1914 and no payments had been made since then. That left unclear the possibility that the agreement was still legally binding. Vickers continued to produce the fuse and to record the number that it made.

So far so good. But after the fighting had ended, Krupp filed a claim for £260,000 as payment for Vickers' wartime manufacture of *KPz*. The British company contested the number of *KPz* shells which Krupp estimated it had used, but not the legality of the claim, and eventually (in August 1926) a compromise was reached. Vickers paid £40,000 to Krupp for their use of the patent and the case was closed.

This chapter opened with 1919 praise by the Prime Minister for the city's munition companies. He saw that Germany's 'battered shield [...] of militarism' had been crushed by Sheffield steel. He might have added 'with some help from Germany's own fuses'.

CHAPTER 5

The University and the Cutlers' Company

Adding to the enormous contribution to the war effort made by the city's people and factories, the long established Company of Cutlers in Hallamshire and the more recent university also made available their own special skills and resources.

The University of Sheffield

A 'University College of Sheffield' had been formed in 1897 from three separate institutions – Firth College, the local Medical School, and the city's Technical School. By 1902, local enthusiasm and successful fundraising led the City Council to apply to the king for a university charter. This was granted and sealed in 1905, by which time buildings had been designed and constructed in Western Bank[119].

The new university's income and students came almost exclusively from within the city and its neighbourhood, rather than from the national and international sources of today. This local base led to the provision of many part-time (mainly evening) courses for people employed locally, and by 1914 about 1,700 such students were enrolled. The number of full-time students was much smaller – around 350. When war was declared, many of those immediately volunteered to serve in the army, and by 1916 there were only about 150 full-time students[120]. Similarly, around a third of full-time staff volunteered or were called-up for war service, and teaching had to be taken over by remaining colleagues or newly appointed women and non-enlistable men. Most of the athletic ground was let out for grazing in the absence of a groundsman.

The university's considerable contribution to wartime life in the city was much enhanced by its recently appointed vice chancellor, H. A. L. (Herbert) Fisher (1865-1940). Mr Fisher was a distinguished historian who moved from Oxford University to take up the Sheffield position in 1913. He was well placed as a member of the nation's establishment, having the Prince of Wales as a godfather and many links to senior Liberal politicians and members of the aristocracy. His transition to Sheffield had been delayed by membership of a royal commission with the Indian civil service, but with his wife and young daughter he moved to the city in the summer of 1913[121].

Herbert Fisher was vice chancellor of Sheffield University from 1913 to the end of 1916. He then became a member of parliament and president of the government's Board of Education.

Herbert Fisher was responsible for many innovations and worked tirelessly to expand the university's role in the city. For example, he delivered a large number of public lectures, both to encourage local recruiting and to review the background and development of recent events[122]. These were extremely well-received, often by capacity crowds, and his ideas were widely reported and discussed in local and other newspapers. His patriotic enthusiasm undoubtedly added to Sheffield's early positive response to the war. After he had discussed national needs and aims in a lecture on 2 September 1914, the *Sheffield Daily Independent* reported that 'the vast audience rose, and, with fervour, sang "The National Anthem", "Rule Britannia" and Watt's fine hymn "O God our Help"'. The new vice chancellor also contributed in other ways and served on many local committees, for example as president of the city's thrift week early in 1916. His wide involvement in the city led to the 1915 *Sheffield Yearbook* describing him as the 'Stimulator-General of Sheffield'[123].

Herbert Fisher was also active in national affairs. For example, in December 1914, he was appointed to the government's committee examining claims of German brutality and law-breaking, and in May 1915 was elected a trustee of the British Museum. In April 1916, he was sent to France to study that country's use of propaganda. His continuing links with government departments and contributions to the development of education policies led in December 1916 to an invitation to serve as president of the country's Board of Education[124]. As a result he left the university, but the family retained their Sheffield house for at least two more years. The position of vice chancellor was filled by William Ripper, the long-time Professor of Engineering[125].

Professor of Engineering William Ripper took over as the university's vice chancellor from 1917.

In conjunction with Pro-Chancellor Sir Henry Stephenson, H. A. L. Fisher arranged for distinguished painter William Rothenstein to be appointed as an honorary part-time professor of civic art. The two were long-time friends, and, although William Rothenstein was 'at first reluctant to go so far'[126] into the north, his annual lectures were well-received. Another innovation was a new Department of Russian, financed for seven years by steel company Vickers with an explicit aim of helping the city's trade with that ally of Britain.

MAPPIN ART GALLERY. SHEFFIELD.

"ON THE PERONNE FRONT"

Paintings & Drawings by William Rothenstein.

(One of the Official Artists on the Western Front), Professor of Art, Sheffield University

JUNE 3rd to JUNE 30th, 1918.

ADMISSION FREE.

WEEK-DAYS, 10.0 a.m. to 8.0 p.m. (except Friday); SUNDAYS, 2.0 to 5.0 p.m.

William Rothenstein served in Sheffield as part-time Professor of Civic Art. He also painted scenes on the Western Front as an official war artist.

On Sunday 2 August 1914, two days before Britain entered the war, vice chancellor Fisher received a request from the War Office for a list of staff or student members of the university willing to accept officers' commissions in the Territorial or Reserve forces. Letters and telegrams were immediately sent out and advertisements were placed in the press. The large number of positive replies included forty from current staff, and from that initiative and its follow-up emerged the Sheffield City Battalion, often referred to as the Sheffield Pals. Over the next few months, this and other units drew from the university about 1,100 students and staff[127].

The university's Officer Training Corps (OTC, founded in 1911) already provided instruction and military practice to prepare men for army commissions, and it immediately welcomed applications from non-students. By the end of the war, around 350 ex-OTC men from Sheffield had been appointed as junior army officers. Rifle instruction for the corps was provided by local clubs, and (to supplement the city's Totley Range) a miniature rifle range was established within the Applied Science Department.

The dangers facing junior officers on the Western Front were recognized in a letter to local newspapers from the vice chancellor and the OTC commanding officer in May 1915:

> The loss of life amongst officers in the present war is most serious, especially in the junior ranks, and unhappily we must look forward to the loss increasing rather than diminishing. It is imperative that there be a continuous supply of young men of good education and ability to replace those who have given and will give their lives for their country.[128]

The following year, Mr Fisher sent a memorandum to the War Office pointing out the dangers of sacrificing so many future national leaders and requesting that high-achieving educated men should more often be employed in non-combatant roles. The response was not encouraging.

Scientific applications Despite losing key members of staff to the war, the university played a substantial role in the application of science to military needs, and in addition several of its departments worked closely with industries in Sheffield and beyond[129]. Within a few weeks of the war's outbreak, a scientific advisory committee was created from members of several departments. This worked, usually without charge, to assist local and other enquirers through information about technical literature and research findings and by collaborating with some companies to develop and test new materials or procedures, for instance through a series of applied experiments.

In its first year, the Scientific Advisory Committee received exactly 100 enquiries, but by March 1916 it was decided that requests were more effectively met by individual investigators. Within the university's Department of Applied Science Professor William Ripper was an energizing and expert leader and Professor J. Oliver Arnold had long

The university's Department of Applied Science was in St George's Square, on what is now Mappin Street.

worked to improve the composition and manufacture of steel. Already closely involved in the city's industry, Professor Arnold and his team now expanded their activities to study a range of pressing problems. For example, they experimented to increase the effectiveness of electric arc furnaces and they developed alternative furnace linings to take advantage of available but previously-unused materials[130].

Other technical innovations from Sheffield University in conjunction with local companies included new tool steels, improved foundry practices, more effective scrap usage, new methods of annealing, and a range of easily used pyrometers for assessing the temperature of metal[131]. Throughout the war, Metallurgical Department staff conducted thousands of different product tests for local industry and jointly with Admiralty technicians. (The Admiralty had a main inspection office in Janson Street and a section within the university's Department of Applied Science.) Other university technical contributions included the manufacture of many thousand measurement gauges, as well as the design and testing of master gauges requiring accuracy up to a 10,000th of an inch. Magnet steels, essential for aeroplane engines, were tested, and measuring instruments were calibrated in the Electrical Engineering Department, and the Metallurgical Department developed new ways to melt and manipulate brass for cartridge discs. That department also experimented with the composition of cupronickel, needed, for instance, in bullet sheaths and shell base-plates, perfecting a method of production that could be used in local factories. In addition to providing firms with advice and guidance, training around 450 men, the Metallurgical Department made and rolled large quantities of new material. From 1917, the Electrical Engineering Department worked with the local Anti-Aircraft Corps to improve equipment and techniques for aircraft detection. A training simulator was, for a period, erected in the university's Firth Hall, which included a 'travelling Zeppelin searchlight'.

One notable development was the establishment, in 1915, of an entirely new department of glass technology, led by Dr William Turner. Before the war, optical and other specialist glass had almost all been imported from Germany and Austria, but those imports were now blocked. South Yorkshire was home to a large number of the nation's glass companies, but their methods remained old-fashioned, limited to basic forms of the product, and largely untouched by scientific experimentation. The new department worked with the Ministry of Munitions and with companies in the region to improve manufacturing procedures, to train technicians, and to meet wartime needs for all kinds of glass.

Components for anaesthetic drugs previously imported from Germany were produced in large quantity by the Chemistry Department, assisted by volunteer female dispensers from the Children's Hospital and with contributions from women lecturers and students. The Department of Geology carried out research to locate and assess raw materials for steel furnaces and, in 1917, established a new section to study refractory operation, helped by finance from local companies and trade associations.

As well as these many links with industry and the production of war-related material, the university provided a range of scientific and medical staff for other wartime contributions. Bacteriologists used their expertise in active warzones, staff from the Medical Department served in local and

Professor W. Palmer and assistants in the chemistry department worked long hours to make anaesthetic drugs for use in military hospitals.

other hospitals, Physics staff turned their skills to X-Ray work, and the Departments of Pathology and Physiology were called upon for many thousands of military-patient medical investigations and pathology tests.

Lectures and courses Immediately, from the autumn of 1914, vice chancellor Herbert Fisher introduced and promoted two types of war-related lecture for the people of Sheffield and its neighbourhood. Initial priority was given to a military recruiting campaign in which the university set out to demonstrate the urgency of the country's situation. Speakers were made available to companies, local groups and military units, and in the first two years of war the university organized about 400 meetings of this kind in the city and neighbourhood. Display Box 5.1 illustrates the approach that was taken during the first months of war.

A second lecturing activity continued for a longer period, but mostly during the war's first two years. More than 500 talks for the general public about the war's historical background and current issues were sponsored and delivered in Sheffield and nearby[132]. Principal events in the 'University War Lectures Programme' took place in the city's Victoria Hall[133] or other large meeting places, and attracted many distinguished and well-known speakers as well as large numbers of listeners. For example, writer Hillaire Belloc spoke about the strategy of the war, and the under-secretary of state for India described the state of India. Other topics included the Belgian

Display Box 5.1
THE UNIVERSITY'S RECRUITING LECTURES

Sheffield University arranged nearly 1,000 community talks during the war. One set of lectures started on 5 September 1914 with this letter to the Editors of local newspapers:

> Sir,
> At a meeting held at the University this afternoon it was decided to make a great effort to bring to the notice of everyone in Sheffield and the neighbourhood the gravity of the present crisis and the country's urgent need of help.
>
> To deal with this work a committee has been appointed, with the Vice-Chancellor as chairman, two secretaries elected, and an office arranged at the University. It was decided to take the following steps: (1) To hold meetings in the dinner hour at the leading works in Sheffield and district. (2) To provide lectures in the evenings both in Sheffield and in the neighbouring towns and villages in the West Riding of Yorkshire, in Derbyshire, Lincolnshire, and Nottinghamshire. (3) In dealing with the villages it was decided to arrange a motor car recruiting campaign, a motor car carrying a lecturer, a magistrate, and a medical man visiting in the course of an evening two or three villages.
>
> The operations of the committee will commence at once, and be continued for three to six months, or longer if necessary.
>
> In order to carry out this important work about twenty lecturers have already promised their services. The secretaries will be glad to hear from those who are willing to lend motor cars, from medical men willing to examine recruits after the meetings, from the directors of works, from chairmen and clerks of local authorities, and others who would arrange facilities for the holding of meetings in their respective districts.
>
> Yours etc., H. A. L. Fisher, Chairman. A. J. Arnold and W. S. Purchon, Hon. Secretaries.

struggle, Turkey and the war, the political situation in Europe, German diplomacy, financial aspects of the war, in the heart of France, and Russian bureaucracy. The use of lantern slides was prominently advertised, and tickets were in great demand. In total, 130,000 tickets were sold[134] and proceeds were passed to Belgian and other relief funds. Similar lectures about the current situation were given to troops in local units and camps.

Over and above these recruiting meetings and the broad-ranging war lectures, the university added to its routine teaching some instruction specifically to meet wartime requirements. Some members of staff were concerned about the city's likely first-aid needs in the event of air-raids, and within a week of the declaration of war the vice chancellor's wife and others arranged for basic first-aid courses to be provided for the public by volunteers from the university and the city. From February 1915, academic staff and fifty volunteer ladies provided classes in English language, and sometimes history, for Belgian refugees. No fees were charged and several dozen classes were run for more than 500 of the recent arrivals.

Among many other new courses during the war, Sheffield University provided basic instruction in metalworking for women.

More technical, munition-related instruction for the public was initiated in the Applied Science Department. Lecture series were provided for groups of workers, for example covering German technical terms in 1916, coal carbonization in 1918, and factory welfare supervision in 1918.

Extremely important for many would-be munition employees were the university's brief courses in lathe work. From the spring of 1915, 'able-bodied and non-recruitable men' wishing to work in munition companies were offered seven to ten days of lectures and practical work in the basic operation of lathes. Demand for this training was considerable, as hundreds of novices sought to help the nation's productive effort. At one point the course had a waiting list of almost 500 people[135]. By 1916, some women were also receiving basic instruction in manual tasks for munition work.

Through the Committee on Munitions of War, the Engineering Department trained around 1,200 militarily-ineligible men to produce shells, itself delivering eighty each week to the Ministry of Munitions. By 1917, the growing need for junior analytical chemists in Sheffield factories led to the introduction of chemistry courses for women, and around 100 female workers were trained for chemists' jobs in the steel industry.

In addition, the university provided technical training for army officers. At least 150 attended lectures in laboratory work and around 200 others learned about field telephone systems. Longer courses in mechanical engineering and in metallurgy were made available to wounded officers

A large number of would-be munition workers received initial lathe training at the university.

who were no longer able to serve in an active role, and many of those moved on to jobs in the army's equipment repair shops. In addition, several hundred soldiers and ex-soldiers of all ranks, including many disabled, were taught how to produce the cupronickel strips needed for shell cases or learned how to operate machine tools for factory work.

Other voluntary activities Staff and students helped the community in other ways[136]. Following the sudden influx of Belgian individuals and families after the German invasion of their country, there was an urgent need for accommodation and day-to-day support. In November 1914, two university houses in Western Bank, previously Stephenson Hall Church Hostel, were made available and became known as the University Belgian Hostel. University staff were among those working to support around twenty occupants, who were originally planned to be 'of the educated class'. They were helped financially through donations from local people, including more than 300 regular subscribers, and the hostel was in use until mid-1916[137].

A second major voluntary contribution, from November 1915, was the establishment and operation of the university's 'Hospital Supply Depot'. Co-ordinated by wives of medical and other academics, 500 women worked at different times, with a daily average of seventy-five, to prepare bandages, medical dressings, operation sheets and other items for dispatch to military hospitals. The depot was registered as a charity and money to purchase material and to fund the delivery of finished items came through flag days, concerts and donations from hundreds of local people. As was usual in the period, donors and their contributions were listed in the city's

The university converted Stephenson Hall Church Hostel in Western Bank into accommodation for newly arrived Belgian refugees.

Voluntary workers in the university's hospital supply depot delivered nearly 500,000 items to more than ninety military hospitals.

newspapers. In the summer of 1916, the depot established a section to prepare and dispatch surgical dressing pads made of sphagnum moss collected from moorland in the neighbourhood and elsewhere. Across all its work the depot supplied nearly 500,000 items to more than ninety hospitals in the United Kingdom and abroad, with most sent locally[138].

Part of the university's hospital supply depot was a separately housed surgical supply branch operating with close involvement from civil engineering staff. Around forty-five volunteers, including several of the city's schoolteachers, worked throughout the war, often in evenings or at weekends, to design and manufacture hundreds of wooden and metal surgical aids, instruments and appliances, and items of hospital furniture. Products were sent to more than forty military hospitals. Some of the surgical items were tailor-made for individual patients in the city, requiring special measurement and personal fitting.

In these and other ways the city's fledgling university contributed significantly to wartime Sheffield. As described in the *Sheffield Daily Telegraph* in June 1915, 'The University is entering into every department of our civic life. It displays imagination and leadership. It is serving the city as well as the nation.'

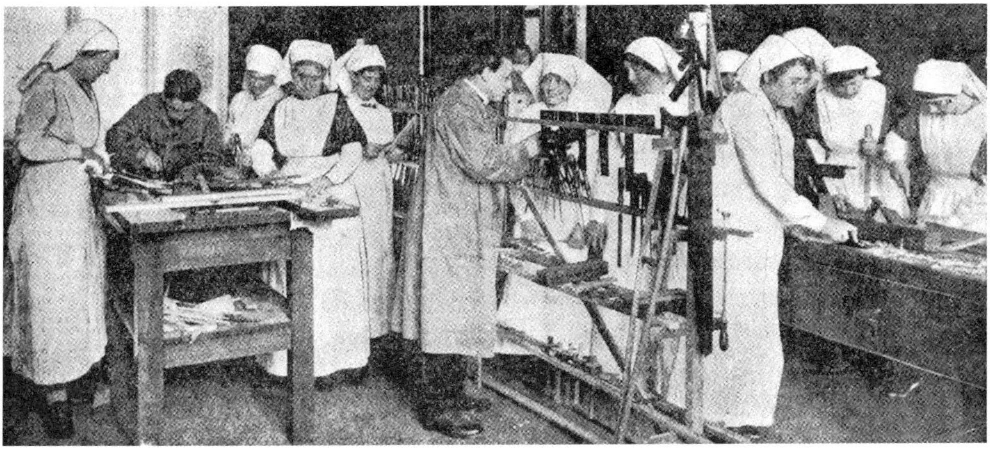

Other volunteers in the depot's Surgical Supply Branch constructed wooden and metal surgical aids and provided tailor-made appliances for individual patients.

Sheffield Committee on Munitions of War

It was not until the spring of 1915 that the government recognized the scale of the country's munition problem – production of ammunition and weapons was too feeble to win the war. Several developments in Sheffield at this time came together to transform the city's achievement.

First, in response to a request from the War Office, a local committee was created, drawing upon the city's large employers and principal trade unions[139]. The government was still hoping that sufficient munitions could be obtained through its small number of traditional suppliers. Following an informal meeting in the Cutlers' Hall on 21 April 1915, an invited delegation visited the War Office and met Lord Kitchener himself[140]. The group was encouraged to set up a joint Sheffield Committee on Munitions, with equal numbers of employers and employees. That met on 30 April 1915, under the chairmanship of Herbert Hughes, the President of Sheffield Chamber of Commerce[141].

Herbert Hughes was the initial chairman of the university-based Sheffield Committee on Munitions of War.

Simultaneously, the Applied Science Department of the university, led by William

Ripper, was considering ways to involve a wider range of producers in government work. Sheffield was home to many hundreds of small and medium-sized companies creating metal products of all kinds, and very few of these had previously considered producing items for military use. As it became clear to the government that their favoured large producers were already over-committed with orders and that potentially adversarial committees of both managers and trade unionists, as initially suggested, were likely to be slow and inflexible, a second Sheffield committee emerged as the primary mechanism to expand the city's munition work. With the blessing of the earlier committee, this smaller group comprised only employers and it retained Herbert Hughes as chairman. Starting work at the beginning of May 1915, it became known as the Sheffield Committee on Munitions of War.

The new committee accepted the university's offer of accommodation and facilities in the Applied Science Department, and Professor William Ripper was elected as its vice chairman and Albert Davidson as honorary secretary[142]. An initial meeting resolved to 'obtain as complete a list as possible of all the firms in Sheffield and immediate district who have machinery which could in any way be used in the manufacture of Munitions of War or auxiliary to such manufacture'. The city's main armament companies were not to be included as they were already contracted to the military authorities. Instead they were informed of progress and they offered practical assistance to smaller firms if needed.

Consulting engineer Albert Davidson became the first honorary secretary of the Sheffield Munitions Committee.

By now the Ministry of Munitions was encouraging throughout the country the formation of 'Co-operative Groups' of companies in order to expand local munitions production. Within that structure, the Sheffield Committee on Munitions of War operated as one of the ministry's forty-one 'Boards of Management'[143], falling within its Area 3 whose head office was in Leeds.

The committee's initial review of potential munition contributors drew on work already done by the local labour exchange and the inspector of factories, and by the end of May 1915, it had identified nearly 150 local firms to be checked as possible additional providers of war material. The committee mounted an exhibition in the Cutlers' Hall for silverware and other firms to learn about shell-making, and visits were made to local companies in order to discuss possibilities and to suggest equipment modifications. Several firms were soon able for the first time to meet requests for war production, and in August 1915 the Sheffield Committee on Munitions of War signed its first contracts with the Ministry of Munitions, acting as an intermediary between the ministry and local producers. Initially, the committee would deliver each week 3,000 18-pounder shells, 400 6-inch shells, 2,000 primers, 1,000 shell fuses and 1,000 gaines (metal tubes to be attached to a fuse). Orders for these items were placed by the committee with local companies, who now had to learn about products previously outside their range, and a substantial administrative workload soon built up. As early as September 1915, the university was visited by King George V, who attended a meeting of the Munitions Committee as part of a more general tour of the city. Excerpts from a local newspaper account are in Display Box 5.2[144].

Display Box 5.2
THE KING, THE UNIVERSITY AND THE MUNITIONS COMMITTEE

On 28 September 1915, King George V paid a visit to the university before later inspecting works in the city's East End. The *Sheffield Daily Telegraph's* account on the following day included the following:

> The King came on no state occasion but to pay a private visit [...] He came unheralded and carried out this tour with as little ceremony as possible [...]The very element of surprise gave the city an opportunity to show what it could do in the way of a spontaneous welcome [...] Wherever the King went, there were outbursts of enthusiasm, which showed that [...] the sentiment of loyalty to the Throne is deeply seated in the minds of the people. Crowds gathered as if from nowhere [...]
>
> As with the gatherings of the public, so it was with the decorations. Early in the morning Sheffield was a dull city, pursuing the usual tenour *[sic]* of its way under a lowering sky which suggested anything but King's weather [...] But soon the Union Jack and the flags of our Allies began to shoot up on most of the principal buildings [...] Even in the poor streets near the Applied Science Department, flags fluttered gaily [...]

In the entrance hall of the department were a good number of leading citizens, and soon after twelve o'clock the sounds of growing excitement told them that His Majesty was approaching. Presently a storm of cheering was heard rolling up the streets, and, with the waving of hats and handkerchiefs, and many expressions of loyalty, the King arrived at the department. He was received by the Pro-Chancellor (Dr George Franklin), who presented the Vice-Chancellor (Mr H. A. L. Fisher), the Registrar (Mr W. M. Gibbons), and the Bishop of Sheffield (Dr Burrows). The Lord Mayor presented [the named members of the Munitions Committee and others ...]

His Majesty spent more than half-an-hour in a tour of the department, and, in the well-equipped laboratories, tool rooms and machine rooms saw the progress of that course of instruction in metallurgy and engineering which has given the Sheffield University a foremost place in the applied science schools of the world.

A subsequent internal document of the Munitions Committee expressed great satisfaction with the visit, and reported that the chairman 'gratefully presented to the Honorary Secretary the pen used by His Majesty'.

From that autumn, a substantial number of contracts with local companies was drawn up by the committee and authorized by the Ministry of Munitions, usually its Trench Warfare Supply Department, or in a few cases by the Admiralty. Orders were placed with silverware and cutlery companies, spoon and fork makers, iron foundries, woodworking firms and small engineering works. Most contracts stipulated that necessary component materials would be supplied to the company at a fixed price[145], and the Sheffield Committee also had to arrange the transportation of these materials around the city. At certain periods, the government's orders were indicated to be especially urgent. For example, in the initial manufacture of shrapnel-proof steel helmets, 'it is imperative that you clear these consignments with the greatest possible speed [...] Please therefore arrange to work both day and night shifts.' Product samples had to be submitted from each firm for testing by the ministry and inadequacies had to be followed-up and rectified. As the war developed, so did the Committee's workload, and its office staff were supplemented by evening and weekend help from members of the university's Registrar's Department[146].

The Committee on Munitions of War brought into military production the facilities of 116 firms in Sheffield and neighbouring towns such as Chesterfield, Worksop and Matlock [147]. Initial company orders were for a specified number of items or weeks, but later they were often issued as open-ended running contracts for weekly quantities but without a fixed overall total. Details of ninety-five of those companies, the ones in Sheffield only, are summarized in Appendix One, where contracts through the committee are identified by abbreviation 'SCMW'. That list also shows that many Sheffield companies working for the government did not depend upon the committee. The Ministry of Munitions gradually developed systems and expertise that permitted its own direct issue and management of contracts. The Sheffield Committee on Munitions of War encouraged this shift to direct agreements between the government and individual companies, and it moved out of its intermediary role. It was thus earlier in the war that the committee's work to guide new munition producers was of particular importance.

Overall, the Sheffield Committee was responsible for the production of almost 500,000 shells, nearly 1,000,000 grenades, and almost 1,000,000 steel helmets. It also made around 27,000 measurement gauges, both through local companies and in the university itself, and some of these were extremely sophisticated. Its many products are summarized in Display Box 5.3, with a total output of almost 12,000,000 items[148]. These items are in addition to Sheffield's production of large weapons, forgings and steel plate, which was described in Chapter Four. Instead, the committee worked primarily to produce smaller but equally essential components.

One or more of its sub-committees met daily in St George's Square during most of the war, and the full committee came together weekly or fortnightly. The co-ordination of production from smaller companies remained its primary activity throughout, but it also had three other functions – providing technical advice to the government, negotiating on behalf of all the city's employers, and acting as a local problem-solver for the Ministry of Munitions. In the first case, linked to the university's more general role as technical adviser, the Munitions Committee, for example, successfully responded to requests for new methods to reduce the steel industry's use of sulphuric acid and it carried out essential research into the machining and production of rifle barrels.

Second, for the city as a whole the committee pressed the Ministry of Munitions to increase the quantity of petrol made available for companies to convey materials around the city. Other city-wide activities included

Display Box 5.3
PRODUCTS FROM THE SHEFFIELD COMMITTEE ON MUNITIONS OF WAR

Here is a simplified version of an overall summary produced in May 1924. For each item the total value of contracts was also indicated, with an overall sum of £1,565,583 14s 6d.

Adapters, steel	12,034
Base plates, steel	378,306
Bombs for trench howitzers, complete or part	730,221
Boxes for trench howitzer bombs	186,427
Brass rod	147 tons
Burster containers, steel	4,122
Cartridge discs	308,250
Exploder containers, steel	1,160,330
Exploder containers, tubes or rings for	24,127
Friction tubes, brass	372,842
Fuses, brass or cast iron	587,196
Fuse bodies, brass stampings or iron castings	1,120,521
Fuse-hole plugs, brass or cast-iron	1,111,062
Fuse-hole plugs, wood for transit	1,156,798
Friction tubes, brass	372,842
Gaines, steel	632,271
Gauges	27,371
Grenades	897,018
Gun forgings, rough bored	48
Helmets, steel	972,657
Primers, percussion, brass	270,649
Shrapnel discs or sockets, stamped	782,799
Shrapnel discs or sockets, machined	315,353
Shell, high-explosive or smoke: 18-pounder, 6-inch or 4.5-inch	465,887
Shell heads: 60-pounder or 6-inch	90,564

work to provide war service badges and to obtain the release of serving soldiers. Badges were issued, first by individual firms and later by the government, to indicate that a person was employed on essential war work outside military service; see Chapter Two. As early as June 1915, the committee urged the government to provide these badges to appropriate Sheffield workers and even submitted a design and cost quotation (which was not followed up). However, in September 1915 the Ministry of Munitions agreed that all requests for war service badges from within the city should first be examined by the Sheffield Committee on Munitions, with recommendations for allocation being passed to the Ministry[149].

At this point in the war the large number of previously-issued badges (provided directly to companies) were to be replaced by a new issue to specified individuals. All of the city's requests within this programme, in practice mainly through employers on behalf of their workers, were examined and processed by the Sheffield Munitions Committee, and the committee's approval led the ministry to issue new badges to as many as 19,500 named Sheffield workers. Following the introduction of conscription in January 1916, badge-issuing procedures changed again, and local decision-making, based on a frequently-changed list of scheduled occupations, passed mainly to the city's recruiting office. However, several hundred appeals for exemption from call-up were passed to the committee for examination and recommendation in the early months of 1916[150].

The Sheffield Committee on Munitions of War also served local companies in negotiations with the ministry about releasing men from the army for essential munitions work. In July 1915, committee member Arthur Balfour met the minister of munitions and senior officials to plead for the return to Sheffield of skilled munition workers now in the army. As a result, the committee was asked to submit written details about local needs, and it was decided that all Sheffield companies' requests for the return of essential men should be made through the committee. As many as 2,750 specific investigations were carried out from St George's Square and, as a result, more than 2,000 men were released from the army back into local factories.

Industrialist Albert Hobson was honorary treasurer and later chairman of the Sheffield Committee on Munitions of War. His two sons were killed in the war.

Linked to those activities, a third general function of the Sheffield Munitions Committee was as a local problem-solver and a knowledgeable mediator between manufacturers in the city and the ministry in London. A huge number of detailed enquiries were received from both government and

Display Box 5.4
SHEFFIELD MUNITIONS COMMITTEE'S MEMORIAL TO THE FALLEN

The work of the committee resulted in a positive cash balance at the end of the war, and the chairman wrote to collaborating companies as follows:

> We are now engaged in winding up the activities of the Committee, and the final adjustments with the Ministry of Munitions are almost complete. It is anticipated that there will be a credit balance in hand [...] The Committee hope that the contractors will agree to forego any interest they may have in the distribution of the balance in order that it may be handed over to the University of Sheffield for educational purposes [...]
>
> The Committee and the contractors alike are under a deep obligation to the University. At the cost of much inconvenience the University placed rooms at the disposal of the Committee to serve as their headquarters. The advice and help of the University scientific and technical staff have always been at the command of the Committee when faced with problems of manufacture, and the University administrative staff has borne a large share of the administration [...]
>
> The War has been won through the sacrifice of the young manhood of the country. University students freely gave their lives in the cause of liberty. Those who have survived the great struggle now throng to the laboratories and classrooms; the duty to provide them with a training that they may become established in life is paramount, while the value and importance of these young men as assets of the country cannot be overstated. It is not speaking in terms of exaggeration to say that to them and their successors are committed the destinies of the nation.
>
> If the Committee's suggestion as to the disposal of the balance in hand is approved by the contractors, it could be devoted to a purpose which would serve as a memorial to the fallen, and at the same time provide for the educational advancement of the survivors of the Great War and future generations of the country's youth.

companies, and the committee's staff, numbering fifteen at its busiest period, sent out in total well over 10,000 letters[151]. Committee members, all unpaid, made frequent visits to the ministry's Whitehall offices and were in regular contact with local ministry officials.

After the armistice in November 1918, the committee was, of course, no longer required. From December of that year outstanding contracts were liquidated, and in December 1919, chairman Albert Hobson wrote to all contractors with a request to use the committee's remaining money as a 'memorial for the fallen'[152]. Among those deceased were Chairman Albert Hobson's two sons and a nephew of vice chairman William Ripper. Excerpts from the chairman's letter are in Display Box 5.4.

Surviving records do not indicate how widely this request was accepted. The committee's minute book contains very little beyond that date except for a final entry on 3 June 1928, merely the signature of 'W. M. Gibbons, Secretary'.

The Company of Cutlers in Hallamshire[153]

Like the city's university, the Cutlers' Company had no direct role in the governance of Sheffield but its influence and status were considerable. The company's importance came from its close involvement in local affairs over many centuries (it was founded in 1624), and the fact that many of its members also held key positions in principal organizations of the city. It became usual for the Master Cutler, elected by company members for a year, to be appointed *ex officio* to a range of important Sheffield positions[154].

With the arrival of war, many customary activities had to be abandoned and changes had to be made. The annual Cutlers' feast was cancelled and a single Master Cutler, William Ellis, served for the entire war[155]. Some members left to fight and others turned their expertise to the production of munitions. Nevertheless, the company and its hall continued to serve in traditional ways, adjusting these to assist the national effort.

Wartime in the Cutlers' Hall In August 1914, the Mistress Cutler, Mrs Lucy Ellis, formed and chaired an 'Army and Navy Aid Committee' (later called the 'Sheffield Voluntary Aid Association' or the 'Sheffield Voluntary Association'), which was made up of ladies who met regularly in the hall to prepare and dispatch clothes and other items to the War Office and directly to military hospitals. Members of the public and local working groups were asked to bring articles to the hall, and committee members also made or repaired items. Up to 3,000 items (mittens, socks, mufflers, nightshirts, etc) were dealt with each week and, overall, the committee provided more than 200,000 articles for serving troops or those being treated in hospital.

The Cutlers' Hall was also made available for a stream of other war-related activities. For example, in early 1915 cutlery made in Germany (no longer imported) was exhibited for possible replacement production by local firms and a similar exhibition was mounted the following year by the Board of Trade. Subsequently, detailed specifications of government-required products were stored in the hall for manufacturers' consideration. At other times, for instance, a meatless cookery exhibition was held by the *Sheffield Daily Telegraph* for local housewives, a national welfare and economy exhibition included thrift competitions, and the city's Soldiers' Comforts Society offered for sale handicraft items made by wounded men in local hospitals.

Also among fundraising events in the hall, several groups held bazaars for the Third Northern General Hospital, and the city's auctioneers sold items in aid of a new Star and Garter Home in Richmond for wounded soldiers. Sheffield Ornithological Society was there in November 1917 with a 'Grand Exhibition' of canaries and other birds and, in May 1918, the Sheffield Society of Artists presented a variety of local scenes. Other activities in the hall raised money for a soldiers' leisure hut at Ripon camp and for 350 additional beds in the Ecclesall base of the Third Northern General Hospital. In September 1917, as food was becoming scarce, a war vegetables exhibition was held, and also in that month a display of photographs and parts from destroyed German aeroplanes and Zeppelins raised money for wounded members of the flying services, attracting nearly 45,000 visitors.

A second Cutlers' Company activity helped troops in a different way when, in December 1914, the previous year's Master Cutler, Thomas W. Ward, initiated a scheme for unwanted razors to be donated through the Cutlers' Hall for soldiers' use.

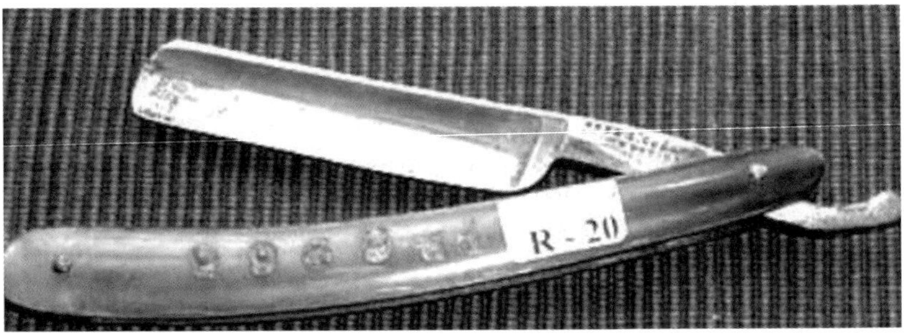

The Cutlers' Company collected and repaired used razors of this kind for servicemen, sending more than 300,000 to the War Office.

Following a very successful local campaign, the War Office requested a nationwide appeal for which it would pay essential costs. The Master Cutler immediately placed advertisements around the country in newspapers, post offices and elsewhere, and requests were sent to all local councils and similar bodies. When required, renovation work to blades or handles was carried out on the premises or in local cutlers' workshops, and more than 300,000 were dispatched through the Company for military use[156].

Throughout much of the war, the Cutlers' Company served as a principal decision-maker in the export of alloy steels and associated products. The government's War Trade Committee had quickly banned the export to Germany of high-speed steel containing tungsten or molybdenum, but by May 1915 had become concerned that products could nevertheless reach Germany through neutral countries. The committee asked the Cutlers' Company to examine all new applications for steel exports and to certify those that were free from tungsten and/or molybdenum and, thus, exportable to neutral countries. The company set about devising an effective procedure and documentation, and these came into operation at the beginning of July 1915[157].

All proposed exports of steel and steel products had to be submitted for approval, and the work soon expanded into a major responsibility for the Cutlers' Company. Certificates of exemption from the export ban had to be signed by two members of its Export Committee, or by one member and the law clerk or one of his deputies, and the initial committee of five available signatories was expanded to sixteen by the end of 1916[158]. The Cutlers' Company was at first asked to handle applications from all over the country, but after a few weeks a national framework was established in which it dealt only with those from a broadly defined Sheffield area.

The Export Committee worked hard to make decisions on the day of application, and the company's 1919 annual report reported that 'during this period of three years and eight months *[i.e., from May 1915 to December 1918]*, 205,462 Certificates were granted by the Committee involving 821,818 signatures, or 720 signatures per working day of six days per week'. At one stage no less than 2,000 assessment-based signatures were required each day, and of course many additional activities became necessary – recording and filing certificates and correspondence, sending certificates by mail or by hand-delivery, and discussing cases that fell near the margin of acceptability. 'Lady clerks' were employed to handle much of the administration. Fees for a certificate were set by the government and, overall, the company received a total of £15,777[159]. In addition, at several points during the war the Export Committee proposed changes and simplifications to the national regulations or reviewed technical proposals from the Ministry of Munitions, and its members were often called on to provide specialized advice to one government body or another.

Sheffield's own aeroplane The Cutlers' Company made a different kind of contribution in 1917 when the city came to acquire its own named aeroplane. Although in later years a naval cruiser became HMS *Sheffield* (from 1936) and a destroyer with that name is well-known from the 1982 Falklands War, the city's the First World War *Sheffield* has largely been forgotten – one of the nation's earliest aeroplanes. The first controlled flight in Britain had been in 1908 and the use of planes for military activity was unfamiliar in 1914[160]. But as design and technology advanced they became greatly valued for reconnaissance, bombing and aerial fighting.

From within Britain and the empire, the government sought additional funds to build more aircraft. Donations came from individuals and groups, and twelve British cities were also asked to provide aircraft for a newly established 'Imperial Air Fleet'. This was made up of planes that were given to Australia, Canada, India, New Zealand, Newfoundland or South Africa. Each one bore the name of its donor city and was held in trust by the Imperial Air Fleet for its owning nation until the end of the war. They were not sent to their new country, but instead served in Allied operations on that nation's behalf, usually on the Western Front.

In June 1917, the Master Cutler was asked by the Imperial Air Fleet committee to finance a plane from Sheffield. He sought funds from key manufacturers in the city and the required sum (a little over £2,000) was quickly raised through the company without a public appeal. The plane was offered to Newfoundland, Britain's oldest colony, which remained separate from Canada until 1949. It was an RE8, a two-seater model that had been introduced in 1916 and that, for a while, became the nation's standard reconnaissance aircraft[161].

On 29 September 1917, the city's plane was ceremonially named *Sheffield* and formally presented to Newfoundland. The presentation took place at Coal Aston Airfield[162] and attracted a large crowd. Newspaper reports indicated that as many as 80,000 people attended; additional trams and special buses were provided. The ceremony was graced by a guard-of-honour from the Royal Flying Corps and music from the thirty-strong Newfoundland Band, which had travelled to this country with their

An RE8 aircraft of this kind was financed through the Cutlers' Company and dedicated at Coal Aston Airfield on 29 September 1917.

mascot, a very large Newfoundland dog. The name *Sheffield* was already in place on the new plane, which was formally offered by the Master Cutler via the city's lord mayor to the vice president of the Imperial Air Fleet. It was then named by the Mistress Cutler:

> I name you 'Sheffield'. May you bring honour to Sheffield and Newfoundland and to the Empire. May our enemies tremble and our friends rejoice when they see you. May those who fly in you do their duty to their country, their King, and their God, and may God have you and those who fly in you safe in His keeping.

The Mistress Cutler names Sheffield *at Coal Aston Airfield watched by a large crowd, note-taking press reporters, and a cameraman from Pathé News.*

Sheffield was next presented by the Imperial Air Fleet to the government of Newfoundland, and Lady Isabel Morris, wife of the colony's premier, attached to it a bronze badge in the shape of a caribou's head bearing Newfoundland's motto and that of the Imperial Air Fleet. Members of the crowd, most of whom had not previously been close to an aeroplane, were then treated to an hour's display of flying. Several official guests, but only men, flew as passengers in the second cockpit[163] and half-a-dozen other planes also took to the sky.

Sadly, the Mistress Cutler's hopes for the new plane's safety and success were soon dashed. As so often on the Western Front, the aircraft's service came to an abrupt end when its two-man crew, one British and one Canadian, were killed in action near Ypres on 28 November 1917. The city's name lived on in a prompt replacement, but this too was lost and its crew also killed on 25 April 1918. A third *Sheffield* was still held by the Royal Air Force in January 1919[164].

What happened to the city's aeroplane when the war ended? The country then faced a novel problem – a huge surplus of unwanted military equipment. Around 15,000 planes and 35,000 aeroplane engines remained without a use, and these were rapidly becoming obsolete and in danger of decay and rust. Many were soon turned into scrap, and those probably included the plane from Sheffield[165]. The city's name graced the skies only briefly.

The wife of the premier of Newfoundland places a bronze motto on Sheffield, *ready for its take-off. The Master Cutler is left of her in the picture.*

CHAPTER 6

1917 and 1918: A troubled city

The last two years of war were increasingly difficult for Britain and its allies. Despite some significant victories, overall military progress was poor and by the spring of 1918 German advances made a British defeat very possible. At home conditions were steadily getting worse and the public, dulled by deaths and disablement, was becoming weary of war. Food, fuel and other essentials were increasingly scarce, some rationing had to be introduced, and military conscription took more and more men away from their families. Adding to the pain, Britain was, in 1918, hit by a major epidemic of influenza. Although most politicians, newspapers and churchmen continued to argue in favour of war, some Labour MPs and others were now pushing for negotiations and an early peace with Germany.

Darkness before the dawn

Britain's troop losses in 1917 were even worse than in previous years, and casualties from Sheffield mirrored the national pattern. The city suffered around 1,500 and 1,700 military deaths in each of 1917 and 1918, up from about 800 and 1,250 in the two previous years, and the high number of disabling injuries increased in the same way.

During this period, Germany acquired new destructive equipment, including improved submarines and powerful aeroplanes that were able to bomb London in daytime as well as at night. Both Britain and Germany had applied blockades at sea to prevent supplies reaching their opponents, and by 1916 both countries were suffering domestic shortages as a result of the other's activity[166]. Historians generally view the British blockade as particularly effective, but at the end of January 1917 Germany announced that its submarine warfare would in future be without restriction: all vessels approaching Britain – merchant as well as military – were now open to underwater attack without warning[167]. In the following months a huge number of vessels, including a hospital ship and its patients, were sunk with dreadful loss of life, and essential supplies to Britain were reduced still further. Among the dead from indiscriminate submarine attacks were a number of American citizens. Until then the United States had remained neutral in the conflict, but Germany's unrestricted submarine warfare and other developments provoked a change of policy. On 5 April 1917, the US joined the war in support of the Allies.

Less encouragingly for Britain and France, they lost the support of Russia, a key ally on the Eastern Front. The tsar was forced to abdicate in March 1917, localized street demonstrations and troop mutinies grew into a national revolution, and in November 1917 Vladimir Lenin and Bolshevik colleagues came into power. The following March, Russia made peace with Germany and withdrew from the war, allowing some German troops fighting in Eastern Europe to be transferred instead to the Western Front. Part of the German Army in the west now mounted a substantial attack and breached a section of British lines. Wider losses seemed inevitable and the outlook was poor. However, the Allies' defence held at great cost, and a counter-movement in July succeeded in reversing the enemy's progress.

Other military news in the second half of 1918 also turned positive for Britain. Recently-arrived American soldiers had by now gained valuable experience and were making their presence felt, the British Air Force had further improved reconnaissance and attack, the army was well supplied, and German air-raids on London were contained. The submarine threat was reduced by grouping vessels into convoys, and the Allied position was further improved a few months later by the capitulation of Germany's east-European allies Bulgaria and Turkey. From late October 1918, mutinies in the German Navy spread more widely and peace discussions now seemed realistic. On 9 November, colleagues forced the German kaiser to abdicate and he fled to neutral Holland. An armistice was signed on 11 November, initiating a period of non-combat for terms to be discussed and agreed.

In these last two years of war setbacks in battle were accompanied by unending pressures at home. Particular problems arose from widespread shortages. By late-1917, long queues outside food shops were common and stock often ran out before every customer could be served.

Life was also made difficult in other ways. Lighting regulations were firmly enforced by policemen demanding the blackout of houses and other buildings, retail shop displays were darkened, illumination was reduced in churches and public buildings, and most streetlamps were extinguished[168]. Petrol shortages reduced travel by car and the city's road surfaces were in a poor state. The council was short of money and men to repair its streets, and half its steam-rollers and many lorries had been sent to France for military roadwork[169]. Passenger travel by train was also a problem, as military and goods transport now took priority. In May 1918, the number of available passenger journeys was further reduced by around 40 percent and many ticket prices were increased yet again. Housing was in short supply and living costs continued to rise. The budget in April 1918 once more increased taxes on income, alcohol, sugar, tobacco and matches, as well as raising postal and other charges. Across all the war years the cost of living more than doubled, with greatest increases in the price of food – particularly affecting poorer families. Furthermore, by mid-1917, even people in work were finding it difficult to pay for what they needed and conflict between industrial workers and their managers was common.

Workers' problems were accompanied by concern about the frequent introduction in their factory of substitutes and the use of 'comb-outs' and 'clean cuts' to obtain still more men for the forces. The number and intensity of factory disputes and strikes increased throughout 1917 and into 1918, often encouraged by locally elected shop stewards rather than through established trade union channels. Sheffield's munition firms were among the thousands of companies that experienced disruption or temporary closure, which was often brought about by members of the Amalgamated Society of Engineers[170]. Many people in the city became irritated by repeated interruptions to their daily life and the impaired production of munitions. During a strike in the spring of 1917, the *Sheffield Daily Independent* reflected a common perspective when on 18 May it published on its front page a poem entitled *Engineers!*. Two of the three verses were:

While idle stand your lathes and gears,
And red rust on your tools appears,
Hark to the German gibes and jeers!
Do you like them, engineers?

By your country's hopes and fears,
By your children's future years,
By the dead upon their biers,
Get your coats off, engineers!

As described later in the chapter, exemptions from call-up were progressively withdrawn from skilled workers, and the new military service tribunals became inundated with appeals against conscription. In addition, the city's munition tribunal continued to receive hundreds of allegations each month, as companies brought actions against men who had broken work rules, lost working time, gambled in the factory, or refused to obey an order. For example, in March 1917 three machine-shop workers in the city were summoned to the tribunal for refusing to work with women dilutees employed on shell production. A different kind of industrial problem emerged in the spring of 1918 as government orders for munitions began to dry up (stocks had at last reached an adequate level), and women employees in Sheffield and elsewhere started to lose their jobs. By the end of that year the trickle of losses had become a flood.

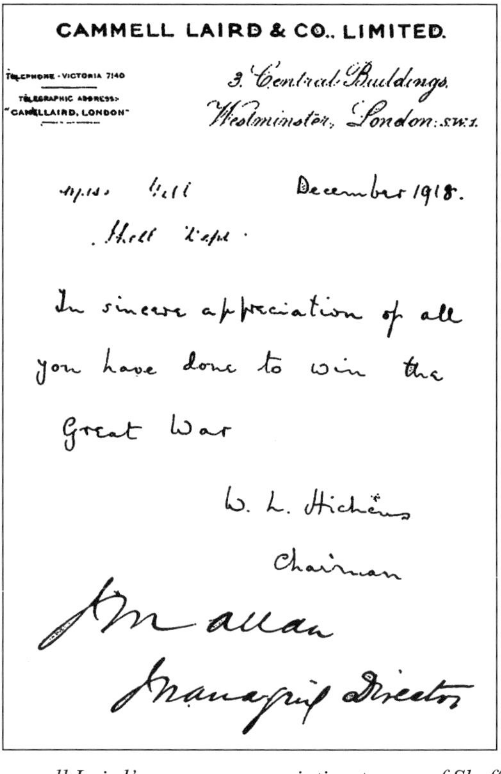
CAMMELL LAIRD & CO., LIMITED.

TELEPHONE - VICTORIA 7140
TELEGRAPHIC ADDRESS:
"CAMMELLAIRD, LONDON"

3. Central Buildings,
Westminster, London: S.W.1.

December 1918.

In sincere appreciation of all
you have done to win the
Great War

W. L. Hichens
Chairman

J M Allan
Managing Director

Directors of Cammell Laird's express appreciation to one of Sheffield's munition workers as she loses her job.

National Projectile Factory, Templeborough, Sheffield.

An Appreciation of loyal services rendered by … during the Great War, 1914-1918, as … from … to … at the NATIONAL PROJECTILE FACTORY, where 2,500,000 SHELLS were turned out to Feed the Guns.

Thos. Firth & Sons, Ltd.,

Christmas, 1918.

Many hundreds of redundant shell girls at Firth's national factory received one of these certificates.

The war was, of course, on everyone's mind – it could not be avoided. Huge numbers of letters and parcels were posted to serving troops. In return many official letters and telegrams contained bad news, and all neighbourhoods knew some families' grief. Furthermore, the city was now home to a large number of hospitalized soldiers and men discharged from the services as disabled. Each day invalids filled the streets and public buildings – convalescent hospital patients as well as mutilated ex-soldiers. Also unavoidable were the National Federation of Discharged Soldiers and Sailors and the Comrades of the Great War, both of which were very prominent through regular meetings and fundraising campaigns[171]. The human cost of war was by now horribly obvious.

Reminders of war also came through widely advertised exhibitions. During the summer of 1917, the Mappin Art Gallery exhibited more than 100 drawings of the Western Front by renowned artist Muirhead Bone, and those were followed in subsequent weeks by more than 400 British and Allied war photographs and then by sixty-six lithographs of the 'Great War – Britain's Efforts and Ideals'. In September 1917, the Cutlers' Hall provided (in the words of the *Sheffield Daily Independent*) 'the most interesting exhibition of modern times' – a collection of items and materials from German Zeppelins and aeroplanes. Visitors could see parts of aircraft used in the war, some unexploded bombs and German bomb-dropping equipment, as well as viewing detailed photographs of aircraft and other items of war. Into October 1917, the Mappin Art Gallery presented a Ministry of Munitions' exhibition of women's war work, carried out, as the *Independent* reminded its readers, 'under the supervision of skilled men', and in September 1918 it displayed large coloured photographs of Western Front battles. In August 1918, the Empire Theatre showed government-sponsored films about the war, and earlier that year a film entitled *The Kaiser* at the Albert Hall displayed the German emperor's life and emphasized his country's continuing barbarity.

Wartime fundraising activities were also hard to avoid. Many factories encouraged weekly deductions from workers' pay or extra donations to special relief causes. Flag days were held almost every week, with hundreds of sellers around the city – mainly women and hospital patients.

MINISTRY OF MUNITIONS.

EXHIBITION of Official Photographs and Samples of Women's Work at the MAPPIN ART GALLERY, Sheffield

(By kind permission of the Art Gallery Committee),

Illustrating the various types of Work upon which WOMEN ARE EMPLOYED IN ENGINEERING & OTHER INDUSTRIES ON MUNITIONS OF WAR.

Open Daily, from 11 a.m. to 8 p.m. until October 9th. Admission FREE.

Female munition workers were recognized in this 1917 exhibition at the Mappin Art Gallery.

MAPPIN ART GALLERY, SHEFFIELD.

EXHIBITION OF BATTLE PHOTOGRAPHS IN COLOUR

From the Ministry of Information, depicting Scenes and Incidents on the Western and Eastern Battle Fronts.

The "TANKS IN ACTION" is the Biggest Coloured Photo in the World.

FREE DAILY (Friday excepted) 10.0 a.m. to 8.0 p.m.
SUNDAYS. 2.0 to 5.0 p.m.

From AUGUST 24th to SEPTEMBER 22nd, 1918.

'Tanks in Action' is one of the photographs in this 1918 Sheffield display.

Prominently advertised campaigns like Tank Week (December 1917), Cruiser Week (March 1918), War Weapons Week (July 1918) and Feed the Guns Week (October 1918) included displays, bands and speeches in Fitzalan Square and elsewhere. And schoolteachers were persistent month after month in encouraging children to buy still more war savings certificates.

American troops also put in an appearance, preparing for service in Europe and elsewhere. A small number of US doctors gained experience in the city's military hospitals and in May 1918, around 450 airmen arrived for attachment to Coal Aston Airfield and Repair Depot[172]. On 16 May, these were treated in the Town Hall to afternoon tea with the lord mayor and civic dignitaries, followed by speeches, patriotic cheers and singing of the two countries' national anthems. American Independence Day (4 July) saw a baseball game between two American teams at Bramall Lane. This event, watched by around 20,000 people with proceeds to American and British charities, also included an athletic competition between US and UK troops, singing and folk-dancing by Sheffield schoolchildren, and military and popular music from the two countries. It closed with *The Star-Spangled Banner* and *God Save the King*.

Public reminders of active or deceased soldiers were springing up around the city. In March 1917, donations were sought and trees were planted along part of Oxford Street on behalf of ex-pupils now at war from Crookesmoor Council School. Support for the national effort was boosted by many public meetings and church activities. Religious services regularly contained prayers for the troops and often included sermons praising the nation's cause. Nationwide, intercession days were held at the beginning of each year and on the day that war had been declared. Support from outside the city included several more visits from suffragette Emmeline Pankhurst. For instance, in April 1918 her Sheffield speeches praised women munition workers and boosted the government's substitution campaign by urging older men to offer themselves in place of called-up workers. As elsewhere in the country, by May 1917 the city council had established a national service committee to encourage and channel volunteers for factory work.

Despite the nation's depressed mood, everyday leisure activities of course continued. The city's two remaining cycling clubs and two athletics clubs survived the war, as did more than a dozen each of bowling and tennis clubs. Ten golf courses were still open, but parts of the Hallamshire course had been ploughed for oats and allotments and the Dore and Totley

From 1916 the city's recruiting office was based in the Corn Exchange in Sheaf Street.

course was in part used for hay and grazing. Occasional good news included the declaration in August 1917 that Sheffield was no longer a 'closed area' under the Defence of the Realm Act. Since August 1914, people in closed areas had been prohibited, for instance, from carrying a camera or taking photographs in a public place, but at last pictures for pleasure were once again permitted. This was a mere drop of comfort in the city's ocean of problems, but perhaps a normal life could at last be glimpsed.

Conscription, tribunals and conscientious objectors

By late 1915, the flow of military volunteers had become inadequate to meet the army's need and, as a result, Military Service Acts in January and May 1916 took away personal choice by introducing large-scale conscription. Men between 18 and 41 were now to be called-up to fight, and by 1918 that upper age-limit had (with some variations) been increased to 50[173].

This shift to government control meant that administrative procedures had to be transformed. Accurate details of all eligible men had to be gathered and monitored, and conscription procedures for selected groups

Captain George Barnsley was promoted to major after becoming the area's recruiting officer in mid-1916.

had to be developed. Sheffield's recruiting office, now installed in the Corn Exchange, took on more civilian staff under the supervision of military officers. In November 1917, responsibility for recruiting was transferred from the War Office to a new Ministry of National Service but remained under military supervision. The area's recruiting officer, Captain (then Major) George Barnsley, was retitled as an assistant director of national service.

However, even with compulsory call-up the number of new soldiers remained below military needs. One reason for this was poor physical condition. Only around half the men examined in 1917 and 1918 were passed as fully fit for immediate combat service. Some were considered acceptable after 'hardening' by route-marches and other physical activity, and others were taken on for more sedentary work only. Many were rejected entirely[174]. Early in the war medical examinations were mainly carried out by civilian practitioners on a part-time basis and some variation between doctors and regions had occurred. By the middle of 1916, assessments had become more standardized and were now explicitly linked to different kinds of military needs. Display Box 6.1 shows that men were henceforth placed in one of thirteen medical categories, each of which defined a person's suitability for a particular kind of role. These categories became especially important for individuals and decision-makers in 1917 and 1918, and men in low-importance jobs who were placed in a high medical grade were almost certain to be called-up.

Throughout the war the government struggled to tighten its definitions of 'nationally important' work and to assess how essential was the job of every potential serviceman. Schedules of 'protected', 'exempt' or 'certified' jobs were repeatedly refined and came to form the basis for individual call-up decisions by a local recruiting office. The period saw many comb-outs of entire firms, as recruiting authorities trawled through complete workforces to locate more men who could be enlisted[175]. In these ever-tightening conditions, many workers objected to a decision that they should be sent to war and claims for exemption became common.

Military tribunals The Military Service Act of January 1916 had established military service and appeal tribunals around the country. The Sheffield Military Service Tribunal (sometimes referred to as the Sheffield

Display Box 6.1
WAR OFFICE MEDICAL CATEGORIES

From mid-1916 War Office medical examiners were required to place each man in one of the following precise categories and sub-categories. These formed the basis of call-up and assignment decisions, and for many men became central to life or perhaps death.

Category A: Fit for general service
A(i): Fit in all respects for overseas service
A(ii): Will be A(i) after training
A(iii): Now sick or wounded but will be fit after treatment when hardened by marching and other activity

Category B: Fit for service abroad but not for general service
B(i): Fit only for overseas garrison or provisional units
B(ii): Fit for overseas labour units or in regimental outdoor work
B(iii): Fit only for overseas sedentary work, for instance as a clerk, storeman, batman, cook, orderly, or on sanitary duties

Category C: Fit for service at home only
C(i): Fit only for home garrisons or provisional units
C(ii): Fit only for home labour units or regimental outdoor work
C(iii): Fit only for home sedentary work, as illustrated in B(iii)

Category D: Temporarily unfit for Categories A, B or C
D(i): Placed temporarily in command depots
D(ii): Placed temporarily in regimental depots
D(iii): In any unit while awaiting medical or dental treatment

Category E: Unfit for any other category and unlikely to be fit within six months

Recruiting Tribunal, the Sheffield Military Tribunal or simply Sheffield Local Tribunal) was chaired by city solicitor and alderman Sir William Clegg, who was also responsible for the completely separate Munition tribunal. The city's military service (recruiting) Tribunal became extremely busy and operated as two parallel courts. Its second court was chaired by

Sir William Clegg was chairman of the local military service tribunal and held several other key posts in the city.

a prominent councillor or alderman, as was the first court in Sir William's absence, and clerk for the tribunal as a whole was William Hart, the city's town clerk. Overall, Sheffield's two military service courts handled almost 35,000 claims for exemption in more than 250 sessions before closing in November 1918. They often met several times a week, starting at five o'clock in the afternoon.

Men wishing to challenge the decision of this legally lower court could apply to an appeal tribunal. Sheffield appeals were heard by the South Yorkshire Tribunal, which covered a wide area of the (then) West Riding, including Doncaster and Rotherham. Sometimes meeting in Sheffield's Town Hall, this was chaired by the Earl of Wharncliffe, who held the rank of commander in the Royal Navy. From time to time this tribunal also needed a second court, which was chaired by a local councillor. Up to its closure in November 1918, the South Yorkshire Appeal Tribunal dealt with almost 6,000 cases from its area.

An objector's case was sometimes presented by a local solicitor, and a representative from the city's recruiting office was also present – almost always urging conscription. He was not himself a member of the tribunal. Cases usually concerned individual men, but sometimes an employer argued for a group of his workers. On other occasions the military representative proposed that a current exemption should be withdrawn, for instance because a man had changed his job or because the nationwide schedule of protected occupations had been modified.

Most conscripted men accepted their position and joined the services when ordered, so that only a minority came before a tribunal to request exemption. Court sittings were described in the local newspapers and reports reveal that the most frequent outcome in Sheffield was a temporary delay of conscription – usually for between three and six months conditional on circumstances not changing[176]. A small number of applicants received an absolute exemption without an expectation of later call-up, but the military representative might later request that this be changed. It is also clear from newspaper reports that in only very few Sheffield tribunal cases was immediate call-up required.

The majority of Sheffield's tribunal claimants eventually joined the services as instructed. On what basis did they previously claim exemption? Three general arguments were used: family need, business requirements, and conflicts with conscience. In the first case some men pleaded that their assistance and income were essential for an elderly parent or family members in difficulty. For example, in 1916 a 19-year-old carter was temporarily exempted from call-up so he could continue giving wages to his widowed mother and two younger brothers and two sisters. Similar temporary exemptions were granted to a spring-knife cutler supporting his mother and her family of twelve and to a married fruiterer with a wife and eight school-age children. However, claims for family reasons were concentrated in the first months of conscription. As allowances for soldiers' families became more widely known and perhaps acceptable, call-up exemption was rarely sought on the grounds of family need.

A second basis for objection was in terms of business requirements. Some claimants argued that their call-up would destroy a company engaged on nationally-important work or would throw people into unemployment. On that basis, three-month exemptions were awarded in Sheffield to a builder constructing new houses for the city's workers and to decorators painting munition factories; several single-person coal merchants were also deferred for three months. Other men were granted temporary exemptions to allow them to complete export orders. A self-styled 'missionary', who worked to help troops passing through Sheffield stations and to support soldiers' families in their homes was allowed to continue, as was the manager of the Edgar Allen Institute, which treated military and civilian patients, and the chauffeur to the commanding officer of the Third Northern General Hospital.

During 1917, accountants and solicitors in the city obtained exemptions by arguing they were overwhelmingly busy because of extra demands created by the Ministry of Munitions and because many of their staff had already been called-up – more than half the accountants and around a third of solicitors. In addition, several manufacturing and other companies were allowed to retain a small number of key workers temporarily on the grounds that almost all their employees had moved away. Cutlers Joseph Rodgers claimed to have lost nearly 1,000 workers to the army or munition companies, and the Corporation Tramways lost 500[177].

Only a minority of applications to Sheffield Military Tribunal were immediately rejected, including those from a group of instructors on a coalmining course and several steelworkers not engaged on munitions.

Those were called-up straightaway. However, men exempted temporarily or permanently from military service were not freed from all responsibilities. They were required by the tribunal to undertake military drill and musketry training with the city's Volunteer Defence Corps, and were instructed to undertake work considered to be of national importance. Such work, perhaps arranged through the labour exchange, could be (for example) in a munition factory, on a farm, or in a fever hospital or an asylum. Other possibilities included taking non-combatant military service or working with the Friends' Ambulance Unit; see below.

In the absence of published overall figures and in view of the fact that an unknown number of men applied again at the end of current exemption, it is not possible to cite the total numbers of Sheffield claimants exempted versus those who were called-up. However, it is clear that very few tribunal applicants in Sheffield were immediately required to join the services and that absolute exemption from conscription was also rare. Most Sheffield applicants were conditionally deferred for a few months, and presumably a large number of these subsequently became troops[178].

Conscientious objectors The 1916 Act accepted that some men would have a genuine objection of conscience to fighting and possibly killing other people, and such men were to be treated leniently. Conscientious objection was introduced above as the third possible basis of a claim for exemption, and it appears from Sheffield newspapers to have been relatively unusual in the city. There was no requirement that a claim of this kind should be based on religious belief, and at least one person seeking exemption through the Sheffield Military Tribunal argued that socialism was his religion. Nationally, it is likely that around 16,000 British men refused to fight on grounds of conscience, but published numerical estimates are inconsistent and unreliable. Detailed information about individual objectors and their later opinions and treatment is restricted to only a small minority[179].

Conscientious objectors (less politely referred to by some as 'conchies' or 'cuthberts') thus comprised only a small proportion of claimants before a tribunal in Sheffield. Like others, if excused from a fighting role they were required to contribute to the war effort as a non-combatant. Nationally, around 3,300 such men joined the army's Non-Combatant Corps (NCC) – occasionally disparaged as the 'No Courage Corps'. The corps was created in March 1916 and its members, uniformed private soldiers, were subject to military discipline and were supervised by army officers. However, they were not required to carry rifles or take part in combat, instead working to repair or construct roads, railways and army buildings and assisting in other practical ways.

Some conscientious objectors at the Sheffield Military Tribunal were offered work with a medical service, for example with the Red Cross or in one of the local hospitals. Several agreed to join the Friends' Ambulance Unit (FAU). This national organization had been set up in September 1914 by volunteers from the Quaker religious group the Society of Friends, but the unit had no formal attachment to the Society. The FAU transported and cared for wounded men in its own ambulances and operated a number of hospitals near the Western Front as well as providing orphanages for children who had lost their parents. Its uniformed members worked in semi-military units alongside the army but not under military control. However, their senior officer held a commission in the British Army. Members of the unit (eventually around 1,200) received no wages, and funds and equipment were raised from public donations. Although most FAU work was in France and Belgium, a few hundred members served in Britain and several dozen were in hospital ships.

Membership of the Friends' Ambulance Unit was not restricted to Quakers, and recruits came from a variety of backgrounds both religious and non-religious. Some were Christian pacifists, others drew an anti-war position from socialist principles, and many were indeed Quakers. In practice, the unit was a hybrid and effective compromise, described by one member as 'an attempt to have the cake and eat it, to go to war and be a pacifist [...] to share in the common ideal and to make some kind of protest against the common folly'[180]. The number of Sheffield members of the unit remains unknown.

More generally, although Quakers had always argued for non-violent pacifism and continued to do so[181], they also advocated individual freedom of conscience. As a result Friends were free to respond to the war in their own way. A minority, perhaps about a third of those eligible, accepted the need to fight in one of the services, often with considerable distinction. In Sheffield, Herbert Barber (Master Cutler in 1909) lost two of his sons who had become army officers[182]. Other Quakers worked during the war in non-military ways, for example helping British families of German men who had been interned as enemy aliens.

Among conscientious objectors accepting a move into the FAU was a tribunal applicant described on 8 June 1916 in the *Sheffield Daily Independent*: 'He was not willing to take work under the naval or military authorities or in any way aid in the prosecution of the war, believing that human life was sacred and all war contrary to the principles of Christianity. Applicant had attended the Church of England until about twelve months ago, but had ceased to do so because he disagreed with its attitude in respect of the war.' He was given a fortnight to join the Friends Ambulance Unit or the British Red Cross.

Although many conscientious objectors considered a non-combatant role to be acceptable instead of fighting, a small minority refused to be 'part of the war' machine in any way. If those men refused all work defined as nationally important for the war, they were liable to be imprisoned. It has been estimated that in total around 1,000 absolutist conscientious objectors were imprisoned for two or more years and maybe around 5,000 others for shorter periods. Twenty or thirty persistent law-breakers (estimates of the number vary) were given death sentences, which were later commuted to penal servitude[183].

Sheffield newspapers appear to contain no information about conscientious objectors from the city who were imprisoned[184], but other sources identify as jailed absolutists two brothers working as cutlery bone-cutters – Joseph and William Parkin of Gleadless Road. Both were imprisoned in Wormwood Scrubs and then Dartmoor jails, and William's hard labour in prison is said to have caused his early death. Before the war, John Bonsall lived in Duke Street and operated a haulage business from Bond Street. His absolutist objection to call-up also resulted in imprisonment in Wormwood Scrubs, but he subsequently chose to join the Non-Combatant Corps and served as a cook in army units.

National protest groups included the No Conscription Fellowship (NCF), founded in December 1914 and open to all men of military age who were not prepared to take a combatant's role. The NCF contained many Quakers and other religious pacifists, but most of its members had secular or socialist objections. The Fellowship produced thousands of libertarian and anti-war leaflets, despite some printing presses being confiscated or disabled and several authors being prosecuted. Local branches included one in Sheffield and several objectors before the city's military service tribunal, both religious and non-religious, declared that they were NCF members.

Other cases reported in the local press included members of the anti-war Christadelphian Church and 'a specialist in vegetarian foods' (in the words of the *Independent*) who refused to fight because of his close adherence to the gospel of Jesus Christ. 'If Jesus Christ were in England at the present time [...] he would be put into prison under the Defence of the Realm Act.' Another man objected to being called-up because: 'I feel that war is entirely forbidden by the teachings of Jesus. He has shown that evil can only be cured by doing good.' A 'member of a Friends' Adult School, a Wesleyan, a member of the No Conscription Fellowship and the Fellowship of Reconciliation' was asked whether he would leave a soldier to die on the battlefield rather than help him. He replied (but did not answer the question) that 'if everyone did as I think they ought there would be no war'. These and similar claims for exemption, including a few suspiciously recent converts to a pacifist group) were disallowed and the applicants were ordered to undertake public service or join the army.

Similar decisions were reached about a number of avowed socialists in the city. The Socialist Party objected to the war for its large-scale killing of workers, considering all working people to be members of an international brotherhood. The war was seen as being waged for the benefit of the capitalist class to the harm of working people. One prominent local tribunal claimant in September 1916 was yeast dealer Alfonso Samms – a socialist member of the Sheffield Board of Guardians who was well-known for his anti-war activities. A year previously he had been sentenced to two months in prison for attempting to cause disaffection among wounded soldiers in the Guardians' hospital. The South Yorkshire Appeal Committee now ordered him to join the Non-Combatant Corps, but he refused. It is not clear what happened next.

Objections to the war were also raised by people who had no cause to appear before a military tribunal, perhaps being older, unfit or otherwise ineligible for military service. For example, Cecil Wilson, the chairman and works manager of the Sheffield Smelting Company, felt in November 1915 that it would be wrong for him to help his company to produce war material. The company had, in 1914, shared the general enthusiasm for fighting, encouraging its workers to enlist, offering them a financial incentive, and providing an allowance to soldiers' dependants. However, in April 1915, after the firm started to roll brass for shells and cartridges, Cecil considered it wrong for him to have 'any part in the manufacture of something the sole object of which was to destroy human life'. He resigned his leading position in the company, but continued to work on the firm's non-military projects[185].

By the middle of the war, the government was concerned that anti-war feelings were spreading and reducing the nation's will to fight. A growing number of people, including around thirty Labour and other MPs, were questioning the wisdom of continuing a costly and painful conflict that appeared to be getting nowhere. In June 1916, Sheffield police prohibited a 'stop the war' demonstration in the city, and it was frequently emphasized that any public statement thought to be prejudicial to military discipline could be treated as an offence under the Defence of the Realm Act.

The following months saw several Sheffield men charged on that basis. For instance, in June 1917, Charles Storey of Coniston Terrace was accused of 'attempting to cause military sedition and dissatisfaction among members of His Majesty's Forces'. Aged 67, he had been in the habit of settling himself on a seat near the military hospital at Carter Knowle School and declaring that solders were fools, murderers and so on: '[C]onscientious objectors were ten times better than they.' He was bound over for twelve months.

In addition to men of military age who claimed exemption, some others of all ages also opposed the war in private or in public. By 1917, doubt was growing within parts of the community as well as merely among many of the conscripted men who appeared before a military service tribunal[186].

A small number of men who had accepted their call-up subsequently left their unit without permission or did not turn up in the first place. The handwritten report-book of an unknown Attercliffe policeman describes no fewer than thirty-seven arrests of deserters from UK units that he had made in the twelve months from February 1917 – more than three a month. Some of these men had settled into jobs in a local factory and others were extending their leave in the city. A few appear to have fled immediately after being called-up instead of reporting as required to their initial unit. Overall, there may have been several hundred deserters from the city, but most periods of absence were brief. Nevertheless, the majority of British people had no doubt – the war must be continued until victory is achieved.

Shortages and rationing

War-weariness also came from the daily struggle to cope with the scarcity of essential items, particularly of food at a time of rising prices. The country had long needed to import much of its food, for instance around two-thirds of its sugar and four-fifths of its wheat, and German submarine activity was now ensuring that less and less was available.

Lack of food During 1916, the authorities tried to improve food production and reduce consumption in several ways. A Regulation of Meals Order set limits on some servings in restaurants and hotels, a

Milling Order required the extraction of more flour from the available wheat, and the public was urged to have one meatless day in each week – those were by now obligatory in public eating-places[187]. Fines were introduced for wasting food by feeding it to pigeons or stray animals.

By 1917 the country was desperately short of wheat, and posters like this were widely displayed.

In October 1916, the government took control of all wheat purchases from abroad and its Corn Production Act of April 1917 guaranteed farmers minimum prices for wheat and oats, thus hoping to increase the country's own output. In May 1917, the king instructed churches to read out a proclamation in which he stated that 'abstention from all unnecessary consumption of grain' was the most effective way to defeat the enemy. He requested families to reduce their bread consumption by at least a quarter and not use flour in pastry and other non-bread items. The king also asked people to sign his pledge: 'We the undersigned members of this household hereby pledge ourselves on our honour to respond to His Majesty's appeal.' The government appointed a national food controller with (eventually) a large staff. His department urged restraint through advertisements and posters, by publicizing ways to avoid waste[188] and by encouraging voluntary self-rationing in terms of maximum amounts to be eaten each week. Food economy was included in school lessons and it was forbidden to throw rice at weddings.

The Food Economy Department within the Ministry of Food in conjunction with the National War Savings Committee and its many local groups organized economy-oriented events around the country. In May 1917, Sheffield's Cutlers' Hall housed a two-week 'national economy and welfare exhibition', which provided lectures and demonstrations about how to save and produce more food and gave detailed advice about growing vegetables. Also in the exhibition were displays of labour-saving devices, items for sale, and war exhibits. The event was linked to a programme of children's competitions and practical work in all the city's schools. In the same month, the Town Hall entrance was draped with an information sheet reminding people of the food controller's recommended scale of voluntary rations.

The national economy campaign also gave rise to several songs about food-saving, among which was *Wear a Purple Ribbon* – a public symbol of support for the cause. Needing to save more of the nation's wheat, government regulation bread, widely known as 'war bread', was introduced, in which a proportion of white flour was replaced at different times by barley, rice, oatmeal, beans or potatoes. Food hoarding became an offence that was vigorously pursued by the authorities, with several local prosecutions reported in the city's newspapers.

The government's Cultivation of Land Orders included new authority for councils to take possession of land for allotments[189]. The city's own land cultivation committee took over several sites and released additional areas it already owned. Many Sheffielders took this opportunity to grow their own food, paying a monthly rent for their plot, and in the course of the war the number of allotments in the city, including some from a private landlord, increased from about 1,600 to around 10,000. Despite a formal prohibition, much allotment activity took place on a Sunday.

Local produce exhibitions and competitions were frequently held around the city with a city-wide show in Weston Park in September 1917. In addition, local and national newspapers provided advice on how to get the best from an allotment, and households were bombarded with suggestions for improving the content and preparation of their meals. For example, the *Sheffield Daily Independent* published wartime housekeeping leaflets which recommended economical meals, and in the autumn of 1917 city schools and cookery centres offered adults free lessons about how to preserve fruit at home. The Ministry of Food issued several war cooking recipes, including a 1917 war Christmas pudding which used only those materials then available. Another suggestion was for wartime soup, shown in Display Box 6.2.

In August of that year, Sheffield established its own food control committee, which gave rise to at least four sub-committees – the flour, bread and potatoes sub-committee, the meat sub-committee, the sugar and butter sub-committee, and the milk sub-committee. Made up of councillors and suppliers, these worked to fix prices for all the city's retailers, often on a weekly basis[190]. Much of the main committee's effort went into improving supplies to the city and monitoring local allocations so that individual retailers received amounts that matched their estimated numbers of customers. From September 1917, it introduced schemes to allocate fixed amounts of sugar to families of different sizes. The meat sub-committee checked (with the help of special constables) that all retailers

Display Box 6.2
WARTIME SOUP
One of the 'War Cooking Recipes' published by
the Ministry of Food in 1917

Every economical housewife should have Wartime Soup constantly going: it is both delicious and nourishing and, above all, cheap.

Ingredients: All outer leaves and peelings and tops and tails of vegetables, all fruit peelings, stones and cores, all sauce-pan and dish rinsings, bread crusts, remains of suet, batter and milky puddings (but not jam or sweet puddings), cheese and bacon rinds, skim milk, sour milk, remains of sauces (not sweet sauces) or gravy, vegetable water, margarine (if liked), pepper and salt, water.

Preparation: Wash thoroughly all vegetable peelings and leaves (do not use potato peelings); use the outer leaves of cabbage, cauliflower, broccoli, curly kale, lettuce, leeks, and onions; the tops and peelings of turnips, carrots, parsnips, swedes, kohlrabi. Put all into a cooking box saucepan with plenty of water, bring to the boil, boil for twenty minutes; add some or all of the other ingredients; season to taste; boil ten minutes without removing cover, and place in cooking box two to three hours. Take out and rub through a sieve and, if necessary, reheat on gas ring.

displayed a notice of their prices. Rabbits were in great demand, with butchers' prices determined by yet another unexpected regulation – the government's Wild Rabbits (Prices) Order. Even horse-flesh shops had queues from time to time, and around ten were now flourishing in the city.

The 1918 edition of the *Sheffield Yearbook and Record* includes considerable detail about the prices set in Sheffield in the previous year. Separate levels were required for different kinds of meat, and the *Yearbook* cites fixed prices for no less than twenty separate cuts of beef, fifteen of mutton and lamb, and eight of pork. Beef joints ranged from the currently familiar steak, brisket and kidney to others of the period like 'bosom' and 'bedpiece'. Despite all these efforts, food became increasingly difficult to obtain during the second half of 1917. The 1918 *Yearbook* saw it like this:

> Sugar was short throughout the year [*i.e., 1917*]. Most people had to give up taking sugar in their tea [...] Although the authorities

> denied that there was any such arrangement, sugar could not be obtained without the purchase of a stated quantity of other groceries [...] 'No Sugar' became a frequent notice in shop windows[191].
>
> By August there was also a shortage of butter, and later on of tea; and long butter and tea queues became common outside the shops of the poor, especially on Saturdays[192].
>
> There was also a beer problem. Owing to the fact that corn was needed for food, the government restricted the amount of barley that could be used for beer. Public-houses were open only a portion of the day, and closed at 9.30 each evening, but even so they could not get sufficient beer to supply their customers. 'No Beer' was in the windows of most public houses. This generally meant that there was no beer for stray customers, and barely enough for the regular thirsts.

The year 1917 also saw the opening of communal kitchens in the city, providing at moderate prices prepared food that could be taken home to eat. First (in February) came a small outlet close to the Moor, which was operated by the city's Salvation Army, and in May 1917 the council opened its own public kitchen in Gibraltar Street, run by volunteers and two paid part-time cleaners. The scheme became very successful as the cost of food continued to rise and supplies became scarce. In the following spring other low-price outlets, now within a countrywide framework of 'National Kitchens', opened in Burngreave and in Mowbray Street, and by November 1918 the city had a total of seven kitchens within the scheme[193].

Continuing shortages and food queues continued to create irritation, anxiety and sometimes anger; a long wait might result in only a meagre purchase or total failure, and favouritism by shopkeepers was widely suspected. Retailers' prices were regularly checked by officials against the allowed level, and fines were levied for over-charging.

By 1918 the food situation was grim and on 7 January the *Sheffield Daily Independent* reported that 'some thousands of people' were queuing for food. Meat was in particularly short supply. Retired scissor-smith John Dyson wrote in his diary for 10 January: 'Mr Oates' butcher's shop had but little meat in it and was full of people and a small queue standing outside at 10.30. About thirty minutes later he closed his shop and exhibited a sign "No meat. Sold out".' On the next day, 'I called at our provision merchant F. E. Thompson Ltd., but he had not a scrap of bacon or butter or margarine or any kind of fat in the premises. Maud *[the family's maid]* had early in the morning been to Oates the butchers but there was such a long queue she gave up'[194].

For a week in January the Cutlers' Hall housed an SOS exhibition – Save or Starve. Part of a national programme, this was organized by Sheffield Women's Committee of Food Experts, a temporary group of senior canteen staff and cookery teachers together with the lady editors of the city's two newspapers[195]. The exhibition had a single-minded focus on potatoes as those were readily available. It promoted cookery with potatoes rather than flour or other material – demonstrating (with free samples) the use of potato bread, potato soup, potato scones, potato butter, potato and apple pudding, savoury potato roll, and meat and potato pie with a crust made of flour and (surprise, surprise) potato. The exhibition also urged food economy more generally through talks by Mrs C. S. Peel, a well-known writer in the field, for instance of the book *Eat Less Meat*, who was on the staff of the Ministry of Food[196].

The government now tried to equalize the amounts available to everyone by rationing principal foods. Details changed slightly as experience led to improvements, but in outline each household had to

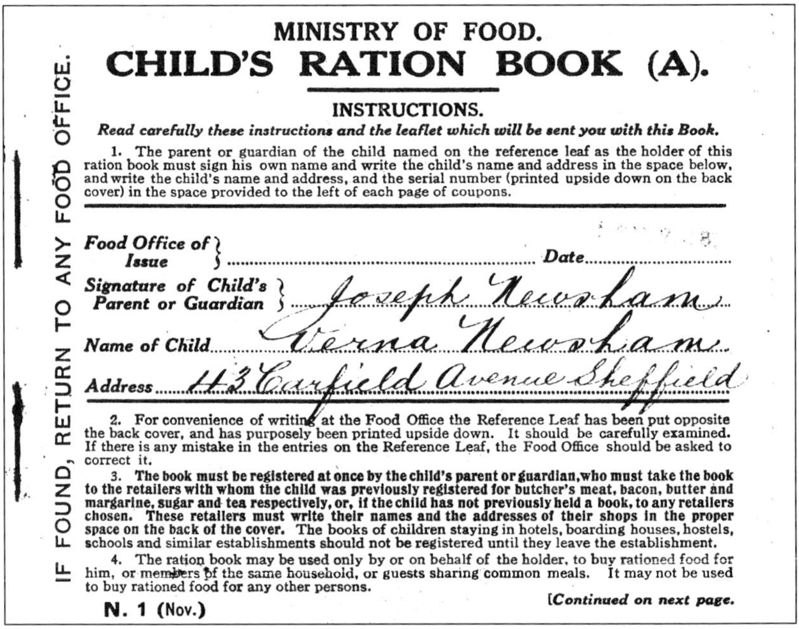

IF FOUND, RETURN TO ANY FOOD OFFICE.

MINISTRY OF FOOD.

CHILD'S RATION BOOK (A).

INSTRUCTIONS.

Read carefully these instructions and the leaflet which will be sent you with this Book.

1. The parent or guardian of the child named on the reference leaf as the holder of this ration book must sign his own name and write the child's name and address in the space below, and write the child's name and address, and the serial number (printed upside down on the back cover) in the space provided to the left of each page of coupons.

Food Office of Issue .... *Date* ....

Signature of Child's Parent or Guardian Joseph Newsham

Name of Child Verna Newsham

Address 43 Carfield Avenue Sheffield

2. For convenience of writing at the Food Office the Reference Leaf has been put opposite the back cover, and has purposely been printed upside down. It should be carefully examined. If there is any mistake in the entries on the Reference Leaf, the Food Office should be asked to correct it.

3. **The book must be registered at once by the child's parent or guardian, who must take the book to the retailers with whom the child was previously registered for butcher's meat, bacon, butter and margarine, sugar and tea respectively, or, if the child has not previously held a book, to any retailers chosen. These retailers must write their names and the addresses of their shops in the proper space on the back of the cover.** The books of children staying in hotels, boarding houses, hostels, schools and similar establishments should not be registered until they leave the establishment.

4. The ration book may be used only by or on behalf of the holder, to buy rationed food for him, or members of the same household, or guests sharing common meals. It may not be used to buy rationed food for any other persons.

N. 1 (Nov.) *[Continued on next page.*

Some food rationing was introduced in 1918, requiring the issue of different ration books to adults and children.

register for each type of rationed food with a retailer accepted by the local food control committee[197]. Based on a family's size and membership, the control committee determined its weekly allocation of a particular food and worked to provide every retailer with the total amount required by all of its registered customers. Books of coupons were issued to each family[198], entitling every member to a specified quantity each week of butter, margarine, lard, sugar, tea, bacon (briefly) and jam (later). First within the scheme was sugar in January 1918, and the other items followed during the spring and summer. In the middle of the year the city also introduced meat coupons based on the value of a purchase[199].

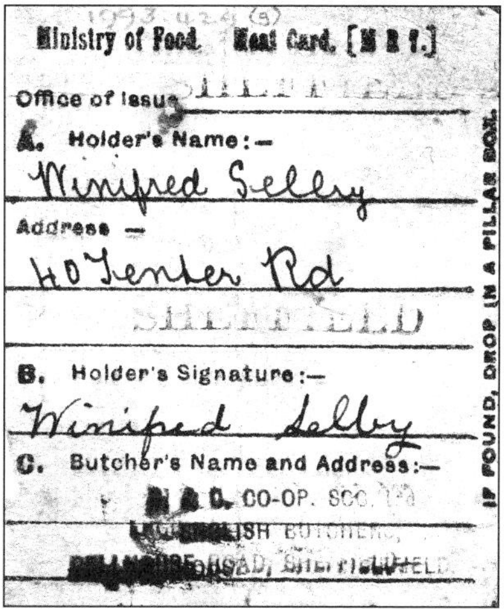
Ministry of Food. Meat Card.
Office of Issue
A. Holder's Name:—
Winifred Selby
Address —
40 Tenter Rd
SHEFFIELD
B. Holder's Signature:—
Winifred Selby
C. Butcher's Name and Address:—
CO-OP. SOC.
IF FOUND, DROP IN A PILLAR BOX.

From mid-1918 each person's meat card had to be registered with a named butcher to obtain a fixed quantity each week.

The administration of rationing was an enormous task for the city's food control committee and its staff, especially in the absence of computers, and for many families it was at first difficult to cope with the procedure. However, in general it worked smoothly and queues in the city and nationwide were gradually removed. Bread was never rationed. Sheffield's food control office was in the Wesleyan Schools at the West Street end of Carver Street, with an information centre in High Street and other offices elsewhere in the city. For each period of administration, 479,000 separate ration books (initially cards) had to be sent out, all based specifically on the details of a recipient family. Depending on the food category, different amounts were allocated for different people – adults, expectant mothers, children, boys between 13 and 18, certain medical categories, and the city's 50,000 'heavy' workers and 35,000 'very heavy' workers. In addition, emergency ration books were required for troops temporarily in the city on leave and for other visitors, and different arrangements had to be made for hotels and restaurants, special events[200] and changes of address. Furthermore, the city's food producers had to be granted their own bulk permissions for each item. As well as ration books themselves, almost all of Sheffield's rationed food was distributed by the committee, for example through its newly-established margarine clearing house, as retailers had to be sent the appropriate quantities of each product to match their registered customers.

Regularly during 1918, this local committee published detailed lists of each kind of personal ration for the next week.

Everyday life had moved a long way from the *laissez-faire* traditions of pre-war Britain. Controls on food, like other forms of wartime centralized regulation, created more and more committees, public servants and bureaucratic activity – and also a lot of new jobs for female clerks[201].

Other government controls Household problems other than food were dealt with by yet more centralized regulations. For fuel, a national controller of coal mines was set-up to maximize supplies and to reorganize coal transport arrangements. In the middle of 1918, domestic coal rationing was extended from London, where it had been introduced in October 1917, to Sheffield and the rest of the country. In July 1918 the city appointed its own coal controller and a fuel and lighting committee to ensure that permitted quantities were allocated to each house in terms of its number of rooms. Gas and electricity allowances were fixed similarly. As in the case of food, the price of each kind of coal was specified by the authorities, separately for either bagged or loose, and every household had to register with a particular supplier[202].

Lighting in shops and factories was cut back under the Defence of the Realm Act, and by the autumn of 1918 many weekday church services had been abandoned to save fuel. Petrol had been rationed since 1916 and the scarce supplies were now mainly directed to military and munition needs. As an alternative, a few gas-driven taxis and lorries made their appearance in the city from the autumn of 1917 – gas was carried in a large container on top. The City Council acquired ten electric vehicles for its refuse collection, and its remaining working horses felt the impact of restrictions. The government's Horses (Rationing) Order of April 1918 substantially cut back the maximum weekly grain allowance for horses employed on sanitary and cleaning work, and by June the city's animals had lost so much weight that it was feared 'they will not be able to carry on the work in a hilly district

Conditions were particularly difficult by 1918, and the city then appointed its own coal controller to ration scarce supplies.

like Sheffield'. The hunt for fuel even extended to looking for oil, and some drilling started in around half-a-dozen wells in Derbyshire. Most were quickly abandoned, but in May 1918 oil was struck at Hardstoft near Hardwick Hall and a small regular supply appeared possible. However, the end of fighting and many technical difficulties meant that the scheme was before long abandoned.

In addition to food and fuel shortages, the city suffered from the nation's lack of paper. Paper bags became scarce, newspapers and magazines were reduced in size, and books became less available and more expensive. Schools suffered so that, for example, in the autumn of 1917 the log book of Ranmoor Council School reported that 'we are quite without exercise books for writing [...] but the difficulty of supply is so great that it is not likely that [an] order will be fulfilled early'. Some Sheffield Sunday Schools postponed their annual prize-giving as no suitable books for prizes were available. Wastepaper now increased greatly in value and was collected from the city's houses and offices by the council, local newspapers, the Salvation Army and other groups. The government issued a schedule of prices to be paid.

Tobacco, glass containers and other items for household use were also scarce and controls and committees extended even to the humble match. The government set up a Tobacco and Matches Control Board with a national Match Control Office and from 1917 maximum prices were set. As there were many different brands of either traditional or safety matches, and as these were sold in boxes of different sizes or joined together in books, the list of prices, which had to be displayed by every retailer, was long and complicated. Sheffield shops were starved of match supplies and customers were granted only small quantities. Instead, mechanical cigarette lighters became popular, with a resultant surge in prices.

The multiple strains of family bereavement, bad news about the war, long hours of work and widespread household shortages were increasingly blamed for a range of war illnesses. Local newspapers contained articles about 'war neuroses', 'war anxiety', 'war headaches' and similar problems. In May 1917, the *Sheffield Daily Independent* was concerned about the city's 'thousands of sickly anxious-looking men, women and girls with muddy complexions', and in the next month it told its readers that 'thousands of people are feeling worried because of the uncertainty of the future, and thousands are working long hours on war work; consequently the War Headache is common'.

The period also saw many suggestions and advertisements for cures and remedies. Recommendations included an assortment of pills, potions and powders, or perhaps a glass of hot water containing a teaspoonful of limestone phosphate before breakfast. Zox powders were alleged to remove headaches 'in a minute or two', and several creams were advertised to help women munition or canteen workers care for their skin. For instance, 'Ven-Yusa, the Oxygen Face Cream for Munition Girls' was specially formulated 'to give the skin a real invigorating oxygen bath' so that 'war-work will not spoil the skin'. Oatine Face Cream was also advertised for munition girls and those helping in the buffet or canteen. It was 'used in National Factories and may be obtained from many Munition Canteens and all chemists'.

The British Electric Institute promised to revive war-weary individuals and cure a wide range of complaints.

Great benefits were promised from the remarkable powers of electricity. During 1918, Sheffield newspapers carried large advertisements from the British Electric Institute based in London. For example, a drawing of a pitiably listless man was followed by suggestions that: 'your vitality is ebbing away. You are in urgent need of a radical remedy to regain your

Troops at Coal Aston Airfield included members of the Royal Naval Air Service.

strength and manly power.' Luckily, a 'remedy is at hand'. 'Electricity, all-powerful in its curative properties, just as it is irresistible in its force, will give you back the strength you have lost. It will make a "man" of you again. The "Ajax" Dry Cell Body Battery pours a stream of new life into your weakened body, and Courage, Ambition and Energy will fire your soul again. It cures Nervous Debility, Neurasthenia, Neuralgia, Rheumatism, Sciatica, Stomach, Liver and Bladder Troubles, Paralysis, &c., &c.' In later months a similarly optimistic advertisement assured Sheffielders that the Pulvermacher Appliance delivers its 'curative supply' without causing electric shock. Whether or not any of the suggested remedies made any difference, Sheffield in 1917 and 1918 was in a poor state.

Two more arrivals: Prisoners-of-war and influenza

As the war developed, both sides captured more and more enemy troops. By the end of 1918, around 150,000 German, Austrian and other prisoners-of-war (97 percent German) were being held in more than 400 camps around Britain[203]. Two of these camps were in Sheffield – at Coal Aston and at Redmires.

In February 1917, around 300 German prisoners-of-war arrived at Coal Aston Airfield, and that number was probably increased later. Many were put to work under military guard on construction projects at the camp and elsewhere, but little information is available about their activities. The publication of military details would have been contrary to wartime regulations. However, cases brought before civilian courts of law could be reported in the press, and several of these appeared in Sheffield newspapers.

For example, in September 1917 a Sheffield man working as a labourer at Coal Aston camp was charged under the Defence of the Realm Act for passing a tin of condensed milk to a German prisoner. The accused man said he was helping the German after his plea 'For God's sake give me a drop of milk for my tea'. In another case, in March 1918, a Sheffield member of the Women's Army Auxiliary Corps based at Coal Aston was fined £5 for communicating with a German prisoner. According to the *Sheffield Daily Independent*:

> Corporal H. G. Smith (Royal Flying Corps) stated in Court that when a party of Germans were being marched to a quarry where they worked he saw one of them write something on a piece of

> paper which he put into a matchbox and placed near a water pipe. Later he saw the girl defendant fetch this. She fetched five notes in all, and then he took her to Adjutant Hudson.
>
> Winifred Dean, of the W.A.A.C., said that about three weeks ago the matchbox was thrown from where the Germans were working near, and she saw one of the German prisoners looking over the wall and smiling. The defendant picked it up and found a note inside, which began 'My Darling Unknown'. There were about five notes in all, which the defendant read to them [...] There was no secrecy about all this, and they treated the matter as a joke, and nothing more.
>
> Adjt.-Lieut. Hudson said that what had occurred was a breach of discipline [...] If the girl got information to the German by love letters, he did not know whether she got anything else to him [...] The defendant said she [...] only did it to cheer him up.

'Cheering up' was not the intention of some farmers near the city's other prisoner-of-war camp, at Redmires. On 19 October 1918 the *Independent* reported: 'Carl Braun, Richard Kummeth and Emile Frank, German prisoners-of-war, were seen at two o'clock yesterday morning in a potato field in the occupation of Mrs Marsden, near Redmires Camp. Mrs Marsden's son James, and his cousin Benjamin, were keeping watch. The Germans were carrying bags, and, when they found that they were detected, ran away, dropping the bags. James Marsden, who had a gun, fired into the air. As the men did not stop running, he fired at their legs and hit Franke. One of the others came forward shouting "Kamarade". He was arrested', as were the others.

Redmires Camp had only recently (on 9 October 1918) opened for prisoners-of-war. From its early days as the first base of Sheffield City Battalion to the departure of Royal Engineers in March 1918, the camp had accommodated a series of army units. However, after modifications it was now used to house captured German officers and their orderlies. In January 1919, the camp received a routine inspection by a Swiss delegation based in London, at which time it housed 501 German and four Austrian officers together with 150 orderlies. The camp, like others, had its own hospital and recreation rooms, and the prisoners reported that they were well-treated[204]. Prisoners were held at Redmires and other UK camps until the autumn of 1919[205].

It gradually became usual for some prisoners, maybe as many as half by the end of the war, to work in factories, quarries, farms or similar settings[206]. A painting by Charles Holmes of part of Vickers' works shows a military guard in an official stance[207]. He and others were required to watch over prisoners for an entire shift and supervise them from and to their camp. At the end of May 1918, a charge of giving cigarettes to prisoners working at Vickers was dismissed by a local court on the grounds that this was a common occurrence[208].

Prisoners-of-war made a less dramatic impact on the city than did another arrival – an influenza virus. Just when the war seemed at last to be going Britain's way, grief and anxiety hit the country from a completely unexpected direction. A world-wide epidemic, sometimes called a pandemic, of flu reached Sheffield in the summer of 1918. Its origin has never been clearly identified – perhaps birds from India or another Asian country, from unsanitary conditions on the Western Front ('French fever'), from an army camp in Kansas USA (an early incidence site), or even from somewhere in Spain ('Spanish flu').

The pandemic killed millions of people around the world and at least 150,000 in Britain alone[209]. It reached Sheffield in three main waves – in July 1918, November 1918 and, with less intensity, in the early months of 1919, and overall caused nearly 3,000 deaths in the city, often from linked bronchitis or pneumonia. For a period in the autumn of 1918, 300 deaths were occurring in the city each week from influenza and associated pneumonia, and at its Sheffield peak in November the disease caused around 750 deaths in a single week.

The 1919 edition of the *Sheffield Yearbook* summarized the attacks: 'The worst influenza epidemic Sheffield has ever experienced occurred in the autumn of 1918. People in the prime of life died so rapidly that queues almost developed at the cemeteries. Many bodies remained unburied for nearly a fortnight. Coffins were difficult to get; grave-diggers were few; undertakers were working night and day. Many funerals took place after dark.'

Grave-digging problems were made worse by the increasingly urgent call-up of men for the military services. On 5 July 1918, the *Yorkshire Telegraph and Star* reported a request from the city's deputy town clerk to the South Yorkshire Appeal Tribunal that three grave-diggers working for the corporation should not be conscripted: 'Owing to the present epidemic the death rate has leaped up, and we are unable to cope with the orders. People are lying dead in their houses seven days, and sometimes even nine [...] The position is very serious indeed.'

Among the city's deaths from influenza was Private F. B. Bower of Hawksley Avenue, who died in November. He had lost an eye from a shrapnel attack in December 1915, and flu now caused the wound to re-open. Also in November, one of the city's Australian munition workers died from the disease. Henry Ryan had volunteered to leave his home country in February 1917 and arrived in Sheffield in August of that year. He had since been employed at Vickers' Brightside Works and was living in one of the temporary huts in Petre Street. Around eighty fellow Australian workers attended his funeral. Among other deaths from flu was 25-year-old Lucy Castledine from Mount Pleasant in Stocksbridge. Lucy had worked as a nurse in Firvale Hospital since 1916 and in October 1918 caught flu from a soldier in her care. She rapidly succumbed and was buried in Bolsterstone Cemetery. Around thirty soldiers from the hospital escorted her coffin, which was draped in a Union Jack. Her military patient also died.

The deadly impact of influenza was often very rapid. Inquests reported at the end of October 1918 included one for Albert Mallinson of Woodside Lane. Albert had continued in his job until Wednesday when he complained of a cold. He was dead by Friday. Domestic servant Florence Shepherd of Morpeth Street suffered head pains on Thursday night and died on Sunday morning. Around the same time, Florence Jacques of Bamforth Street also died. Her sore throat had started on Friday evening.

In addition to the hundreds of deaths, thousands more people suffered but gradually recovered. Life in the city was widely disrupted. Police court cases were postponed, at one point more than a third of the fire brigade was stricken, several collieries stopped work altogether, patient-visiting in some hospitals was banned, and many schools in the neighbourhood were closed. However, almost all Sheffield schools remained open, albeit with much reduced attendance. In October 1918, theatres, music halls and cinemas, where infection was thought to spread, were placed out of bounds to troops in the city.

By that month illness among hospital staff made it necessary for the authorities to ask for help from the city's people. The Third Northern General (military) Hospital was short of forty nurses and could not accommodate more patients, but Lodge Moor Fever Hospital, with a third of its nurses ill, could take more if volunteer helpers would come forward. Newspaper articles described the need for assistance in both hospitals, and parts of a more specific letter by city health officials are shown in Display Box 6.3. Very quickly volunteers met the needs.

Display Box 6.3
VOLUNTEER NURSES NEEDED

Excerpts from a letter to local newspapers on 31 October 1918

At the present moment there are many households in Sheffield, every member of which is suffering from influenza. In many cases they have no-one to help them [...]

All the hospitals in the city are full and overcrowded except Lodgemoor, where additional wards could be opened if nurses and staff could be obtained [...] Nothing further can be done unless the women of the City are willing and able to come forward and volunteer their services in this very great emergency. Two forms of service are open:

1. To nurse and give assistance to families in the homes of patients under the supervision of trained nurses.

2. To undertake to serve at Lodgemoor as temporary nurses or ward maids. Anyone volunteering to serve at Lodgemoor must realise that they may come into contact with patients suffering from scarlet fever or diphtheria.

The Corporation [...] offer remuneration for these services, but the appeal is really to the public spirit, and the willingness to serve others, that has been so abundantly shown during the last four years of war.

Workers' illness meant that many Sheffield factories had to stop working for short periods, and at other times production was interrupted by the flu-created absence of essential workers. Munition output was inevitably affected. At Vickers Holme Lane factory, Septimus Bennett's work suffered from his own illness and from frequent absences among his co-workers: 'On Monday I hadn't a single girl with the afternoon shift'[210].

Chemists and doctors were under siege and queues were to be seen around the city. Many remedies were suggested, including various forms of the then-popular quinine, 'Capsules of Cinnamon and Quinine', and other types of pill. Advertisements for previously established products were now adjusted to show their benefits against the new ailment. 'Oxo fortifies the system against influenza infection.' 'Protect yourself from the Flu by taking a few Peps every day.' 'Pinkobolic Soap is a sure shield against influenza.' The Milton Manufacturing Company of London advertised its antiseptic product's uses against flu in the home and offered its spray and sprayer to companies: 'A representative will call at your works to advise.'

Illness and death from the influenza epidemic darkened further the city's mood into the autumn of 1918[211]. News from the battlefield was beginning to improve, but optimism was still in short supply. Nevertheless, the military worst was indeed over, and on 11 November an armistice was signed. The fighting had stopped, and a permanent peace could now be sought.

'Hearts were full and tears were many'

During the first few days of November, newspapers reported a sequence of events in Europe that at last pointed to an end to the struggle. When the Allies demanded Germany's acceptance of peace terms by Monday 11 November, that country could see no alternative and signatures from both sides were placed on an armistice document at 5.10 am that morning. Hostilities were to cease at 11 am[212].

Sheffield and the rest of the nation were waiting for that signature. The city's newspaper offices received the news at around 10.30 am, just in time for the proposed ceasefire at 11.00 am. By then, in the words of next day's *Sheffield Daily Independent*, 'the city right out to the suburbs had undergone a remarkable transition from the grey of a November morning. Flags were unfurled, colours flying, and smiling faces and laughter bespoke the message – Peace. Bells that had been silent for the greater part of the war clanged in measured refrain, as they do on royal occasions; and the air-raid buzzers that had been wont to break in like a nightmare on the sleep of citizens told to all far and near the glad message of the hour.'

The city centre bells of the (Anglican) Cathedral and (Catholic) St Marie's rang in turn throughout that Monday, and thanksgiving services were held there, in the (Methodist) Victoria Hall and in churches around the city[213]. The *Independent* pointed out that in the churches: 'perhaps better than anywhere else in public, one grasped in a fuller sense the mingling of joy in the hour of triumph and of pathos in the memory of those who had fallen. Hearts were full and tears were many.' The *Yorkshire Telegraph and Star* offered a different story: 'Up at Redmires in the camp there, for ever a memory of the much-loved City Battalion, are some 300 of our soldiers and a considerable number of German prisoners, and, as the sound of cheering came down, wonder was expressed about which of these bodies was cheering the loudest at the coming of peace.'

The city's newspapers described scenes on 11 November and subsequent days in great detail. For example, different sections included:

> Union Jacks and flags of the Allies came out with astonishing prodigality, and were suspended from windows and points of vantage, babies and children everywhere were almost smothered with colours [...] With the tension of four years of war gone everybody was gripped with a new excitement.
>
> The procession of convalescent wounded from the Base and Wharncliffe War Hospitals was doubly impressive from the fact that they sported colours, carried their heads high, and 'made light' of the woes war had visited on them. They were conspicuous everywhere in the city [...] and not uncommonly the recipients of kisses to the victors which their admirers gladly gave. Many paraded in bath chairs and spinal carriages bedecked with flags.
>
> A group of wounded soldiers were to be seen in High Street formed in a circle, and a dainty girl passed round the circle kissing each in turn, while a comrade rang a bell to denote each kiss.
>
> Bands associated with some of the works commenced to play.
>
> University students in their O. T. C. [*Officer Training Corps*] uniform paraded the streets blowing whistles and toy trumpets. They halted in front of the Victoria Monument opposite the Town Hall and sang patriotic songs.
>
> Barrel organs were kept busy in side streets adjoining the main thoroughfares, playing for those who wished to dance in glee[214].

Shops did a great trade in fireworks (quickly sold out) and in hooters and red, white and blue ribbon. They soon closed, as did the city's schools and nearly all factories. Conscription notices and military tribunal cases were immediately cancelled, and on the next day the Home Office announced that many restrictions were withdrawn. Public bells could now be rung, clocks could strike at night, and streetlamps could be unmasked – but only half could be lit, to save electricity. The Town Hall clock was again illuminated. As usual, retailers coupled the mood with a commercial intent. Cockayne's department store in Angel Street held a 'patriotic concert to celebrate the end of the war' in its restaurant daily for about a fortnight, and advertised 'peace frocks' in which to welcome home-coming troops.

For women workers the writing had been on the wall for a while. The 'shell girl' was doomed, and many had already lost their jobs. Septimus

Bennett described the morning of 11 November in the Vickers Holme Lane factory: 'Girls in particular started singing all the patriotic and topical songs of the day, one of which struck me as having great merit. It was new to me, and I can only remember one line of it. "When the war is over, the women will all be men"'[215]. Septimus was not yet in a position to read the next day's *Yorkshire Telegraph and Star*. After reviewing a great victory, the paper turned to the nation's workers: 'and the men! Those [...] who had been left behind to supply the munitions of war; those men who had toiled day after day and night after night [...] for four long years without murmuring.' There was no mention of women. Although the nation's working men indeed deserved praise, the paper's traditionally narrow gender focus was a stark warning: female contributions were already fading from view.

For Britain as a whole, feelings of relief were, of course, paramount. But would these feelings last into the future? Sadly, the next few years were not happy ones.

CHAPTER 7

Remembrance, riots and disability

As 1918 passed into 1919, Britain was still officially at war. It was assumed that the ceasefire would become permanent, but so far peace was only temporary. Some troops had been demobilized, but most were still waiting impatiently in their units[216]. Industry's war-work had almost disappeared, and employees – especially women – were losing their jobs in growing numbers. International discussions about peace arrangements were scheduled, but those did not start until mid-January and proved to be complex and lengthy.

Celebrations and mourning

However, at last on Saturday 28 June 1919, Germany and the Allies jointly signed the Treaty of Versailles and the First World War formally came to an end. Germany was required to accept harsh conditions and make substantial payments to its enemies[217], and a League of Nations was envisaged, which would aim to settle disputes by international discussion rather than by combat.

Celebrating the peace It had been clear for some days before the treaty date in June that signature was imminent, and Sheffield's morning papers on that Saturday suggested that the signing would be at 3 pm. By then, the city centre had been decorated and around 20,000 people had gathered in the centre, jamming many streets. The news arrived by telegraph at 3.40 pm (signatures had been finalized at 3.12), and rockets were fired, buzzers and sirens sounded, and bells rang out from the cathedral and other churches. Speeches were made outside the Town Hall, hymns were sung, and cheers were raised for the king and prime minister. The lord mayor then led a procession along Fargate to the Cathedral Yard, where around 15,000 people joined in a non-denominational service[218]. Other services were held around the city including in Endcliffe Park, and many shops closed their doors for the rest of the day. The next day (Sunday) saw Thanksgiving services in many churches and in open-air settings such as Sheffield Wednesday's football ground. Despite the positive mood, for many families peace had come too late. Grief and mourning for lost young men were also widespread.

The next few days saw many celebrations. For example, on 5 July 1919, James Dixon and Sons held a 'Fete in Celebration of Victory and Peace' at Stumperlow Hall, the home of managing director James Dixon. This ran from 12.30 to 8.30 pm and included lunch and tea. Thanksgiving speeches were given and the afternoon was devoted to athletic sports of both a serious and a frivolous kind. In addition to handicap races and separate competitions for ladies, boys, and men over 50, there were obstacle- and sack-races and a ladies' 100-yard skipping race. The company choir sang patriotic and other songs, and music was provided by a military band from the local Comrades of the Great War. Other events at the fete included a comic football match and an hour's social dancing[219].

Among celebrations after signature of the Treaty of Versailles on 28 June 1919 was a fete held at the home of managing director James Dixon.

On Thursday 17 July, more than 50,000 elementary schoolchildren held a peace pageant in the city centre and in six different parks, presenting tableaux ('living pictures') of societies around the world, displaying the city's patriotism and saluting the national flag. Some 8,000 pupils enacted *Merrie England* outside the Town Hall, Hillsborough Park was the setting for songs, music, Morris dancing, physical exercises and flag displays by 9,000 children in front of 23,000 spectators, and nearly 8,000 children sang and danced in Meersbrook Park watched by an audience of 15,000.

Sunday 6 July was declared Empire Thanksgiving Day, when church services were held throughout the country including all over Sheffield. The government sought fitting public tributes and celebrations for what was widely referred to as the Great Sacrifice or the Great Deliverance, and decided to mark the war's newly confirmed end with a national peace day on Saturday 19 July. A major parade would be held in London and this needed a central point of homage. However, preparation time was short – only about three weeks were available. Recently knighted architect Sir Edwin Lutyens was asked to design a national memorial, and on the appointed day his temporary monument was unveiled in Whitehall. He ensured that it was non-denominational, and named it a cenotaph by combining Greek words for 'empty' and 'tomb'.

Despite poor weather, London's peace parade on 19 July 1919 was a great success with huge crowds watching troops from Britain and the empire march through the city. The marchers passed and saluted the new memorial, and moved on to Buckingham Palace. There they were greeted by the king and queen, who were accompanied by members of parliament, wounded soldiers, war widows and bereaved mothers. Throughout London there were parties, pageants, plays, music, dancing, games and fireworks.

London's peace parade on 19 July 1919 saluted the temporary cenotaph.

Crowds of people fill Fargate as Sheffield celebrates peace on 19 July 1919.

July 1919 peace celebrations in Amy Street, Crookes.

Preparing for peace celebrations in Summer Street, Netherthorpe.

Sheffield also had its peace parade and celebrations on that Saturday. Streets were decorated with flags and bunting, and many thousands of spectators gathered in the city centre for a parade of bands and troops, some women as well as men, who marched past the lord mayor and other dignitaries at the Town Hall. A white memorial cross was placed at the junction opposite the cathedral, encircled by a Union Jack flag and surmounted by a laurel wreath. This was treated with great reverence by individual citizens and members of the passing parade. After the march-past, schoolchildren presented tableaux of Victory, Peace, Britannia, Liberty and Progress on platforms outside the Town Hall. Subsequently, more than a dozen bands played in parks, teas were served to around 5,000 widows and orphans of the war[220], and bonfires were later lit at five of the city's highest points. Local newspapers on the following Monday contained detailed reports about individual events, and a general account is included in Display Box 7.1.

The city's hospitals organized a special day for their patients. For example, Wharncliffe War Hospital (still housing soldiers) offered entertainment, a whist-drive and fireworks on the parade ground. Local neighbourhoods contributed in their own way. Teachers in Norton organized a children's sports day and tea, a bonfire was lit, and fireworks and rockets were set off. A dinner was held on the following Monday for

Display Box 7.1
PEACE CELEBRATIONS OVER FOURTEEN HOURS

Excerpts from a report in the *Sheffield Daily Independent* of 21 July 1919

Sheffield gave itself up on Saturday to fourteen hours' expression of relief that the years of war weariness had at last ended. The predominant note was one of light-heartedness and gaiety which infused people of all stations of life from irresponsible youths to invalids in bath-chairs, for whom the crowd considerately made room.

People with war sorrows hid their feelings, and it was only momentarily that the thoughts of the thousands who thronged Fargate to watch the march-past of war heroes were directed to a sense of sorrow, when the troops and demobilised turned "eyes right" as the temporary cross to the memory of the fallen was passed [...]

The city on no other occasion has presented such a gay appearance. The striking feature was that the most effective colour schemes had been carried out in the poorer localities, where many hours must have been spent in designing and erecting triumphal arches and decorating dingy dwellings with festoons of flags and flowers [...]

When the exuberance of the crowds had reached a high point in the early evening, torrential rain fell, but very few were deterred from *[sic]* cutting short their programme of festivity. Rain had been falling incessantly for nearly four hours when anti-aircraft guns gave the signal for the lighting of the bonfires at Bole Hills, Parkwood Springs, Ringinglow, Sky Edge, and Wincobank. Thousands toiled in the rain to the scenes of the fires [...] to watch the official firing of the piles of timber at eleven o'clock.

In spite of the rain, thousands of rockets and other fireworks were sent up as night fell. Searchlights stabbed the darkness, and wheeled and flashed in a manner reminiscent of the days of air raid alarms.

returned Norton soldiers and their friends, and the Sunday of that weekend was an occasion for special church services there and across the city.

In the days before 19 July, Sheffield newspapers carried advertisements from the town clerk. 'It is proposed as part of the Peace Celebrations to present the Discharged and Demobilised or Serving Soldiers, Sailors and Air Force Men residing in Sheffield and V.A.D.s, W.R.N.S. and W.A.A.C.s

Sheffield City Council offered commemorative cards to all city men and women who had served in the war.

etc. with COMMEMORATIVE CARDS, thanking them for their services during the War.' Individuals were asked to register their details in order to receive the card, and this was then inscribed with their name and details: 'In grateful recognition of services to his King and Country rendered during the GREAT WAR, the citizens of Sheffield present this memento'.

The city's retailers took advantage of the cheerful mood. Clothes and food shops were busy despite the continuing shortages, and G. H. Crossley (with four shops in Sheffield) advertised: 'Flags for Peace Celebrations. Flags of All Nations. All Flag Poles and Flag Sticks. Red, White and Blue Ribbons'. Jointly with the city's new development corporation, Vickers'

The new Vickers Vimy commercial aeroplane visited Coal Aston Airfield as part of Sheffield's flying exhibition in July 1919.

Aviation Department organized a flying exhibition at Coal Aston Airfield between 23 and 26 July. Two-seater aeroplanes were on display and brief flights in the passenger seat could be booked for two guineas (£2.10). These turned out to be very popular with women as well as men. A large Vickers-Vimy commercial aircraft also put in an appearance and attracted great interest. This was one of the world's first planes for commercial passengers, containing eight chairs and a couch for reclining. At the time, Vimy aircraft were of particular public interest because one had recently made the very first flight across the Atlantic Ocean, from Newfoundland to Ireland. That plane's pilots, John Alcock and Arthur Whitten-Brown, also visited Coal Aston and the city at this time.

Between 4 and 9 August 1919, a large 'pageant of peace' was held in Hillsborough Park in support of St Dunstan's Fund for Blinded Sailors' and Soldiers' Aftercare[221]. With 500 volunteer choir-members from the city and soldiers from local regiments, the pageant contained episodes such as *Belgium – the Flight* and *The Empire and her Allies*. The period also saw special religious services in many of the city's churches. For instance, leading up to a commemorative mass at St Vincent's Church on

19 August 1919, more than 1,000 servicemen of all denominations marched behind a drum and fife band from Paradise Square to Solly Street, entering the church through a military guard of honour.

The next two years The first anniversary of the Armistice (Tuesday, 11 November 1919) recalled the end of the First World War in a spirit more of sadness than of celebration. It was also viewed in Sheffield as League of Nations Day to mark the international agreement now considered central to the maintenance of peace[222]. Religious services were held across the nation and London saw parades pass the cenotaph. In Sheffield, a civic thanksgiving service was held in the cathedral, and events – sombre as well as social – were held around the city[223]. In the late evening a torchlight procession of around 10,000 soldiers with bands and banners was organized by the Comrades of the Great War and the Federation of Discharged and Demobilised Soldiers. Starting at the bottom of Hawley Street, this wound its way around the city centre to Leopold Street, with applause along the route from crowds of spectators.

Also on that first anniversary another important event took place all around the country. Four days before, on 7 November 1919, newspapers carried a request from the king that the nation should come together on 11 November in a 'simple service of Silence and Remembrance'. In order to

Sheffield's band within the national charity Comrades of the Great War. This group became part of the British Legion when that was formed in 1921.

'perpetuate the memory of the Great Deliverance and of those who have laid down their lives to achieve it' he proposed 'for the brief space of two minutes a complete suspension of all our normal activities' at the moment of armistice – the eleventh hour of the eleventh day of the eleventh month.

The public had very little time to take in this completely unexpected idea[224]. Quickly named the Great Silence, it was widely discussed in newspapers and everyday conversation, and there was considerable advance uncertainty about how people would respond. In the event, Sheffield had little doubt. Almost all public activities paused for two minutes at eleven o'clock, cued by city-centre buzzers or suburban church bells. From the Town Hall steps the lord mayor introduced the pause, and buglers from the York and Lancaster Regiment brought it to an end by playing *The Last Post*. Men removed their hats and women stood with

This permanent version of the cenotaph was unveiled in London's Whitehall on 11 November 1920.

bowed heads. 'Tramcars [...] carts, motors, vans, cycles, and all, halted all over the road, while pedestrians stood their ground regardless of the proximity of vehicles. It was a beautiful and almost unreal silence, just like the stopping of a stopwatch.'[225] In the cathedral, in many churches, and spontaneously in shops and factories, the two minutes pause was followed by a short service of remembrance and thanksgiving with communal singing of the national anthem.

What about the temporary cenotaph erected in London so hastily in July 1919? This was taken down in the following January, after making an enormous impact on a country lacking other memorials to the war's dead. It had been decided early in the war that men who fought and died together would stay together in death. All bodies thus remained in their war-zone, and very few families could visit a grave for personal mourning[226]. Since the cenotaph's unveiling in July 1919, it had become a place of pilgrimage as well as a national monument. Families from all over the country (including from Sheffield) travelled to Whitehall to lay a personal tribute at its base, and the government soon decided that the temporary wood, plaster and canvas construction should be replaced with a permanent monument. Sir Edwin Lutyens made very slight adjustments, and a new stone-built cenotaph was unveiled by the king on 11 November 1920. Explicitly for people of all faiths and of none and bearing only the words 'The Glorious Dead', this drew an unprecedented number of mourners. Within a couple of weeks of its unveiling around 100,000 wreaths and bunches of flowers had been placed around its base. Feelings on unveiling day are described from an anti-war perspective in Display Box 7.2[227].

Another important symbol of the nation's respect for wartime sacrifice was also introduced on 11 November 1920. A former military chaplain was concerned about the huge number of soldiers who had no known grave[228], and in the autumn of that year he argued for one representative of all those deceased men to be returned to his home country. The government agreed and arrangements were made for an unidentified body to be brought back to Westminster Abbey and reburied with full military honours.

On 9 November 1920, four bodies[229] of unknown men were exhumed from four different battle areas in Flanders and France and placed in fresh coffins. A senior officer, said in some reports to have been blindfolded, selected one of these randomly, and that body – symbolizing thousands more – was returned to London. In the morning of 11 November 1920, it

Display Box 7.2
THE CENOTAPH ON 11 NOVEMBER 1920

A report in the following day's issue of *The Herald*

At eight o'clock the people stood eight deep in a double line from the cenotaph to Trafalgar Square. From here, the queue stretched down Northumberland Avenue to the Embankment and along the Embankment to Westminster. From there it doubled back to Trafalgar Square.

These were no mere sightseers, these men and women slowly moving along in that great pilgrimage, tired and drooping with the long waiting. They were the mothers and the fathers and the wives and the children of the great army of the dead.

There were old mothers in dingy black, down whose furrowed cheeks the tears trickled; there were young women who carried in their arms the little ones grown sleepy on the long trail. And all along the way the air was heavy with the pungent earthy odour of white chrysanthemums and the strong sweetness of the lilies that so many of the pilgrims carried.

At last, through the mist, the noble lines of the cenotaph appeared, now standing twelve feet deep in flowers. Here the policemen gently marshalled the pilgrims into double file, and with bowed heads they passed, the men with bare heads, and the women, many of them with their faces buried in their handkerchiefs.

At either end of the enclosed space more flowers were banked high. And then were piled higher and higher as woman after woman, and here and there a child, stooped to add their tribute. Many of the women, bowed and broken, were overcome with weeping as they were led away.

was drawn by gun-carriage in a procession of more than 1,000 troops to the rebuilt cenotaph for the monument's unveiling and initial ceremony, followed by the country's first two-minute silence. After transfer to Westminster Abbey, the coffin was formally interred with the simple inscription 'An Unknown Warrior', being placed in soil that had also been brought from the Western Front.

The dead soldier's presence in Britain made a tremendous impact and the tomb immediately and subsequently drew a huge number of mourners.

In its initial week almost 1,000,000 people made the pilgrimage from all over the country, and mourners often moved on to lay their personal wreath at the cenotaph. Since then the unknown warrior's tomb and the cenotaph have retained their central importance to the nation. The tomb now represents unknown lives lost in all the country's wars.

Poppies from the Western Front

Among fatal casualties at the second Battle of Ypres in May 1915 was a friend of Canadian medical officer Major John McCrae. Moved by the horrors he had seen and the death of his friend, John McCrae composed a poem that has since had a wide-ranging impact – well-beyond expectations at the time. Originally titled *We Shall Not Sleep* and later renamed *In Flanders Fields*, this has touched many people across many generations:

> In Flanders fields the poppies blow
> Between the crosses, row on row,
> That mark our place; and in the sky
> The larks, still bravely singing, fly
> Scarce heard amid the guns below.
>
> We are the Dead. Short days ago
> We lived, felt dawn, saw sunset glow,
> Loved and were loved, and now we lie,
> In Flanders fields.
>
> Take up our quarrel with the foe:
> To you from failing hands we throw
> The torch; be yours to hold it high.
> If ye break faith with us who die
> We shall not sleep, though poppies grow
> In Flanders fields.

The poem's contrast between fresh poppies and slaughtered soldiers leads the reader into a strong demand that lost lives should not have been wasted: do not 'break faith with us who die'[230].

The poem was published in 1915 and subsequently widely reproduced in Allied countries. Three years later an illustrated version in the *Ladies Home Journal* came to the notice of an American YMCA worker, Moina Michael, who was then in New York. She had read the words before but

The body of an unknown warrior starts its journey on 9 November 1920 from the Western Front to Westminster Abbey.

now 'the last verse transfixed me' – 'if ye break faith with us who die we shall not sleep, though poppies grow in Flanders Fields'. She determined that within USA people should wear a red poppy as a sign of remembrance and an emblem of keeping the faith with the men who died.

Moina Michael set about trying to persuade American agencies and the country's War Department to adopt this symbol, but her campaign was in vain. In 1919, she moved from her New York role to continue working with ex-servicemen at the University of Georgia, and from that base she eventually managed to persuade a local branch of the newly-formed American Legion to take up the proposal. That branch expanded the fight and succeeded in gaining nationwide acceptance of the idea. From September 1920, the Flanders Field Memorial Poppy became the American Legion's national emblem of remembrance.

These developments remained almost unknown in Britain, where chrysanthemums were a common memorial flower. However, Anna Guérin, a representative of the French YMCA, had been impressed by the American development and organized in her own country the sale of artificial poppies to fund rehabilitation and support for French ex-servicemen. During 1921, she also set out to persuade other countries to sell poppies for those purposes and to adopt the flower as a national symbol[231].

Britain soon took up the idea and the country's first poppy day was held three years after the armistice – on 11 November 1921. It was organized by the British Legion, which had just been formed to help discharged and demobilized troops and their families[232]. The legion combined three earlier ex-servicemen's groups, and a Sheffield branch was registered as a charity on 1 July 1921. Previous (now combined) groups in the city had included the Sheffield Discharged Soldiers and Sailors Fund (officially formed on 9 April 1917) and the Sheffield branch of the Comrades of the Great War (from 21 October 1917). The latter had an office in Pond Street and became based in Comrades Hall in Townhead Street, within what had until recently been the Temperance Hall. Among its activities was an enormous 1919 Christmas party in Comrades Hall for 5,000 war widows and orphans, organized jointly with the newly-formed Sheffield Rotary Club.

Since 1921, the British Legion's annual sale of memorial poppies has been particularly important as a source of income and a public reminder of lives cut short on behalf of the nation. In 1946, the second Sunday in November was confirmed as 'Remembrance Sunday' to cover fatalities from all wars, and the Royal British Legion Festival of Remembrance is still held annually on the preceding day[233].

'We will remember them'

Other support groups did their best to help. The King's Fund for the Disabled sought funds for wounded ex-soldiers, for instance through a 'Gratitude Week' in the city and elsewhere in January 1919. Previous members of the Twelfth (Sheffield City) Battalion of the York and Lancaster Regiment (the Sheffield Pals) formed the Twelfth Club, taking part in annual memorial services close to 1 July, the initial day of slaughter in the Battle of the Somme, as well as reunion dinners, concerts, dances and other events. Firms, trade unions and other groups in the city organized their own commemorations and celebrations. For example, the Sheffield Typographical Society held a Branch Reunion on 22 November 1919 in the Cutlers' Hall. Its 530 members and apprentices had provided 214 troops, of whom twenty-six had died.

Tyne Cot is one of many military cemeteries created and maintained by the Commonwealth War Graves Commission (www.cwgc.org).

Since Victorian times, many people in Britain had come to value elaborate funeral ceremonies[234], but these were not possible for deceased soldiers in the First World War as all bodies remained in their battle-zone. Subsequent mourning at a graveside far away was similarly ruled out. However, soldiers' graves had been recorded since October 1914 (originally by the Red Cross), and this process became increasingly formalized through the creation of War Graves Registration Units. In May 1917, these units came within a new Imperial War Graves Commission, which was later renamed the Commonwealth War Graves Commission. That now commemorates around 1,700,000 deceased men and women from all Commonwealth countries and two world wars. The commission has designed and built a large number of dedicated cemeteries in many countries, each with a standard gravestone irrespective of rank, race or creed[235].

Soon after the First World War, visits to the Western Front became possible for families able to afford the cost[236]. These were often described as pilgrimages by bereaved relatives and ex-servicemen. From 1919, the Salvation Army, the Red Cross, the YMCA, some churches and several other organizations helped with arrangements, Thomas Cook and other travel companies arranged tours, and the Michelin Tyre Company and others produced battlefield guidebooks[237]. In addition, many relatives and friends wished to commemorate and give thanks in their own community.

For example, in April 1919 pupils and parents of Western Road Council School funded the planting of trees for fallen ex-scholars. In March 1919 a cathedral service commemorated Sheffield prisoners-of-war who had died in German hands. And in December a memorial to Sheffield City Battalion was dedicated in the cathedral[238].

There was a widespread desire in the city to construct other reminders of loss and expressions of gratitude, and memorial proposals had been

The city's war memorial in Barker's Pool is here unveiled on 28 October 1925.

discussed on several occasions during the war. Suggestions then ranged from monuments in the warzone to homes in the city for war orphans. A popular 1916 proposal was for a substantial commemorative hall in the city centre, and in 1918 a site in Barker's Pool was selected for this. However, progress after the war was slow, in part because of poor economic conditions, and only in 1929 was the foundation stone laid. By then the building had been named as the City Hall and its design included a second auditorium to be known as the Memorial Hall. It finally opened in September 1932[239]. By then, Barker's Pool was also home to the city's principal war memorial, which had been unveiled on 28 October 1925[240].

Religious services of remembrance and prayers for bereaved relatives had been frequent during the war[241], and it now became common to install rolls of honour and tablets of remembrance in churches, factories and elsewhere. Memorials were erected in many parishes to give thanks to local men who had died for king and country. More than two hundred of these in the city are detailed in www.sheffieldsoldierww1.co.uk. For example, Norton and Stocksbridge unveiled local memorials in 1920 and 1923 respectively, and many others were erected in that decade. In 1921, the previous altar in St Marie's Church (since 1980 the city's Roman Catholic cathedral) was replaced by one dedicated as a war memorial, and on Armistice Day 1922, victims of the Zeppelin attack in September 1916

James Dixon and Sons' memorial to its deceased workers was unveiled in the company's Cornish Place works in November 1926.

Hadfield's commemorative tablet is now on display in Kelham Island Museum.

Dedicating Norton's war memorial in June 1920.

An Armistice Sunday service at Dore, probably on the day its memorial was unveiled in 1922.

were recalled on their own memorial, now located in Effingham Road[242].

In addition to these collective thanks, memorials to individual men also became important. The bell-ringers of St John's Church in Ranmoor wanted to remember their colleague Arthur Ward, who had been killed in July 1917. Arthur had been a private in the York and Lancaster Regiment and was previously a spoon and fork buffer. In September 1919, a plaque to his memory was installed inside the church bell-tower, in a ceremony that was preceded by a half-muffled continuous peal of 5,088 changes lasting a remarkable three hours and nineteen minutes. Also in St John's, local resident Robert Colver and his wife presented a stained-glass window in memory of their two sons who had been killed in separate battles during 1915. Lieutenant Cecil Mays of the Royal Army Medical Corps was another Sheffield man remembered through a stained glass window, in his case in St Thomas's in Crookes.

Some families wanted a personal memorial in words and pictures. In Deepcar, the parents of Corporal Jesse Kenworthy, previously an employee of Samuel Fox, produced a four-page booklet 'in ever loving memory' of their son. On the front cover was simply 'In Memoriam', and inside pages contained photographs of Jesse as a civilian and a soldier, details of his life and work, the original letters reporting Jesse's death to his father, and tributes from his workplace and Stocksbridge Congregational Sunday School. Also printed were excerpts from his final letters from the warzone and a message he wrote to his parents early in the war. This described his concerns about German aggression and affirmed that: 'My heart's desire is to help to overcome this despotism, and we, as a family, should be prepared to make some sacrifice. It is my duty to go [...] With love to all and hoping that all will turn out in the end.' Sadly for Jesse and thousands more it did not 'turn out in the end'. He was killed in action on 17 August 1916.

Remembrance was sometimes through a contribution made to one of the city's general hospitals. As voluntary hospitals, these depended almost entirely on finance from the public, and individual or multiple beds could be endowed through a donation. Endowed beds were made available free of charge to poor patients or those nominated by the donor. After the war, several beds in Sheffield hospitals were endowed in memory of deceased soldiers. In 1920, Lance-Corporal Noel Wilcock of Priory Road, a Sheffield City Battalion casualty on the first day of the Battle of the Somme, was remembered by his sister with a bed at the Royal Infirmary, above which was placed a memorial plaque. In 1922, Sheffield and District

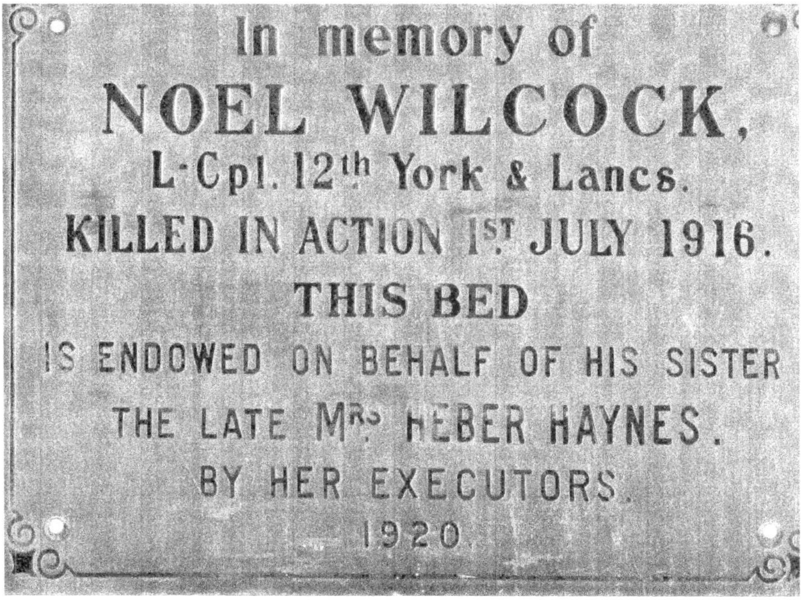

Commemorating a casualty of the Battle of the Somme by funding a bed at the Royal Infirmary.

Cricketers' Association offered their own memorial to the fallen through £1,000 to pay for a bed and treatment in the Royal Hospital. John Kirby of Westbourne Road was also remembered in this way. He had been killed in December 1917, and in 1940 his family financed five beds in the Royal Infirmary.

Many other memorials inevitably remained private to bereaved individuals. For deceased men whose bodies were identifiable, possessions had been returned to the next-of-kin. Typical was a package sent to the mother of bell-ringer Arthur Ward: two identity discs, some photographs, a pocket book, a religious book, a metal mirror and a comb. In addition, the families of fallen soldiers, sailors and airmen subsequently received an individual memento on behalf of the nation – a named bronze plaque.

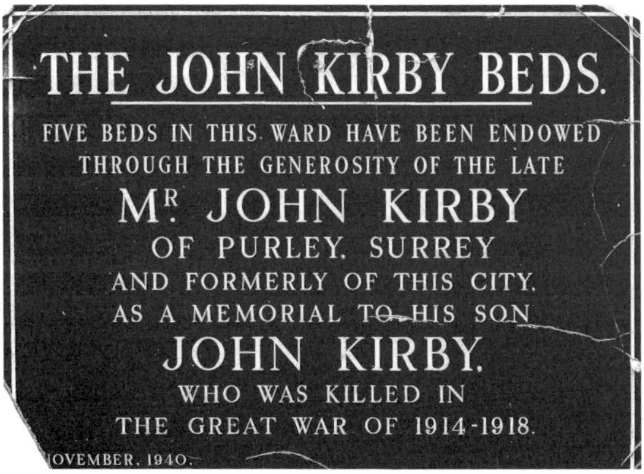

This memorial to John Kirby was placed in the Royal Infirmary several years after the war.

This came to be referred to as the Dead Man's Penny or the Soldier's Penny. Plaques were about 4¾ inches (12 centimetres) in diameter and were accompanied by a letter from the king at Buckingham Palace: 'I join with my grateful people in sending you this memorial of a brave life given for others in the Great War.' The royal coat of arms also headed the accompanying scroll: 'He whom this scroll commemorates was numbered among those who, at the call of King and Country, left all that was dear to them, endured hardness, faced danger, and finally passed out of sight of men by the path of duty and self-sacrifice, giving up their own lives that others may live in freedom. Let those who come after see to it that his name be not forgotten.'

The plaque provided to families of a deceased soldier, sailor or airman became known as a Dead Man's Penny.

All troops, including deceased men, who served through the war or in particular campaigns received a medal for their service. Thus the late Arthur Greensmith's father of Kenwood Park Road received a letter from the Record Office in January 1921: 'I am directed to transmit to you the accompanying [*inserted by hand:* British War Medal] which would have been conferred upon [*inserted by hand:* No 12/934 Private Arthur Clarence Greensmith] had he lived, in memory of his services with the British Forces during the Great War.' For bereaved families this was a stark reminder of what might have been, and for some it may have seemed an additional punishment more than a reward.

Jobs, unemployment and conflict

A fortnight after the armistice in November 1918, prime minister David Lloyd George proclaimed the nation's task: 'to make Britain a country fit for heroes to live in'. That proved to be extremely difficult.

The war had brought some great advances: welfare provisions had improved, many women above 30 now had the vote[243], and technological and medical developments had been stunning. But the country's initial optimism was soon replaced by disenchantment and despair. At a personal level, thousands of men were mutilated, crippled or mentally scarred, families had been torn apart, and reminders of struggle and loss were widespread and painful. Unhappy lives were made a thousand times worse by the economic depression that soon arrived.

The nation's financial state was precarious. The war had been waged largely on borrowed money, and already substantial debts were due for repayment. The government sought breathing space by extending to twice its length the five-year term of earlier saving certificates, thus avoiding having to repay all contributions immediately. Fundraising campaigns remained essential, including Sheffield's 'Victory Week' at the beginning of July 1919, with several days of speeches, band performances, announcements in local theatres and cinemas, and special events and facilities in Fitzalan Square[244]. The government also improved its finances by selling wartime factories, equipment and materials. Around £600,000,000 were raised through more than 1,500 auction sales around the country, including by Eadon, Lockwood and Riddle in Sheffield.

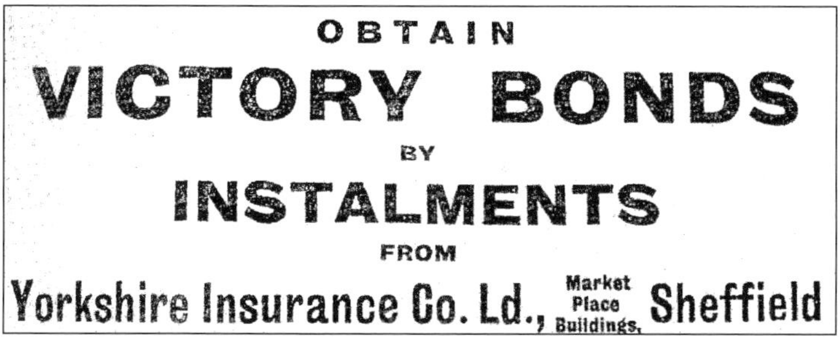

Post-war victory bonds (lending money to the government) could be bought in instalments.

Early 1919 had seen an increase in the city's business activity. Steel was in great demand and non-military orders could now be dealt with. Cutlery and silverware companies experienced a marked improvement, and engineering firms were called upon to re-equip many factories. Generally, the reduction of uncertainty meant that managements could now make investment decisions. Within a widespread mood of optimism, particular firms were able to take advantage of the special circumstances. Scrap processor T. W. Ward was extremely busy with a range of salvaging and dismantling projects, including government work in France. Newton Chambers had some success making cast-iron houses at a time when bricks were scarce and housing was greatly needed.

However, after a brief period of raised activity, employment difficulties became obvious. The demand for many products soon declined sharply, the labour market was being flooded with demobilized troops and munition workers, and not enough jobs were available. Problems were especially severe for women at a time when it was generally accepted that male workers (the 'family bread-winners') should have priority. Munitions were no longer required for the war and many 'shell girls' lost their jobs during the second part of 1918. The city's postwomen were demobilized from February 1919, and Hadfield's last female works employee was paid off in June 1919. The Restoration of Pre-War Practices Act became law in August 1919, prohibiting the employment of women workers in the engineering industry unless so employed before the war[245].

Growing unemployment through 1919 and 1920 was a national problem, but there were signs that Sheffield was losing business because it was not always financially competitive. When Sheffield Corporation Tramways wanted to purchase new rails in 1921, the price quotations obtained from Sheffield firms were substantially above those from Belgian and German companies and higher than other British quotations. The Sheffield order went to Leeds. Tram tyres were reluctantly purchased from Rotherham's Steel, Peech and Tozer, despite the fact that foreign tenders were around 10 percent lower. The city's free library had to desert its customary bookbinder in Sheffield because that company's prices were so much higher than those outside the city. Competitors had reduced their prices, but the Sheffield binder refused to do so. In May 1922, the City Council was told that Sheffield prices for tram-workers' overcoats were considerably above those from elsewhere, and Sheffield Chamber of Commerce reported that 'many orders for railway material for India, which formerly came to this country, are now going to the Continent and America'[246].

Industry gradually moved into stagnation. In the early post-war years households were paying almost three times as much for food and clothes as before the war, and rents, taxes and transport costs had increased similarly. Wages had also grown but to a lesser extent and, by 1920, both wages and the cost of living started to decline. Many workers now accepted reductions in pay, but from mid-1921 Sheffield entered a period of mass unemployment and widespread distress. The city's bankruptcy court was exceptionally busy, and the number of employment exchanges in the city was doubled from three to six.

Jobless people might obtain financial support from three sources – the national government, the local Poor Law Guardians, and some charities. The government's unemployment insurance (introduced in 1911) was available for a maximum of twenty-six weeks in a year, and only for those who had made at least twenty weekly contributions in the last insurance year[247]. In addition, from November 1918, the government provided a new 'out-of-work donation' – widely referred to as a 'dole'. In the following November this 'donation' was withdrawn from individuals who had not served in the war (including 10,000 in Sheffield), but continued to be available to ex-servicemen and women[248].

Separately from these payments made by central government, locally-collected Poor Law rates were sometimes used to help families who made a personal application to their Board of Guardians – either to the Ecclesall Board or to the Sheffield Board[249]. Rather than seeking admission to the workhouse (the original primary Poor Law support), applicants might ask for 'outdoor relief' – a grant of money to help with an emergency or for a brief period. Payments in 1921 ranged upwards from twenty-one shillings (£1.05) depending on family circumstances, but both the local boards followed advice from the Ministry of Health and reduced allowances from June 1922.

A third source of support for jobless families was through local charities or a trade union, but money from these was becoming extremely scarce. One such provider was the Lord Mayor's Distress Fund, which now made use of unspent donations previously given to the city's War Relief Fund. The Distress Fund had committees around the city to distribute groceries and other urgent necessities and sometimes to help with the payment of rent.

Both the City Council and the Poor Law Guardians also provided help through paid work of value to the community, usually on a part-time basis. Thousands of unemployed men were offered temporary jobs making or improving roads, repairing tram lines, clearing moorland paths, laying out recreation grounds, labouring at sewage and water works, and so on [250]. For some unemployed boys under 16, the city's education department opened a recreational centre with a syllabus described as 'singing, physical exercises, outdoor games, lectures, dramatic and musical recitals, map reading, rambling, cobbling, woodwork, and woodcraft'.

The country's financial situation was made worse by a series of strikes with severe impact on businesses and families. For example, a month-long miners' strike in 1919 and shorter ones in 1920 and 1921 stopped or reduced coal production and closed many factories across the country. A tram strike for a week obstructed Sheffielders' journeys to work, and the city also had to cope with strikes by bakers, taxi drivers, and sales-staff of the local co-operative societies. An extended railway dispute in the autumn of 1919 brought almost the entire nation to a halt, created food shortages and led to a number of riots. The situation was so desperate at the beginning of October that Sheffield's lord mayor published an urgent request for 5,000 special constables, and the city's Chamber of Commerce asked for volunteer lorry drivers. At the same time, the Home Office appealed in the city's newspapers for citizen guards to bolster the nation's defences against possible insurrection. Fortunately, the need for these emergency measures was removed on 6 October, when the strike was settled, but industrial conflict continued through the next few years. For example, during 1921 many coalmines were closed through strikes for almost three months, hugely disrupting factories and personal life.

Throughout the city people were short of money. Horse-flesh shops (originally introduced for Belgian refugees) were extremely busy with prices below other butchers, and low-price meals provided by the city's five national kitchens continued to be popular[251]. Local hospitals, dependent on public donations, were struggling. In October 1921, the Royal Hospital reported that more income was essential 'or the work of the institution could not be carried on'. Furthermore, the city was greatly overcrowded and desperately short of houses. Official estimates were that by now more than 15,000 additional homes were needed. Adding to the problems, food was generally scarce, some goods were still rationed, and prosecutions for breaking Food Control Orders were common.

This was not 'the fit country for heroes to live in' that the prime minister had sought in 1918. Discharged soldiers were also suffering. In May 1919 around 20,000 protested in the city centre against their inadequate post-war payments. Mass unemployment (up to 32 percent of the city's registered workers in 1921) became the spark for large-scale demonstrations, protests and occasional riots. Starting in January 1919, meetings and marches of unemployed men in the city centre became frequent. On 13 June 1921, demonstrators from a crowd of 10,000 tried to force their way into the Town Hall, protesting against a proposed cut in relief pay from Poor Law Guardians. Their banner on that day, 'Death is Better than Semi-Starvation', became part of subsequent marches and meetings, as did repeated singing of Communist anthem *The Red Flag*.

For five hours on 12 August 1921, 'central Sheffield was under mob rule' (in the words of the *Independent*) as around 1,000 unemployed men gathered for protest speeches in front of the Town Hall. The building's front doors had already been firmly shut, and entrance from the side was blocked by policemen. Instead, part of the crowd moved on and threw stones and smashed windows in the High Street offices of the *Sheffield*

Daily Telegraph. Attempts to force entry there were followed by a police baton-charge and several arrests, including that of the local Communist Party secretary. More arrests were made a week later at demonstrations organized by the city's communists, and several of the demonstrators were imprisoned[252].

Unemployment continued to rise in 1922, and mass meetings became frequent[253]. On Sunday 30 April, about 500 men tried to commemorate Labour Sunday by attending a service in the cathedral. They were refused collective entry in the form of an organized group, but were accepted into nearby St James' Church. There they joined in some of the service's hymns but refused to take part in the national anthem and many insisted on singing *The Red Flag*. Linked to a national engineering dispute, the next few weeks saw mass pickets sent around the city aiming to dissuade people from working. Starting in May 1922, columns of unemployed men, sometimes several hundred of them, moved between important factories in the city, often being met by police some of whom were mounted on horses. Most of these visits led to no more than verbal threats and arguments, but on 15 May 1922 a large band of men marched to the works of Jessop and Company in Brightside, once again singing *The Red Flag*. Mounted police kept them out but were stoned in response, and windows of the factory were smashed. For assaulting a policeman, one man was subsequently jailed for three months with hard labour. Skirmishes between unemployed demonstrators and the city's police became frequent in this period, and the works of Jonas and Colver, Cammell Laird and several other companies were temporarily shut down by mass picketing.

Prolonged unemployment and increased activity by protesters led to another violent episode on 7 June 1922. A man unable to find work for the previous twelve months could no longer pay the rent for his two rooms in Providence Road, Walkley, and the family, including two sick children, was about to be evicted. Several hundred unemployed men led by two Labour councillors set out to force the landlady to change her mind. After marching from the city centre, with some singing *The Red Flag*, they tried to place back in the house the family's furniture, which had been removed into the yard. Policemen blocking the way were attacked with a shovel, stones and pieces of metal or broken furniture. The police truncheon-charge in response led to panic and a congested rush to escape. Both police and protestors suffered injuries and several had to be taken to hospital[254]. The ensuing court case lasted more than a week, and eleven men and the two Labour councillors were charged with riotous behaviour. Four men were eventually jailed for periods up to two months. The evicted family's only bedstead and their children's pram were smashed in the commotion, but it was later reported that evictions of impoverished families had become less common – perhaps as a result of the Walkley episode.

The city's income could not be expanded by charging higher rates, since many families were already unable to pay. By the spring of 1924, the council was owed £700,000 in unpaid rates, 28,000 rate defaulters, many of them unemployed, had been summoned for non-payment, and poverty was widespread. The Poor Law Guardians were also struggling to cope. Published figures showed that for December 1922 the Sheffield Board had the second highest Poor Law claimant rate in the whole country[255]. The local guardians were forced to borrow huge sums of money, and the Sheffield Board was in debt up to £790,000 by the middle of 1924. On 12 March 1923, the Nether Edge house of the vice chairman of Ecclesall Guardians was attacked. At a time when the building was normally unoccupied, petrol was poured through the letter-box and a lighted newspaper was pushed in. Unusually on that day somebody was at home, and the fire was quickly stamped out. It emerged that the lighted paper had been published by the Communist Party. More generally, Sheffield's industry and commerce were under desperate strain, bankruptcies reached a record level, and no end of the slump could be seen.

The city's disabled men

In addition to the strains of bereavement[256], unemployment and poverty, post-war Sheffield also had to come to terms with large numbers of disabled and mutilated ex-servicemen. During the years of war, more and more troops had been invalided out with impairments caused directly by or aggravated through their war service, and after return to their home city these men became very visible and distressing consequences of the conflict. In the post-war years more than 40,000 out-patient military attendances were recorded at Wharncliffe Hospital before it closed in May 1922[257].

Nationally, several hundred thousand ex-servicemen suffered some form of disability in the post-war years. Some of these recovered sufficiently to be able to work in a paid job, but (like others) they found post-war employment very hard to obtain. A number of local firms joined the National Scheme for Disabled Men, making a commitment to employ handicapped ex-servicemen[258], but a substantial number of them remained physically or mentally impaired. Their lives were now without the income, activity and social position of paid work.

Injury-related pensions were available for war-disabled men, paid in terms of a standard schedule of assessed severity. For example, the loss of two or more limbs or the total loss of sight entitled a man to a full pension, whereas amputation of one leg above the knee was assessed at 60 percent and loss of two fingers at 20 percent. Disability pensions were often granted only temporarily, perhaps for a few months, and men had to submit themselves repeatedly to examination and assessment by a local medical board. A war pensioner's uncertainty about future assessments added to the strain caused by a drastic loss of capability and the need to survive on a very small allowance[259]. Facial disfigurement and dental and head injuries were common, and particular problems could arise with cases of shellshock. Not only were these difficult to assess in terms of severity, but their symptoms might rise and fall in an unpredictable way.

In response to the huge number of disabled veterans, several national organizations were formed to provide support through funds received from the general public. For instance, from 1921 the British Legion was active in helping both the families of deceased soldiers and the disabled men who remained. A separate local development was the Painted Fabrics organization, which originated in an Arts and Crafts Committee established in 1915 by volunteers in the Wharncliffe War Hospital. Men who had been disabled through war service were encouraged and assisted to undertake woodwork, painting, screen-making, pattern-stencilling and other handiwork tasks within their impaired capacity.

The initiative for this form of occupational therapy came primarily from an ex-student from Sheffield School of Art, Mrs Annie Carter. For a period, her artistic input received practical assistance from Edith Sorby, the co-ordinator of the Soldiers' Personal Comforts Depot, which was described in Chapter One[260]. Aided by other volunteers and with financial contributions from the public, these two arranged a series of high-profile exhibitions and product-sales, in London as well as in Sheffield's Cutlers' Hall. The events gained well-publicized support from politicians, businessmen and influential ladies of title[261], and attracted large numbers of customers.

Arts-and-crafts projects had been developed during the war in other local hospitals[262], but Annie Carter's approach was distinctive. She designed and promoted decorative work with varied fabrics, and as well as assisting patients still in hospital she aimed also to support men who had been medically discharged. In parallel with her group's continuing wartime work in Wharncliffe Hospital, around half-a-dozen discharged handicapped men were, by 1916, employed on a commercial basis in a company named as Painted Fabrics. This sold its products both through personal contacts and in exhibitions and sales-of-work in the city and beyond. Applying the principle of 'work not charity', Painted Fabrics employees were paid a small regular wage and the company became financially self-supporting.

By the end of the war, Painted Fabrics was operating from 9 West Bar, there described as a Disabled Sailors' and Soldiers' Mutual Association. In 1923, part of a disused Women's Army Auxiliary Corps camp at Norton Woodseats was bought by the United Services Fund and leased to the company. Some huts became workshops and others were converted to homes for some workers and their families[263]. Up to thirty handicapped men worked with personally-modified equipment to make printed, painted or stencilled items for public sale. Additional funds were raised through garden parties and other social events, and at different times the organization was publicly supported by members of the royal family, by Earl Haig (the first president of the British Legion), by the Red Cross, and by prominent people in Sheffield and beyond[264].

Gunner Arthur Fisher of the Royal Garrison Artillery, previously a labourer at Hadfields steelworks, had considerable cause to thank Painted Fabrics and its organizers. In April 1918, Arthur (helped by a friend) wrote from France to his fiancée Annie Bell in Walkley, saying in part:

> I am so sorry to tell you I got wounded on Sunday 21st [but] do not let it worry you. I am so sorry to say that I have got both my legs off up to my knees but I thank God that I am alive. I volunteered to have them off to save my life [...] Some of my poor chums were killed outright[265] [...] Goodbye from your everloving sweetheart Arthur.

His mother in Albert Terrace Road received a similar letter (both written from a Casualty Clearing Station), and they must have been very distressed. Nevertheless, Annie replied a few days later to 'My own darling sweetheart', including:

> Well darling I can tell you it was a terrible blow when I got the news of you, but do not worry in any way love as I am bucking up now

> dear as the future is not as bad as it seemed at first [...] Well dear you must not think I will turn against you in any way through it, no dear I shall only love you and honour you all the more for it, and I am going to marry you dear as soon as ever it is possible, and if it is your wish I will marry you by your bedside.

Despite Arthur Fisher's double amputation, Annie and he were married in Walkley Parish Church in May 1919. He became an employee at Painted Fabrics' Meadowhead workshop, lived in their accommodation, and contributed to their success over many years. Daughter Nancy was born in 1924, and she later had her own daughter. Nicknamed as 'Stumpy', Arthur remained active and cheerful despite occasional nightmares and flashbacks. For a period he drove a motorcycle with sidecar and later an adapted car, and he enjoyed gardening, fishing, holidays and other leisure activities.

Arthur Fisher lived for nearly forty years after his double amputation, remaining at Meadowhead until 1957. Like the many other ordinary heroes described in this book and its companion *Sheffield in the Great War*, the staff of Painted Fabrics made a contribution beyond value in a painful but inspiring period of the city's history.

LEGLESS BRIDEGROOM

Gunner A. Fisher, R.G.A., who had both legs blown off during the 1918 offensive, and his bride, Miss A. Bell, of Walkley. Fisher, who is a Sheffield man, has been promised a job for life

A year after Arthur Fisher lost both legs on the Western Front, his marriage to Annie Bell was reported by the Sunday Pictorial.

APPENDIX 1

Sheffield's wartime government contracts

The following 360 Sheffield companies received contracts from the government to provide armaments, components or equipment during the Great War. This list has been compiled from company records and histories, newspaper articles, books, committee reports and other sources, but it is no doubt less than complete.

In ninety-five cases below '(SCMW)' indicates that contracts were placed from the Ministry of Munitions through the Sheffield Committee on Munitions of War (SCMW), which is described in Chapter Five. Most other company contracts were agreed directly with that ministry or (less frequently) with the War Office itself, but a few orders for furniture or equipment were received from the government's Office of Works or from the India (or similar) Office. In some cases it is uncertain whether a contract was direct with the government or with another company that was working on a government project. Contracts in Sheffield for medicines, bedding, etc, may have been for local military hospitals.

Many of the companies below were designated as 'controlled establishments'. (Sheffield had around 350 of these. See Chapters Two to Four.) Individual contracts varied in size and length, and some companies were engaged on government work continuously throughout the war whereas others obtained one or more contracts for short periods only.

Most product labels in the list can refer to a range of different specifications. For instance, tools are of many kinds and shells were of varying sizes and design – shrapnel, high explosive, smoke or chemicals. In many cases, a company made or processed only part of a product.

Additional details about several of the medium-size and larger of these firms are provided in Chapters Three and Four. Geoffrey Tweedale has described the broader history of a large number in *Steel City* (Oxford: Clarendon Press, 1995), *The Sheffield Knife Book* (Sheffield: Hallamshire Press, 1996) and his comprehensive *Directory of Sheffield Cutlery Manufacturers 1740-2013* published in 2013 by Lulu.com.

Allen, Edgar and Company, Tinsley: Cast steel, Stone crushers, Tool steel. Also (SCMW) circles and squares of sheet steel for helmets
Allen, Joseph and Sons, Ecclesall Works, 245 Rockingham Street: Clasp knives, Razors
Andrew, J. H, and Company, Toledo Steel Works: Steels, Tools, Wire
Argyle, C. A. and Company, 5-9 West Hill Lane: Tools
Ash, Son and Biggin, Union Lane: Building work
Ashton, A. and Sons, Meadow Street: Tools
Ashton, Thomas A., Sidney Street: Belting, Laces. Also (SCMW) Howitzer shells
Atkin Brothers, Truro Works, Matilda Street: Nickel silver items. Also (SCMW) Machining shrapnel discs
Atkinson Brothers, Milton Street: Clasp knives, Razors, Table knives and forks, Tools
Atkinson, John, 76-90 The Moor: Stamped munition components
Attercliffe Engineering Company, Ardmore Street: (SCMW) Howitzer shells, Tubes for fuses
Axelby, J. H. and Sons, 148 Shoreham Street: Table knives and forks
B. O. B. Company, Ivy Works, Tinsley: (SCMW) Rings for exploder containers
Balfour, Arthur and Company, Dannemora Works, Broughton Lane (Seebohm and Dieckstahl until December 1915): Drills, Munition components, Tools, Tool steel
Barber, I. and J., Wheeldon Street: Clasp knives, Razors
Barnascone, Henry and Son, Empire Works, Mulberry Street: Clasp knives, Nickel silver items, Table knives and forks
Barnsley, G. and Sons, Cornish Street: Boot-making and other tools
Batt, John and Company, 14 Sycamore Street: Nickel silver items
Batt, William and Sons, 17 Sycamore Street: Electroplated items
Baum Brothers, Nursery Street: Clasp knives, Nickel silver items, Razors, Table knives and forks
Beardshaw, A. and Company, 32 Victoria Street: Electroplated items
Beardshaw, J. and Son, Baltic Steel Works, Effingham Road: Tool steel

Bedford, John and Sons, Lion Works, Mowbray Street: Tools
Bell Brothers and Company, Solferino Street: Tools
Bentley, A., Union Lane: Razors
Benton Brothers, Rodley Lane: Knives, Sword handles and grips, Other munitions not yet specified
Bessemer, Henry and Company, Carlisle Street: Steel
Biggin, J., Milk Street: (SCMW) Machining shrapnel discs
Bird and Company, St Thomas Street: Clasp knives, Electroplate and nickel silver items, Razors, Table knives and forks
Blakeley, C. H. and Sons, 165 Napier Street: Tools
Blaskey and Company, Chesterfield Road: (SCMW) Ammunition boxes
Blyde, Edwin and Company, Charleston Works, Lambert Street: Clasp knives, Table knives and forks
Blyde, John, Clintock Works, Milton Street: Surgical scissors, Tools
Boot, Henry and Sons, Moore Street: Furniture
Boots Pure Drug Company, 6 High Street: Disinfectants, Medicines
Booth, P. C. and Company, Sidney Street: (SCMW) Ammunition boxes
Boswell, Hatfield and Company, Hawk Works, Mary Street: Table knives and forks
Bradbury, Thomas, Arundel Street: Nickel silver items. Also (SCMW) Fuse body stampings
Braid, A. E. and Company: Surgical instruments and materials
Bramwell, J. H. and Company, Garden Street: Butchers' steels
Briggs, William and Company, Wentworth Works, Andrew Street: Electroplated items
Brightside Foundry and Engineering Company, Spital Hill: Heating and plumbing equipment. Also (SCMW) Boring gun forgings
Brindley, F. J. and Sons, River Lane: Tools. Also (SCMW) Machining shrapnel discs
Brookes, William and Sons, Howard Works, Woodburn Road: Tools
Brookes and Crookes, Atlantic Works, St Philips Road: Clasp knives, Razors, Surgical instruments and materials
Brooksbank, A. and Company, Malinda Street: Clasp knives
Brooks and Cooper, Mousehole Forge, Malin Bridge: Tools
Brown Bayley Steels, Leeds Road: Alloy steels, Springs
Brown, John and Company, Savile Street: Armour plating, Axles, Springs, Steel, Steel forgings
Burgon and Hall, La Plata Works, Malin Bridge: (SCMW) Plugs for fuses, Tubes for fuses

Burrows, S. H. and Sons, Garden Street: Munitions not yet specified

Bury and Company, Regent Works, Penistone Road: Tools. Also (SCMW) Circles and squares of sheet steel for helmets

Butcher, W. and S., 41 Eyre Lane: Clasp knives, Razors, Table knives and forks, Tools

Butler, George and Company, Trinity Works, Eyre Street: Clasp knives, Nickel silver items, Razors, Table knives and forks

Cadman, Thomas R. and Sons, St Mary's Road: Razors

Cammell Laird and Company, Cyclops Works and Grimesthorpe Works: Armour plating, Gun and other forging, Steel, Shells, Tools. Further details are in Display Box 4.1.

Carr, Wilde and Company, New Enterprise Works, Egerton Street: Razors, Surgical instruments and materials, Tools

Carron and Company, Phoenix Foundry, Furnace Hill: (SCMW) Grenades

Chapman, James A., Woodside Lane: Bayonets, Branding stamps, Swords

Cheeseman, E. W. and Company, Exchange Works, Egerton Street: Table knives and forks

Chesterman, James and Company, Pomona Street: Measuring gauges, rules and tapes, Tools

Christie, J. and Sons, West Street: Clasp knives, Surgical instruments and materials

Clark, J. T. and Company, 63 Norfolk Street: Grindstones

Clarke, J. and Son, Mowbray Street: Clasp knives, Razors, Table knives and forks

Clegg, Henry and Sons, Fitzwilliam Street: Clasp knives, Table knives and forks

Cockayne, T. B. and W., Angel Street: Bedding

Coe, James and Sons, Shiloh Works, Johnson Street: Clasp knives

Colver Brothers, 79 Corporation Street: Tools

Cook, William and Sons, Glasgow Works, Washford Road: Castings, Horseshoes, Steels

Cooper Brothers and Sons, Arundel Street: Dessert spoons, Nickel silver items. Also (SCMW) Machining shrapnel discs

Cooper, Cuthbert and Sons, Creswell Road, Darnall: Boot-making tools

Cooper, George and Sons, Effingham Road: Railway fishbolts and plant

Cooper and Turner, Vulcan Road: Copper rivets

Cotterill and Company, St Thomas Street: Tools

Cravens Railway Carriage and Wagon Company, Staniforth Road: Barrows, Railway wagons, Wheels

Crowley, John and Company, Meadow Hall Iron Works: Wheels. Also (SCMW) Grenades, Iron fuse body castings, Iron Howitzer bomb castings

Crownshaw, Chapman and Company, Penistone Road: Tools

Davy Brothers, Park Iron Works, Foley Street: Boilers, Bulletproof shields, Bulletproof tank plates, Cutting gear, Forging equipment, Presses, Pumping engines, Rolling mills. Also (SCMW) Boring gun forgings

Deakin James, Trinity Works, Matilda Street: Dessert spoons, Nickel silver items. Also (SCMW) Machining shrapnel discs

Dearman, Edward, 9 Edward Street : Branding stamps

Dickinson, E. M., Arundel Street: Clasp knives, Electroplated items, Razors, Spoons, Table knives and forks

Dixon, James and Sons, Cornish Place: Aeroplane piston rings, Components for depth-charges and mines, Cupronickel, Liquid-gas shells, Nickel silver items, Shells. Also (SCMW) Pressing and assembling helmets

Dixon, Peter and Sons, Oughtibridge: (SCMW) Boring gun forgings

Doncaster, Daniel and Sons, Doncaster Street: Munitions not yet specified

Doubied, Edouard, Coleridge Road: (SCMW) Fuses, Plugs for fuses

Drabble and Sanderson, Ebenezer Works, Morpeth Street: Tools

Eadon, Moses and Sons, Alma Street: Tools

Easterbrook, Allcard and Company, Albert Works, Penistone Road: Tools

Ellin, Thomas R., Footprint Works, 31-47 Hollis Croft: Tools

Ellin, Thomas and Company, Sylvester Works, Arundel Street: Clasp knives, Nickel silver items, Razors, Table knives and forks

Elliot, Joseph and Sons, 2-6 Hollis Croft: Clasp knives, Nickel silver items, Razors, Table knives and forks

Ellis, Isaac and Sons, Cavendish Street: Clasp knives, Nickel silver items

Ellis, John Henry and Sons, 294 Queens Road: Tools

Evans, Joseph and Sons, Little London Road: Tools

Farrer, James and Sons, Devonshire Works, 37-43 Division Street: Munitions not yet specified

Fenton Brothers, 6 Earl Street: Table knives and forks

Fenton, Joseph and Sons, 40 Matilda Street: Butchers' steels, Clasp knives, Electroplated items, Table knives and forks

Field, Alfred and Company, Ark Works, Westfield Terrace: Clasp knives, Table knives and forks

Firth, Thomas and Sons, Norfolk Works, Savile Street: Alloy steels, Castings, Drills, Forgings, Sheet steel for helmets, Shells, Tools. Also shells in a government-owned National Factory. See Chapters Two to Four.

Fisher, Harrison and Company, Trafalgar Works, Trafalgar Street: Nickel silver items, Table knives and forks

Fitzwilliam, Earl, Wentworth Woodhouse: (SCMW) Ammunition boxes

Flather, W. T., Standard Steel Works, Sheffield Road, Tinsley: Equipment for aeroplanes and submarines, Forgings, Testing and processing steel

Fletcher, C. W. and Sons, Bramall Lane: (SCMW) Shrapnel discs

Ford and Medley, Arundel Street: Clasp knives, Razors, Table knives and forks

Forncett Engineering Company, Forncett Street: (SCMW) Howitzer shells

Fox Brothers, Delhi Works, Henry Street: Tools

Fox, Samuel and Company, Stocksbridge: Springs, Steels

Foxon, John and Robinson, Henry, Charles Street: Packing cases. Also (SCMW) Ammunition boxes

Gallimore, William and Sons, Arundel Street: (SCMW) Brass conversion from other items

Garlick, C. and Sons, Lynx Works, Charlotte Lane: Tools

Gibbins, J. and Sons, Moore Street: Razors

Granville, F. and Company, 23½ Carver Street: (SCMW) Shell base plates

Graves, J. G., Enterprise Works, Shoreham Street: Nickel silver items. Also (SCMW) Machining shrapnel discs

Greaves, Edward and Sons, 13-19 Gilbert Street: Leather laces

Greaves, Francis and Sons, Radford Works, Radford Street: Table knives and forks

Green, William and Sons, Norfolk Foundry, Ecclesfield: (SCMW) Grenades, Howitzer shells, Metal clips, Plugs for fuses

Gregory Brothers, Bishop Street: Table knives and forks

Hadfields, East Hecla Works, Tinsley, and Hecla Works, Newhall Road: Armour plate, Body guards, Guns, Howitzers, Railway plant, Shells, Steel for helmets and other uses. Also shells, later guns, in a government-owned National Factory. Further details are in Display Box 4.2.

Hale Brothers, Moorfield Works, Snow Lane: Bill-hooks, Clasp knives

Hall, G. and J., Hereford Street: Tools

Hall, Martin and Company, Shrewsbury Works, Broad Street: (SCMW) Fuse body stamping, Shell base plates

Hall, Thomas and Son, Hunter Road, Hillsborough: (SCMW) Rings for exploder containers, Shrapnel discs, Shells

Hall, William, Alma Works, Matilda Lane: Butchers' steels, Tools

Hampton, C. and J., Ouse Road, Attercliffe: Tools
Hand, T. R. and Company, 168 Carr Road: Tools
Hardwick, H., Matilda Street: (SCMW) Fuse sockets
Hardy Patent Pick Company, Mining Tool Works, Heeley: Scoops, Tools
Harrison Brothers and Howson, Alpha Works, Carver Street: Clasp knives, Spoons. Also (SCMW) Machining shrapnel discs, Pressing and assembling helmets, Primers
Harrison, Fisher and Company: Spoons, Table knives and forks
Harrison, Louis, 196 Solly Street: Nickel silver items
Harrop, Absalom, 83 Hereford Street: Forges
Hatfield, J. and Company, Rockingham Street: Clasp knives, Table knives and forks
Hattersley and Davidson, 139 Norfolk Street: Mortar guns
Hawksley, G. and J.W., Carver Street: Leather items. Also (SCMW) Friction tubes
Hawksworth, Eyre and Company, Rockingham Street: (SCMW) Machining shrapnel discs
Hearnshaw Brothers, Sorby Street: Tools
Heeley Silver-Rolling and Wire Mills, Guernsey Road: Nickel silver items
Herriott, F., Son and Company, 113 Arundel Street: Table knives and forks
Hibbert, S. and Son, Charlotte Street: Clasp knives, Razors, Table knives and forks
Hildick, Aaron, Woodside Works, Rutland Road: Tools
Hill, J. and P., Ordnance Works, Bernard Road: Machine tools, Munitions not yet specified
Hobson, Henry and Sons, Express Works, 28 Eyre Lane: Electro-plate and nickel silver items, Table knives and forks
Hobson, Houghton and Company, Don Steel Works, Savile Street: Tools
Hoole, H. E. and Company, Globe Works, Green Lane: (SCMW) Plugs for fuses
Howard and Sons, 151 Meadow Hall Road: (SCMW) Plugs for fuses
Howarth, C. and Company, 9 Eldon Street: Tools
Howell and Company, Brook Hill, Meadowhall: Boilers, Heating coils, Tubes
Hoyland, Charles and Son, 14-18 West Bar Green: Brushes
Hulley, George H., 245 Rockingham Street: Electroplated items
Humphreys, W. R. and Company, Haddon Works, Denby Street: Clasp knives, Nickel silver items, Razors, Table knives and forks
Hutton, William and Sons, West Street: Clasp knives, Nickel silver items,

Spoons. Also (SCMW) Primers, Pressing and assembling helmets, Shell heads and baseplates

Hyde, Robert and Sons, 38-50 Athol Road, Norton Woodseats: (SCMW) Grenades

Ibbotson Brothers and Company, Globe Steel Works: Nuts and bolts, Railway wagons, Shell diaphragm discs, Springs, Tools

Ibbotson, Richard, Shoreham Saw Works, White Croft: Tools

Ibbotson, Thomas, Progress Works, Sudbury Street: (SCMW) Ammunition boxes

Jacobs and Company, High Street: Clasp knives, Table knives and forks

James, J. U. and Sons, Milton Street: Clasp knives

Jessop, William and Sons, Brightside Works: Tool and other steel. Also (SCMW) Boring gun forgings

Jonas, Colver and Company, Continental Steel Works, Bessemer Road: Files, Steel, Tools

Johnson, Christopher and Company, Western Works, Howard Street: Clasp knives, Scissors

Kay and Company, Ecclesfield: (SCMW) Plugs for fuses, Shells, Shell heads

Kayser, Ellison and Company, Carlisle Works, Carlisle Street East: Alloy and other steel

Keates, Albert, Sheffield Organ Works, Charlotte Road: (SCMW) Ammunition boxes

Kenyon, John and Company, Millsands Steel Works, Millsands: Tools

Kitchin, S. and J., Soho Works, Summerfield Street: Butchers' steels, Clasp knives, Machetes, Table knives and forks, Tools

Land, T. and Sons, Colonial Works, Queens Road: (SCMW) Brass component stamping, Fuse body stamping, Stampings for shells

Larder and Burgess, 156 Eyre Street: Electroplated items

Latham, W. and Company, Solly Street: (SCMW) Machining shrapnel discs

Law, W. H., Eyre Street: (SCMW) Machining shrapnel discs

Laycock, Thomas: (SCMW) Plugs for fuses

Laycock, W. S., Archer Road, Millhouses: Aircraft engines, Barrows, Gun carriages. Also (SCMW) Brass component stamping, Howitzer shells, Rings for exploder containers

Leadbeater and Scott, National Steel Works, Penistone Road: Tools

Lee, Arthur and Sons, Love Street and Meadowhall: Aeroplane wire, Steels

Lee and Wigfull, John Street: Electroplate and nickel silver items, Spoons, Table knives and forks. Also (SCMW) Machining shrapnel discs

Linacre, R. and J., Cobnar Road: Bill-hooks
Lockwood Brothers, Spital Hill: Bill-hooks, Clasp knives, Table knives and forks, Tools
Long, H. G. and Company, New Hallamshire Works, Boston Street: Butchers' steels, Clasp knives, Table knives and forks, Tools
Longden, G. and Son, Parkwood Road: Construction work for national factories
Lucas, E. and W., Dronfield Fork and Shovel Works: Tools
Maleham and Yeomans, Bowden Street: Clasp knives, Nickel silver items, Razors, Scissors, Table knives and forks
Mappin and Webb, Royal Cutlery and Plate Works, Norfolk Street: Clasp knives, Metal badges, Nickel silver items, Razors, Table knives and forks. Also (SCMW) Howitzer shells
Marples, Robert and Son, Aizlewood Road: Tools
Marples, W. and Sons, Hibernia Works, Westfield Terrace: Razors, Tools
Marsh Brothers and Company, Pond Works, Forge Lane: Drills, Steels, Tools
Marsden, G. and Son, 112 Carver Street: (SCMW) Brass component stamping
Martin, Hall and Company, Shrewsbury Works, Broad Street: Electro-plated items, Spoons
Mather, Richard and Son, 150 Shoreham Street: Tools
Maxfield, J. J. and Sons, 118-120 Rockingham Street: Nickel silver items. Also (SCMW) Pressing and assembling helmets
McClory, John and Sons, Milton Street: Clasp knives, Nickel silver items, Table knives and forks
Meggitt, Samuel (Sheffield), Effingham Road: Buttons
Mellowes and Company, 40 Corporation Street: Glazing
Midland Manufacturing Company, Celtic Works, Savile Street East: Tools. Also (SCMW) Grenades
Mills, Frank and Company, Division Street: Clasp knives, Table knives and forks
Mills, W. and Company, Woodhouse Mill: Tools
Milner, John and Company, Orient Works, Matilda Street: Clasp knives, Razors
Milns, A. and Company, Stanley Works, Arundel Street: Clasp knives, Nickel silver items, Razors, Table knives and forks
Miris Steel Company, Perseverance Works, Nursery Street: Helmets
Moore and Wright, 137 Trafalgar Street: Tools

Moorwoods, Harleston Iron Works, Harleston Street: (SCMW) Howitzer bomb castings
Morrison, John Edward, Court 4, Lee Croft: Tools
Morton, William and Sons, Rockingham Street: Clasp knives, Razors
Mosley, R. F. and Company, Portland Works, Randall Street: Clasp knives, Electroplate and nickel silver items, Spoons, Table knives and forks
Mudford, J. H., Exchange Street: Ropes
Needham, Veall and Tyzack, Eye Witness Works, Milton Street: Clasp knives, Nickel silver items, Razors, Table knives and forks, Tools. Also (SCMW) Machining shrapnel discs
Neill, James and Company, Napier Street: Magnets
Newton, Chambers and Company, Moorhead and Thorncliffe Iron Works, Chapletown: Container tanks, Disinfectants, Shells, Toluol
Newton, Francis and Sons, Portobello Works, Portobello Street: Clasp knives, Table knives and forks
Nixon and Winterbottom, Pyramid Works, Pond Street: Table knives and forks
Nowill, John and Sons, Scotland Street: Clasp knives, Razors, Table knives and forks
Oates, Albert, Atlantic Works, St Philips Road: Clasp knives
Oates, Turner and Company, Eyre Street: Shrapnel discs
Osborn, Samuel, Clyde Steel Works, Wicker: Castings, Drills, Files, Sheet steel for helmets, Shells, Springs, Tool and other steel
Osborne and Company, 122 Rockingham Street: Nickel silver items
Oxley, James, Toronto Works, Garden Street: Table knives and forks, Tools
Oxley, Thomas, Shiloh Wheel, Stanley Street: Boilers and other equipment
Paget and Senior, 145 Eldon Street: Table knives and forks
Parramore, F. and Sons, Caledonian Foundry, Chapeltown: (SCMW) Grenades, Howitzer shells, Plugs for fuses
Patent Stone Dressing Tool Company, 51 Wicker Lane: Tools
Peace, John and Sons, Well Meadow Street: Tools
Peace, Joseph and Company, Merchant Works, Rutland Road: Tools
Peace, J. H. and Company, 64 Button Lane: Razors, Table knives and forks
Peace, S. and Sons, Well Meadow Street: Tools
Peace, W. K. and C., Eagle Works, Mowbray Street: Tools
Peacock Brothers, 318 Sheffield Road, Tinsley: Tools. Also (SCMW) Plugs for fuses
Pearson, F., 278 Rockingham Street: (SCMW) Ammunition boxes
Pearson, F. G. and Company, Hope Works, Furnace Hill: Tools

Pearson, S. and Company, Eldon Street: Razors
Perkington, George, 113 Broad Lane: Table knives and forks
Petty, John and Sons, Perth Works, Garden Street: Clasp knives, Tools
Pitchford, J. and W., Shude Lane: Razors
Platts, George and Son, 106 Mary Street: Scissors
Portass, C. and Sons, 70 Broadfield Road: Aircraft parts. Also (SCMW) Boxes for howitzer bombs
Potter, J. H. and Sons, Rockingham Works, 65-71 Division Street: Clasp knives, Electroplate and nickel silver items, Razors, Table knives and forks, Tools. Also (SCMW) Fuse body stamping
Princeps and Company, Princeps Works, Matilda Street: (SCMW) Howitzer shells, Shells
Provident Steel and Tool Company, Brown Street: (SCMW) Shells
Radford, H., 69 Arundel Street: Branding stamps
Ragg, John and William, 93-95 Eldon Street: Razors, Trench knives
Ramsbottom, W. and S., Vine Works, Upper St Philips Road: Scissors
Read and Oxley, Watery Lane: (SCMW) Containers for chemical shells, Rings for exploder containers
Redmayne, T. and Company, Little London Road: (SCMW) Grenades
Revitt, Frank, Kenyon Alley: Razors
Reynolds, Frederick, Monmouth Lane: Razors, Table knives and forks
Richardson Brothers, Matthew Street: Tools
Richardson, C. E., and Company, Aizlewood Road: Tools. Also (SCMW) Boxes for Howitzer bombs, Howitzer shells, Machining shrapnel discs
Richardson, Richard, Cornwall Works, Scotland Street: Electroplate and nickel silver items, Spoons
Ridge, W. and Son, Common End, Ecclesfield: Tools
Rippon and Dean, 29 Eyre Street: Branding irons
Ritchie, W. J. and Company, Freedom Works, Arundel Lane: (SCMW) Shells
Roberts and Belk, Furnival Street: Nickel silver items. Also (SCMW) Machining shrapnel discs
Roberts, Percy J. and Company, 18 Rosedale Road, Ecclesall: (SCMW) Primers
Roberts, W. H., Hollin Street: Clasp knives
Robinson and Oates, Challenge Works, 47 Eyre Lane: Table knives and forks
Robinson, Herbert and Company, Canton Works, Young Street: Razors
Robson, Joseph and Sons, Mary Street: Tools

Rodgers, Joseph, 8 Clun Street: Razors
Rodgers, Joseph and Sons, Norfolk Works, Norfolk Street: Razors, Table knives and forks
Roper and Wreaks, 112 Arundel Street: Cartridges. Also (SCMW) Howitzer shells, Shells
Rossell, Henry and Company, Effingham Road: (SCMW) Howitzer shells
Round, John and Son, Tudor Works, Tudor Street: Electroplate and nickel silver items. Also (SCMW) Brass component stamping, Cases for stampings, Fuse body stamping, Pressing and assembling helmets
Rowland, Brindley and Company, Bramall Lane: Tools
Rowlands, T. and Company, North Church Street: Tools
Royse Brothers, 443 Queens Road: Scissors
Sanderson Brothers and Newbould, Newhall Road: Bayonets, Breastplates, Cast steel, Cutters, Swords, Tank plates, Tools, Trench knives
Saville, J. J. and Company: Triumph Steel Works, Shoreham Street: Steels
Saynor, W., Sidney Street: Clasp knives, Razors, Table knives and forks
Schofield, John and Sons, Attercliffe Road: Hair combs, Branding stamps
Seebohm and Dieckstahl: see Arthur Balfour and Company
Sellers, John and Sons, 151 Arundel Street: Razors
Senior, George and Company, Ponds Forge: Steel
Shardlow, Ambrose, Washford Road: Crankshafts, Micrometers. Also (SCMW) Howitzer shells, Tubes for fuses
Shaw and Webster, 20 Cambridge Street: Nickel silver items
Sheffield Engineers, Empire Works, Aizlewood Road: (SCMW) Machining shrapnel discs, Plugs for fuses
Sheffield Flatware Company, 43 Solly Street: Nickel silver items
Sheffield Forge and Rolling Mills, Millsands: Munitions not yet specified
Sheffield and Hallamshire Hacksaw Company, London Works, Bridge Street: Tools
Sheffield Saw and Tool Company, Shoreham Saw Works, White Croft: Tools
Sheffield Scissors and Razor Company, Bishop Street: Tools
Sheffield Silver Plate and Cutlery Company, Priestley Street: (SCMW) Copper banding for shells
Sheffield Simplex Motor Works, Tinsley: Aircraft engines, Mines. Also (SCMW) Howitzer shells, Primers, Shells, Shell nose pieces
Sheffield Smelting Company, Royds Mill and Arundel Street: Aluminium discs, Brass rods, Copper bands, Cupro-nickel sheets, Piston rings. Also (SCMW) Machining shrapnel discs

Sheffield Stamping Company, Solly Street: (SCMW) Machining shrapnel discs
Sheffield Twist Drill and Steel Company, Summerfield Street: Tools
Shipman, Jabez and Company, Attercliffe Steel Works and Wire Mills: Iron, Steel, Wire
Silvester, W. H., 63 Penistone Road: Tools
Simpson, J. R. and Son: Knives and forks
Skelton, C. T. and Company, Sheafbank Works: Garden rakes, Tools
Slack, Sellars and Company, Townhead Works, Lancaster Street: Tools
Slater, Herbert M., Arundel Street: Clasp knives, Razors
Snow and Company, Stanley Street: (SCMW) Adapters for shells, Plugs for fuses
Sorby, E. and Sons, Trafalgar Street: Meat choppers
Sorby, Robert and Sons, Trafalgar Street: Tools
Southern and Richardson, Don Cutlery Works, Doncaster Street: Clasp knives, Razors, Table knives and forks
Spear and Jackson, Aetna Works, Savile Street: Armour plate, Entrenching tools, Saws, Steel, Swords, Tools
Spencer, M. and Sons, Arley Street: Pickaxes, Tools. Also (SCMW) Shells
Spencer, Walter and Company, Crescent Steel Works, Warren Street: Files
Stalker Drill Works, Drill Square, Langsett Road: Tools
Staniforth, T. and Company, Hackenthorpe: Bill-hooks
Stead, J. and Company, Manor Works, Cricket Inn Road: Gun springs and other munitions
Stevens, J. A. and Sons, 68 West Street: Hair combs
Stormont, G. V. and H., 124 Fitzwilliam Street: Tools
Stringer, G. and Company, Wincobank Steel Works: (SCMW) Shells
Styring, Percival Robert, 124 Rockingham Street: Table knives and forks
Sutherland and Rhodes, 35-37 Matilda Street: Clasp knives, Nickel silver items
Swann and Garland, Chippinghouse Road: (SCMW) Plugs for fuses
Swift, J. H. and Sons, 537 Penistone Road: Tools
Swift and Goodinson, 85 Headford Street: Surgical materials
Swift, Levick and Company: Magnets
Swinscoe, John, Norfolk Saw Mills, Mowbray Street: Mallets, Woodwork items
Taskers Engineering Company, Blonk Street: (SCMW) Shells
Taylor, Henry, 92 Arundel Street: Tools
Taylor Brothers, Adelaide Works, Mowbray Street: Tools
Taylor's Sheffield Tools, Bishop Street: Tools

Temporal, Thomas, West End Works, Bolsover Street: Boot-making tools
Temporal, W., 65 Gloucester Street: Razors
Thompson, James (SCMW), 106 Eyre Street: Rings for exploder containers
Thornhill, Bednal and Company, Crispin Works, Sycamore Street: Tools
Thornton, G. W., Trafalgar Street: (SCMW) Machining shrapnel discs
Tinsley Rolling Mills, Sheffield Road: Steel sheets for helmets and other uses, Steel bars
Timperley, Walter A., Prospect Works, Prospect Road: Tools
Turner, Thomas and Company, Suffolk Works, Suffolk Road: Clasp knives, Grinding machines, Nickel silver items, Springs, Tools
Turton, John and Company, Kendal Works, Arundel Street: Electroplated items, Table knives and forks
Turton, Platts and Company, Savile Street: Springs
Tyzack and Holmes, 23-27 Cavendish Street: Measuring tapes
Tyzack, J. and Sons, Valley Road, Heeley: Tools
Tyzack, W., Sons and Turner, Little London Works, Heeley: Tools
University Department of Applied Science, St George's Square: Optical glass. Also (SCMW) Shells
Vickers, River Don Works and Holme Lane, Hillsborough: Armour plate, Artillery weapons, Machine-guns, Shells, Steels. Also (SCMW) Squares of sheet steel for helmets
Vickers, V. B., Sylvester Street: (SCMW) Machining shrapnel discs
Viener, W. and E., Broomspring Works, Bath Street: Breastplates. Also (SCMW) Exploder container tubes, Pressing and assembling helmets, Shell discs
Volola Steel Cask Company, Cobnar Works, Woodseats: (SCMW) Cutting steel sheet for helmets
Wache and James, Trafalgar Street: (SCMW) Machining shrapnel discs, Rings for exploder containers, Shells, Shell heads,
Wain, John, 2 Clough Road: Table knives and forks
Wain, William, 37 Porter Street: Tools
Wales, Thomas and Sons, Queens Road: Tools
Walker and Company, 21 Cambridge Street: Electroplated items
Walker and Hall, Electro Works, Howard Street: Clasp knives, Copper bands for shells, Nickel silver and electroplate items, Table knives and forks
Wall, Kay and Sons, 92 Arundel Street: Nickel silver items, Table knives and forks

Walsh, John, Fargate: Card index cabinets, Furniture
Ward and Payne, West Street: Tools. Also (SCMW) Shell base plates, Shell discs
Ward, Thomas W., Albion Works, Savile Street: Processing scrap metal, Repairing machinery
Wardsend Steel Company: Tools
Watson and Gillott, 26 Eyre Lane: Electroplated items
Watts Brothers, Keeton's Hill, London Road: (SCMW) Cartridges, Shells, Shell base plates
Watts, John, 43 Lambert Street: Clasp knives, Razors, Surgical instruments and materials, Table knives and forks
Wheatley Brothers, Wheatsheaf Works, John Street: Clasp knives, Table knives and forks, Razors
Whiteley, W., Wilkinson T. and Sons, 29 Rockingham Street: Clasp knives
Wilcock, B. and J., Bolton Works, 51 Wicker Lane: Tools
Williamson, S. and Sons, Hollis Croft: Table knives and forks
Willis, Mark and Son, Rockingham Street: (SCMW) Machining shrapnel discs
Wilson, Albert and Son, 41 Bowdon Street: Razors
Wilson, John, 32 Sycamore Street: Knives and forks
Wilson, Thomas, 173-175 Granville Street: Clasp knives, Nickel silver items, Razors, Table knives and forks
Wilson, W. and Sons, Pool Works, Burgess Street: Table knives and forks
Wilson and Frith, 36 Eldon Street: Tools
Wood, B. and Sons, 68 West Street: Clasp knives
Wood, Francis and Son, 67-69 Henry Street: Saws, Table knives and forks, Tools
Wood, J. and Sons, Wisewood: Munitions not yet specified
Woollen and Company, Holly Street: (SCMW) Plugs for fuses
Wostenholm, George and Son, Washington Works, Washington Street: Clasp knives, Razors, Table knives and forks
Yorkshire Engine Company, Meadow Hall Works: Watertight ship doors. Also (SCMW) Boring gun forgings, Shells

APPENDIX 2

Sheffield's businessmen in government service

The following twenty-two company directors and managers from Sheffield have been identified as accepting requests to work for government departments or committees during the First World War. In addition, businessmen serving on the Sheffield Committee on Munitions of War are cited in Chapter Five.

Some of the appointments below were more long-term and time-consuming than others, and a number clearly involved considerable personal responsibility. Some of the individuals named also undertook additional government roles yet to be specified. No doubt others also contributed but details have yet to be located. And of course large numbers of Sheffielders worked indirectly for the government in national factories or in companies fulfilling government contracts.

Balfour, Arthur, of Arthur Balfour and Company: Member of the Ministry of Munitions' Manpower Distribution Board, the Board of Trade's Engineering Committee, the Royal Commission on Railways, the Privy Council Committee for Commercial and Industrial Research, the Manpower Committee, and the Treasury's Industry and Commerce Committee (Later Sir Arthur Balfour and then Lord Riverdale)

Bell, Thomas, of John Brown and Company: Admiralty's Deputy Controller of Supplies (Later Sir Thomas Bell)

Best, F., of Thomas Firth and Sons: Member of the Ministry of Munitions' High-Speed Steel Committee

Clark, W., of Vickers: Member of the Ministry of Munitions' Aircraft Steel

Committee and Member of the Ministry of Munitions' High-Speed Steel Committee

Clegg, Sir William, of Clegg and Sons: Chairman of Sheffield Munitions Tribunal and of Sheffield Military Tribunal

Digman, E. G., of Thomas Firth and Sons: Government work not yet identified

Ellis, Charles, of John Brown and Company: Deputy Director of the Ministry of Munitions, with roles such as Director-General of Ordnance Supply, Chairman of the Central Munitions Labour Supply Committee, and President of the Mission Anglaise de l'Armament (Later Sir Charles Ellis)

Firth, Bernard, of Thomas Firth and Sons: Chairman of the Ministry of Munitions' Aircraft Steel Committee

Franklin, Sir George: Member of Disabled Soldiers and Sailors Committee (Died 1916)

Grant, Allan, of John Brown and Company: Member of the Ministry of Munitions' Aircraft Steel Committee (Later Sir Allan Grant)

Hadfield, Sir Robert, of Hadfields: Member of the Ministry of Munitions' Inventions Committee

Hobson, Albert, of Thomas Turton and Company and Chairman of Jessops: Member of the Board of Trade's Iron, Steel and Engineering Committee and that Committee's Engineering Industries Sub-Committee (Later Sir Albert Hobson)

Kayser, Charles, of Kayser, Ellison and Company: Member of the Ministry of Munitions' Aircraft Steel Committee

McGregor, P., of Sanderson Brothers and Newbould: Chairman of the Ministry of Munitions' High-Speed Steel Committee

Newman, W. F., of Thomas Firth and Sons: Government work not yet identified

Osborn, F., of Samuel Osborn and Company: Member of the Ministry of Munitions' Aircraft Steel Committee

Osborn, S. of Samuel Osborn and Company: Member of the Health of Munition Workers Committee

Ripper, William, of the University of Sheffield: War Office arbitrator in contract disputes

Senior, Albert, of George Senior and Company: Ore-import adviser to the Ministry of Munitions and Member of the Ministry of Munitions' High-Speed Steel Committee

Siddall, Mr, of Sheffield Forge Company: Member of the Ministry of Munitions' High-Speed Steel Committee

Vickers, Douglas, of Messrs Vickers: Member of the Board of Trade's Iron, Steel and Engineering Committee

Ward, Joseph, of T. W. Ward and Company: Chairman of the Ministry of Munitions' Scrap Advisory Committee

In addition, Rotherham-based Henry Steel and J. Peech, of Steel, Peech and Tozer were respectively Chairman of the General Alloy Steel Committee and an executive of the Ministry of Munitions' Iron and Steel Department.

Notes

Chapter One – War on Sheffield's Home Front

1 In addition to many books about the war, websites of a general kind include www.1914-1918.net, www.bbc.co.uk/ww1, www.europeanhistory.about.com/od/world war1/p/ww1101.htm, www.firstworldwar.com, www.historylearningsite.co.uk/ww1.htm and www.spartacus-educational.com/FWW.htm. Additional photographs are at www.gwpda.org/photos and (including original song recordings) at www.ww1photos.com; and some films are at www.britishpathe.com/workspaces/show/jhoyle/ GfYgqoxq/thumb.

The conflict was very quickly dubbed 'The Great War', with 'great' in the traditional sense of 'big'. It started on 4 August 1914 and is usually viewed as ending on 11 November 1918 when an armistice was signed. An armistice is an agreed temporary ceasefire in order to discuss peace terms, and the countries were still formally at war until a peace treaty was signed on 28 June 1919. For that reason it is occasionally referred to as the '1914-1919 war'.

2 Details have been brought together at www.sheffieldsoldierww1.co.uk. The city's earlier (incomplete) Roll of Honour is available at www.sheffield.gov.uk/libraries/archives-and-local-studies/research-guides/world-war-one.html.

3 Some estimates exceed 800,000. All agree that the number of British military deaths in the Great War was without precedent – and more than double those in the Second World War.

4 The overall rate was made up of about thirteen per cent in the army, nearly seven per cent in the navy, and around two per cent for the air force as a whole but very much higher for men who flew the planes. The influenza epidemic of 1918 also killed many troops – possibly 10,000 from Britain. Published estimates of British troop numbers across the entire period range from 5,600,000 to 6,000,000; around eighty-eight per cent of these served in the army, seven per cent in the navy, and five per cent in the air-force. Data have been collated by J. M. Winter in 'Britain's "lost generation" of the First World War' in *Population Studies*, *31*, 449-466. Britain's churches generally supported the war effort, with about 5,000 chaplains serving in the forces, of whom some 170 were killed.

5 The official *History of the Great War* makes it clear that just over half of the troops sent back to UK hospitals were classed as 'sick' rather than 'wounded'; see *Medical Services: General History*, volume 1, page 390 (London: HMSO, 1921).

6 Excerpts from films from the period about the more extreme forms of symptom are available at http://blog.wellcome.ac.uk/2010/11/11/war-neuroses, www.british pathe.com/search/query/shell+shock.

7 Sheffield examples are included in this book's companion publication – *Sheffield in the Great War* by Peter Warr (Barnsley: Pen and Sword Books, 2015). Further details of all of the chapter's themes can be found in that book.
8 Many detailed publications about aspects of the war are cited throughout this book. In addition, Sheffield City Council has published useful guides for investigating Sheffield in the period. These are listed at www.sheffield.gov.uk/libraries/archives-and-local-studies/research-guides/world-war-one.html.
9 The barriers remained in place for approximately a year. Whenever air-raids were threatened, each site was guarded by nominated drivers who ensured that no lights were used on incoming vehicles.
10 A national perspective on the refugees has been provided in pages 217 to 226 of David Bilton's *The Home Front in the Great Wa*r (Barnsley: Pen and Sword Books, 2003). Events in Sheffield have been described by Diana Gascoyne in 'Belgian refugees in Sheffield in the First World War', pages 51 to 56 of the *Sheffield History Reporter Annual*, 1998, which is available in the city's Local Studies Library.
11 Further information about this and other local developments are provided in Peter Warr's *Sheffield in the Great War* (Barnsley: Pen and Sword Books, 2015).
12 Subsequent Military Service Acts were introduced in April 1917, January 1918 and April 1918. The last of these extended the age-range for conscription from seventeen up to (with some variations) fifty years; by then the need for more men was truly desperate.
13 'Northern' refers to the army's Northern Command, not to the north of the city, and the Third Northern General Hospital covered an area outside as well as within Sheffield. The First, Second, Fourth and Fifth Northern General Hospitals were in Newcastle, Leeds, Lincoln and Leicester respectively.
14 In addition to a local section of the British Red Cross Society, Sheffield had two units of the St John Ambulance Brigade – the overall Sheffield Corps and (from 1917) the Heeley Division. These provided uniformed first-aid men for public events, and during the war the Brigade helped in Winter Street and other hospitals by providing night-time cover and was called out as a precaution whenever an air-raid was threatened. Linked to the *Brigade* was the St John Ambulance *Association*, which provided instruction and certification in first-aid and nursing.
15 The Asylum opened its doors in 1872; in 1948 it became Middlewood Hospital, which closed in 1996. See F. T. Thorpe's *A History of the Middlewood Psychiatric Hospital*, published by the Hospital in 1972. A copy of this is held by Sheffield Local Studies Library.
16 This opened in August 1916 with a refreshment room, a games room and a reading/writing room. Paying a nominal rent to the Corporation and operating with money from public donations, the Centre was staffed by volunteer Sheffield ladies. It served free cups of tea and cakes and was soon dispensing around 3,000 teas each week.
17 These and other developments in the city are described more fully in the book cited in Note 11 above.
18 The nation's volunteer defence corps received a small capitation fee from 1917 and the government provided uniforms from 1918.

Chapter Two – Arming the troops 1: Government, employers and trade unions
19 See the official *History of the Ministry of Munitions,* volume 1, part 1, page 8 (London: HMSO, 1922).

20 Early in the war the Admiralty and the War Office operated largely independently of each other, creating separate munition-supply systems for the navy and army respectively. Companies advertised their inclusion in the 'Admiralty List', the 'War Office List' or in both of those.
21 The need for more ammunition was being publicly emphasized by several commentators. On 5 March 1915, historian and poet Hillaire Belloc spoke to a large audience in Sheffield as part of the University's War Lecture series (see Chapter Five). A key theme of his talk was that without more ammunition for its guns the army and the nation would be defeated.
22 Both the *Times* and the *Mail* were owned by Lord Northcliffe, who campaigned vigorously throughout the war for stronger anti-German measures. He was a strident critic of the Secretary of State for War, Lord Kitchener, and on 21 May 1915 wrote: 'Lord Kitchener has starved the army in France of high-explosive shells. [. . .] He persisted in sending shrapnel – a useless weapon in trench warfare. He was warned repeatedly that the kind of shell required was a violently explosive bomb which would dynamite its way through the German trenches and entanglements and enable our brave men to advance in safety. The kind of shell our poor soldiers have had has caused the death of thousands of them.' (Shrapnel shells, containing around 250 pellets for explosion above enemy heads, were Britain's traditional ammunition, but they were ineffective in the novel conditions of trench warfare.) After the shell crisis, *The Times* war correspondent was tried and found guilty of disclosing secret information; he received a fine.
23 The Ministry in fact started work before its formal commencement on 9 June. Newspapers in Sheffield and elsewhere reported staffing and other decisions from late May.
24 Dr Addison later became the third Minister of Munitions, between December 1916 and July 1917. Winston Churchill (the First Lord of the Admiralty in 1914 and a Lieutenant-Colonel in France during part of 1916) took over as the fourth Minister of Munitions from July 1917; after the war, in January 1919, he became Secretary of State for War. Mr Churchill had been a Unionist (Conservative) MP from 1901, but in 1904 crossed the floor of the House to become a Liberal. By 1917 he was a strong advocate of 'land ships' – the tanks that Britain was developing for frontline army activity.
25 This company, based in Ponds Forge, was an established importer of Swedish ore and had extensive contacts in that country, including a strong financial interest in the Forsbacka steelworks.
26 USA was also a vital source of copper and aluminium. The importance of American trade led to offices of the Ministry of Munitions being established in New York and Washington. France, Germany and other countries were also placing orders in USA, and after a while many American factories found it difficult to cope with the hugely increased international demand.
27 The *History of the Ministry of Munitions* (HMSO, 1922) reports that 'by the end of 1916 the Ministry was already the largest selling, as well as the largest purchasing, agency in the world' (volume 3, part 1, page 29).
28 These two worked together as parts of the Alloy Steel Production Committee, also based in Sheffield. Names of members from the city are in the book's Appendix Two.
29 See pages 7 and 99 of the 1923 book by Humbert Wolfe cited in the next footnote. He had previously been a senior official in both the Board of Trade and the Ministry

of Munitions. One early experiment (in the summer of 1915) was the creation of War Munitions Volunteers. Men considered to be in non-essential jobs were invited to volunteer for transfer to munitions work. In Sheffield, an enrolment bureau was opened in the Town Hall in late June 1915, and nationally around 100,000 workers came forward. However, an employer's permission was required for a man's release and many requests were refused. In addition, administrative difficulties of assessment and allocation were considerable, and the scheme was soon dropped.

30 The nation's extended struggle to produce munitions while also providing men for the services has been examined by George Dewar in *The Great Munitions Feat 1914-1918* (London: Constable, 1921), Humbert Wolfe in *Labour Supply and Regulation* (Oxford: Clarendon Press, 1923), and the eight-volume *History of the Ministry of Munitions* (London: His Majesty's Stationery Office, 1921 and 1922). More recent accounts include *The Politics of Manpower* by Keith Grieves (Manchester: Manchester University Press, 1988) which focuses on conflicts between government departments in this period.

31 The estimated total number varies slightly between reports, partly because some factories were subsequently reclassified and others operated on more than one site; in some calculations these were counted more than once. The figures in this chapter are from the detailed listing in the official *History of the Ministry of Munitions*, volume 8, part 2, published by His Majesty's Stationery Office in 1922.

32 However, Cammell Laird declined to accept a fee for either the construction or the management of their Nottingham national factory.

33 Some local developments of this kind were aided by government action. For example, in the spring of 1915 the Board of Trade dispatched to major industrial cities, including Sheffield, an exhibition of shells and fuses for companies to consider the possibility of their manufacture.

34 Munition work was in 1915 defined as 'the manufacture or repair of arms, ammunition, ships, vehicles, aircraft or any other articles required for use in war, or of metals, machines, or tools required for that manufacture or repair'.

Although firms to be controlled were at first all producers of munitions as narrowly defined, the range gradually expanded. For example, to maintain equality of opportunity and restriction within a sector the competitors of controlled firms in the same industry also had to be regulated; some entire sectors became controlled on the grounds that certain member firms were making munitions and thus subject to government restriction. A number of steel companies became controlled in July and August 1915, and all larger firms in the industry were added by November of that year. Railway workers and railway repair companies were also controlled, but less clear was the position of firms supplying materials for (say) uniforms or food for the troops.

35 Restrictive practices were defined as 'any rule, practice or custom not having the force of law which tends to restrict production or employment'. Of particular concern to the government were trade unions' prevention of changes to working methods or hours, and their requirement that many jobs be undertaken only by workers defined by unions as 'skilled'.

In addition to restrictions from the Munitions of War Act, individuals and companies also had to obey many other wartime regulations. For instance, in May 1918 Thomas W. Ward of Savile Street was fined £10 for purchasing second-hand railway lines without a government permit.

36 That restriction was very unpopular, and it had the disadvantage of removing needed munition workers from the labour-force during six weeks of wasted non-employment. Regulations about leaving certificates were modified in January 1916, and the requirement was abolished on 15 October 1917.
37 By July 1915 it was estimated that around twenty per cent of male munition workers had left their jobs to volunteer as servicemen. For the war as a whole, around forty per cent of metal workers served as volunteers or conscripts; see P. E. Dewey's article 'Military recruiting and the British labour force during the First World War' in *The Historical Journal*, 1984, *27*, 199-223.
38 A few national newspapers reported that women had offered white feathers to non-volunteers to symbolize their alleged personal weakness and fear of combat. No such reports have been located in Sheffield, but a letter to the *Sheffield Daily Telegraph* in July 1915 pointed to the possibility of being 'annoyed by the enthusiastic and ubiquitous recruiting female', so presumably some kind of public harassment took place in the city.
39 Between November 1916 and April 1917, decisions about exemptions in the engineering and some other trades were made by unions themselves (under the 'Trade Card Scheme'). This scheme was limited to only some unions, and the government soon came to prefer its own control in terms of a revised Schedule of Protected Occupations.
40 These were manufactured by companies in several cities including in Sheffield by Mappin and Webb.
41 The Ministry was initially reluctant to accept the Sheffield Committee's recommendations about workers not directly producing armaments. (This was a national uncertainty at the time.) For example, only after considerable discussion were the city's cutlers accepted (in October 1915) as potentially eligible for badges.
42 For instance, in September 1916 the government established a Manpower Distribution Board (whose members included Arthur Balfour from Sheffield) to clarify decision-making policies. Within three months, other bodies had instead taken over the Board's responsibilities.
43 In March 1917 recruiting officers were administratively moved into a new Department of National Service, which became the Ministry of National Service in August of that year. On 1 November 1917 responsibility for recruiting was transferred from the War Office to the new ministry.
44 Voluntary enlistment was still possible for militarily-ineligible men in respect of the Royal Garrison Artillery and motor transport branches of the Army Service Corps; these volunteers (usually older or of lower medical grade) were not required to serve abroad.
45 Reduced-price rail travel from and to their family home was available for individuals who offered themselves as munition workers in a different part of the country.
46 As pointed out in a detailed account of the development of the national employment service, this was a confusing period 'in which instructions from Central Office were changing with chaotic frequency as the government tried one expedient after another to solve labour problems'. See page 45 of David Price's *Office of Hope: A History of the Public Employment Service in Great Britain* (London: Policy Studies Institute, 2000).

47 Although originally applied in munition-producing establishments, substitution also occurred in other industries important for the war. Substitution agreements were signed in, for instance, the clothing, boot and shoe, and cotton industries. In many ways substitution was a form of dilution, not only introducing additional workers but perhaps also making changes to job content or introducing machine aids. Adjustments of that kind will be considered in the next chapter.
48 By June 1918 'the best men in the works' had been taken from Vickers' Holme Lane factory; see page 299 of *Septimus Bennett: Artist in Arms* by Martin Phillips and John Potter (Durham: Pentland Press, 2001). Albert Grove of Sheaf Gardens had throughout the war been allowed to remain as a clerk with Sanderson Brothers and Newbould, but he too was among the many called-up in September 1918.

Chapter Three – Arming the troops 2: Dilution, women and health
49 As well as objecting to the possible impact of dilution on their wages, the Amalgamated Society of Engineers and other craft unions were determined to preserve their high status in relation to others. Attitudes in Sheffield have been detailed by James Hinton in *The First Shop Stewards Movement* (London: Allen and Unwin, 1973).
50 Labour Exchanges were officially renamed as 'Employment Exchanges' by December 1916.
51 A circular to controlled establishments in February 1916 summarized the government's requirements at the time. 'The dilution of labour implies that the employment of skilled men should be confined to work which cannot be efficiently performed by less skilled labour or women; that women should be employed as far as practicable on all classes of work for which they are suitable; that semi-skilled and unskilled men should be employed on any work which does not necessitate the employment of skilled men and for which women are unsuitable'. The popular press sometimes referred to female munition workers as 'munitionettes' or occasionally 'the girl behind the man with the gun'.
52 A contract between the Sheffield firm Hadfields and the Ministry of Munitions of January 1918 for high-explosive shells included the clause: 'It is a condition of this contract that any directions of the Minister of Munitions as to the percentage of women operatives to be employed, or as to the number of skilled or semi-skilled operatives to be employed, shall be complied with'.

The expansion of women's work is mentioned among other topics in most books about the Home Front, and more focused accounts have been provided by Arthur Marwick (*Women at War 1914-1918*. London: Fontana, 1977), Gail Braybon (*Women Workers in the First World War*. London: Croom Helm, 1981), Gail Braybon and Penny Summerfield (*Out of the Cage: Women's Experiences in Two World Wars*. London: Routledge and Kegan Paul, 1987), and Susan Grayzel (*Women and the First World War*. Harlow: Longman, 2002). An online version of L. K. Yates's *The Woman's Part: A Record of Munitions Work*, published in 1918 or thereabouts, is available at http://archive.org/stream/womanspartarecor00yate#page/n1/mode/2up, and a brief wider summary is *Women in the First World War* by Neil Storey and Molly Housego (Oxford: Shire Publications, 2011). That extends to coverage of voluntary nursing activities, which are also described (often overseas) in *The Story of British V.A.D. Work in the First World War*, written by Thekla Bowser in 1917 and reprinted by the Imperial War Museum in 2003. *Women in the War Zone* by Anne Powell (Stroud: History Press,

2009) contains vivid first-hand accounts of nurses (qualified and VAD) in the Western and Eastern Fronts.

Production jobs of several kinds are illustrated in *Women's Factory Work in the First World War* by Gareth Griffiths (Stroud: Alan Sutton, 1991), and munition work is described by Peggy Hamilton in *Three Years or the Duration* (London: Peter Owen, 1978) and by Angela Woollacott in *On Her their Lives Depend* (Berkeley: University of California Press, 1994). None of those books contain information about female work in Sheffield, but a local overview has been provided by Sylvia Dunkley in *Transactions of the Hunter Archaeological Society*, 2015, *27*, in press: 'And we, we did our bit: Women's work in Sheffield during the First World War'. A guide to local sources about the city's women workers at the time, also compiled by Sylvia Dunkley, can be accessed through www.sheffield.gov.uk /libraries/archives-and-local-studies/research-guides/world-war-one.html.

53 Estimated national numbers in different sectors vary slightly between reports but the general pattern is clear – an overall increase in women's employment of at least fifty per cent. Statistical tables are provided in Chapter Eleven of G. D. H. Cole's *Trade Unions and Munitions* (Oxford: Clarendon Press, 1923), and in Chapter Six of H. Wolfe's *Labour Supply and Regulation* (Oxford: Clarendon Press, 1923). Chapter One of Gareth Griffiths' *Women's Factory Work in the First World War* (Stroud: Alan Sutton, 1999) includes numerical information about a limited number of employment sectors, and some figures are also in Tables 3 and 4 of Arthur Marwick's book cited in Note 52.

Note that it was not unusual before the war for working-class women to be employed in industrial or domestic jobs. However, they then worked in a limited range of unskilled positions, both before and after marriage, and middle-class women rarely had jobs after marriage. Furthermore, we should not imagine that all women job-seekers could easily find a position. On 26 August 1916 the *Sheffield Daily Independent* reported that 'there are about 5,000 women on the books of the Labour Exchange, ready to undertake munitions work'.

54 The Women's Army Auxiliary Corps (WAAC) and the Women's Royal Naval Service (WRNS) were created in March and November 1917 respectively, and the Women's Royal Auxiliary Air Force (WRAAF) was formed in April 1918. Female troops were employed in catering, driving, store-keeping, telegraphic and office jobs, and numbered almost 100,000 by the end of the war; local newspaper reports indicate that 'some hundreds' came from Sheffield. The Women's Army Auxiliary Corps was renamed as Queen Mary's Army Auxiliary Corps (QMAAC) in April 1918 with the Queen as Honorary Commandant; it was wound down in the autumn of 1921.

A large QMAAC advertisement in Sheffield newspapers in May 1918 asked women: 'Will you come and cook for the men who are defending you and your home?' '7,000 cooks and waitresses are wanted for home service only' and others are 'also wanted for service overseas'.

55 Detailed information is contained in Volume 6 of the *History of the Ministry of Munitions* (HMSO, 1922), Part 1, Chapter 4 (e.g., p.62). In the national shell factories women made up around seventy per cent of the work-force, and in the national cartridge factories that percentage exceeded eighty (Part 2, Chapter 6 of that *History*).

56 Some employers argued against taking on women workers because of the need to provide new rest rooms and toilets, and because the Ministry of Munitions required special treatment for women.

57 See page 128 of Martin Phillips and John Potter's *Septimus Bennett: Artist in Arms* (Durham: Pentland Press, 2001). In many other cases women were taken on for entirely fresh work. For instance, Arthur Lee and Sons hired 180 women as the company moved into the production of aeroplane wire, and Newton Chambers took on around 250 for newly initiated shell-forging work.
58 Craftsmen also suffered from an erosion of their wages in relation to less skilled workers through some national awards, which provided flat-rate increases for all categories of worker – lifting unskilled rates by proportionately more than craftsmen's rates.
59 Many subsequent accounts suggest that the growth of shop-steward militancy was a widespread national development, but James Hinton (see Note 49 above) has argued that a shop steward movement with strong local impact became established in only a few regions, especially in Sheffield, Glasgow and Manchester.

In Sheffield the most radical stewards were in large armament companies, in some cases advocating a Communist-style takeover of the government. Some details are in *Sheffield Shop Stewards 1916-1918* by Bill Moore, published in 1960 in London by the History Group of the Communist Party, which 'exists to forward the study of history from a Marxist standpoint'. See reference 331.88S in the city's Local Studies Library.
60 For example, a strike led by Sheffield's engineering shop stewards in November 1916 after the call-up of an allegedly 'exempt' member received widespread national publicity and led to disputes in factories across the country. In Sheffield itself, enthusiasm for the action spread rapidly and around 12,000 engineering workers stopped work. Further details are in Peter Warr's *Sheffield in the Great War* (Pen and Sword Books, 2015), and this and some other disputes in the city have been reviewed by James Hinton in the book cited in Note 49.
61 In 1916 the Ministry also appointed Time-Keeping Officers to visit companies and recommend possible ways to improve attendance. It is not known whether any such officials were based in Sheffield.
62 The 1915-1916 Directors' Report of Ibbotson Brothers indicates that the business had been running day and night. That was very common in the city.
63 For example, Peggy Hamilton reported that 'when the "big push" was on *[i.e., in the spring of 1916]* many factories worked twelve hours a day for a seven-day week. That meant an eighty-four-hour week, not counting travelling time. At the tool-room [where I worked] we had a spell when we women were working ninety-two hours a week, while the men worked a shift of thirty-six hours over the weekend.' See page 72 of *Three Years or the Duration: The Memoirs of a Munition Worker 1914-1918* (London: Peter Owen, 1978). Women shell workers in Sheffield's Hadfields were at work for around sixty-five hours a week for at least a year from the middle of 1915, and in early 1916 Vickers' Holme Lane shell workers often undertook periods of six consecutive nights of thirteen hours; see page 122 of *Septimus Bennett: Artist in Arms* by Martin Phillips and John Potter (Durham: Pentland Press, 2001).
64 Members of the Health of Munition Workers Committee included Samuel Osborn from Sheffield's Samuel Osborn and Company. In July 1918 the Committee was renamed the Industrial Fatigue Research Board, with a new concern which extended to all (not merely munition) workers. In 1929 that Board changed its name to the more positive Industrial Health Research Board, which continued until 1959.

65 In May 1917, Hadfield's National Projectile Factory dropped one night shift and Saturday afternoon work without losing output. And in the summer of that year its East Hecla Works reduced weekly shell-machining hours from sixty-nine to fifty-seven and a half with either no loss or a slight increase in output.
66 Seebohm Rowntree was a member of the Quaker family which owned the chocolate manufacturers Rowntree and Company in York. He was a strong supporter of the Liberal Party, and had for years worked to improve the conditions of working people. His observational study in York (*Poverty: A Study of Town Life*, published in 1901) had been very influential, and in 1913 he investigated and made proposals about Britain's farming industry. His concerns about jobs and finance were brought together in *The Human Needs of Labour*, published in 1918, and later studies of poverty and living conditions continued up to his death in 1954.
67 See page 74 of Peggy Hamilton's *Three Years or the Duration: The Memoirs of a Munition Worker 1914-1918* (London: Peter Owen, 1978). Firth's national projectile factory at Templeborough employed a female doctor (Lucy Naish) for a period and possibly another woman in that role after she left in 1917.
68 See page 80 of the book about Septimus Bennett cited at the end of Note 63.
69 In describing a new shrapnel machine shop in Vickers, the *Sheffield Daily Telegraph* of 5 August 1915 reported that 'the girls are able to send for food from the canteen or bring in their own meals, which can be heated in a delightful mess room which has been built for them, and adjoining it is a most convenient cloak room'. Similar facilities were provided in the city centre for women tram conductors and in a growing number of other Sheffield factories.
70 Clementine Churchill, the wife of Winston Churchill (Minster of Munitions from July 1917), also publicly supported the YMCA's work to provide factory canteens.
71 In addition to facilities in its national projectile factory, in 1917 Thomas Firth and Sons built a canteen for its workers in Savile Street which could accommodate in one sitting around 600 people.
72 The Vickers Boys Welfare Department organized football, cricket, swimming and other clubs, and provided lectures and other activities. From October 1915 the Sheffield Education Committee followed a recommendation from the Home Secretary to allow boys with definite offers of a munition job to leave school at the age of 13 instead of 14; around 5,000 13-year-old boys moved into Sheffield industry. Girls had to remain at school until they were 14.
73 In 1917, the Ministry of Munitions issued a list of welfare supervisors' duties, pointing out that not all of those mentioned were necessary in every case: (1) Obtaining a healthy staff by assisting with non-technical aspects of selection; (2) Maintaining a healthy staff inside and outside the factory, in five ways: (2a) supervising women's working conditions, (2b) supporting a canteen, (2c) assisting with non-medical aspects of first-aid, (2d) supervising cloakrooms and sanitary provisions, (2e) supervising protective clothing and overalls; (3) Assisting with women's travel, recreation, day nursery and sickness arrangements; (4) Maintaining health, accident and sickness records of women employees.
74 In 1918, welfare supervisors in the Templeborough factory were Miss Britten, Miss Flather, Mrs Prior and Mrs Beatrice Roberts. Laura Flather (1867-1961) also organized the factory's War Savings Association, and at different times served as Company Secretary to the family firm of W. T. Flather, Honorary Secretary of the Sheffield Queen

Victoria Nursing Association and of the Ladies' Civic Aid Society, and as a member of the city's National Insurance Committee. After the war, Beatrice Roberts was employed in a similar role in W. T. Flathers' factory.

75 The London headquarters had more than 18,000 staff, including around 11,000 women. The Ministry also had two offices in USA (in New York and Washington), and one in each of France, Italy and Switzerland.

76 Sheffield was one of nine locations within the Ministry's Area 3, whose general office was in Leeds. A Sheffield 'Branch District Office' of the Ministry was in 17 Foster's Buildings, High Street. In addition, the city also housed (in King Street, in premises requisitioned in May 1916 from the Conservative Association; see below) a national office of the Ministry's Inspection Department. This monitored and advised about output quality from all controlled establishments and national factories, and administered more than thirty local offices throughout the country. A Sheffield branch office of the national Inspection Department was in Telegraph Buildings, High Street, with a Metals Section housed in the University's Department of Applied Science. At least two other Inspection Offices also operated in Sheffield – for the Admiralty in Janson Street and for the Royal Naval Air Service in Surrey Street; both of these worked closely with the University's Applied Science department. Also in the city centre was a War Office Army Contracts Department in St Peter's Close.

The Ministry's take-over of the King Street Conservative Club (above) was based on powers granted by the Defence of the Realm Act. However, the Club took the Ministry to court, claiming illegal trespass and possession of its premises. The King's Bench Division judged in favour of the Ministry, and the Conservative Association had to meet the case's legal costs.

77 From pages xi and xii of G. D. H. Cole's *Trade Unions and Munitions*, published by Clarendon Press (Oxford) in 1923.

Chapter Four – Arming the troops 3: Sheffield get to work

78 David Lloyd George had declared as early as February 1915 that the nation was fighting 'an engineer's war' – to be won in the workshops as well as on the battlefield. In June 1915 he was appointed the first Minister of Munitions, in July 1916 he became Secretary of State for War, and he was Prime Minister from December 1916.

79 Some aspects of this period in Sheffield are described by Geoffrey Tweedale in Chapter Five of his *Steel City* (Oxford: Clarendon Press, 1995).

80 Although the continuing high level of factory business was financially attractive to both employers and workers, it created its own problems. Machines were forced to operate for long periods without pause, so that maintenance and improvements were excessively deferred. And the ready availability of profitable orders led companies to place less emphasis on commercial marketing and civilian product development, so that many were poorly prepared to meet post-war competitive challenges.

81 These were the Royal Arsenal at Woolwich (from about 1695), the Royal Gunpowder Factory at Waltham Abbey (from 1787) and the Royal Small Arms Factory at Enfield (from 1804). In addition, a Royal Aircraft Factory had been established at Farnborough in 1905 and renamed in 1911.

82 Some details are in Allan Grant's *Steel and Ships: The History of John Brown's* (London: Michael Joseph, 1950).

83 The visit of King George V and Queen Mary was originally scheduled for 14 November 1918 as part of a more general tour of the city, but signing of the Armistice on 11 November led to its postponement. The original plans were carried out later, and the visit (incorporating a tour of the Grimesthorpe Works) took place on 20 May 1919.
84 See Chapter 11 in Kenneth Warren's *Steel, Ships and Men: Cammell Laird 1824-1993* (Liverpool University Press, 1998) and Geoffrey Tweedale's *Steel City* (Clarendon Press, 1995).
85 Some details are in *The History of Firth's, 1842-1918*, published in 1924 by the company and written by A. C. Marshall and Herbert Newbould. As in other reports, it is not always clear whether cited production and other figures refer only to Firths' own works or also include the government-owned national factory which the company managed. A 1919 article reports that 'upwards of four million shells were turned out, giving an average of nearly two shells a minute, day and night, Sundays included'. See the magazine *Bombshell* for March 1919, held in Sheffield Local Studies Library.
86 In one extension the company diverted the River Don and its weir alongside its East Hecla Works to provide nearly nine acres of additional land.
87 The company had changed its name to Vickers Ltd. from Vickers Sons and Maxim Ltd. in 1911, having been Vickers Sons and Company Ltd. from 1867 to 1897. The book by J. D. Scott, *Vickers, A History* (London: Weidenfield and Nicolson, 1962), ranges widely over the company's development, but contains little information about its work in Sheffield.
88 This expansion into armaments included the hundred per cent purchase (1897) of the Maxim-Nordenfeld Company (producing machine guns) and of forty per cent of the Chilworth Gunpowder Company (1900). Aeroplanes were manufactured at Crayford in Kent and later at Weybridge in Surrey.
89 See *Septimus Bennett: Artist in Arms* by Martin Phillips and John Potter, published by Pentland Press, Edinburgh, in 2001.
90 Kelham Island Museum holds an informative 23-page booklet which was published soon after the factory's construction. Access to this is free after making an appointment with collections@simt.co.uk but charges apply for photocopying or scans.
91 The term "shirker" was widely used at the time to refer to men who were avoiding military service.
92 Unusually, Cammell Laird declined to accept payment for the company's work on this national factory.
93 A 1919 report refers to the Ministry of Munitions' Metals Supply Department in the city. This worked in conjunction with local companies and the University to develop procedures for making cupro-nickel alloy for small arms ammunition – a completely new venture for Sheffield. That Ministry department may have been based on the Porter Street site.
94 Sheffield street directories of the period describe Kent Smith as 'manufacturers of carbonless metals and alloys', with other addresses as well as in Bacon Lane. In those directories there is no number 50 in Porter Street.
95 The five larger armament firms described in the chapter's earlier sections operated separately from the Sheffield Munitions Committee.
96 This was produced in other local companies according to Flathers' specification, with the letters indicating 'unbreakable axle steel'.

97 See *Pioneers for a Century 1852-1952* by T. Alec Seed, published by the company in 1952.
98 A paravane is a torpedo-shaped device towed from a ship so that its cables will cut the anchors of any moored mines.
99 By 1917 Dixon's workforce of around 750 comprised more than sixty per cent women.
100 Earl Fitzwilliam, principal owner of the company and a Sheffield Alderman, was serving as an Assistant Director of Transport in Flanders.
101 See pages 60 and 61 of W. W. Chisholm's *The Romance of the Moor*, published by the company in 1922.
102 The Company's record book for these transactions is held in the archive of Stocksbridge Historical Society.
103 In 1917, a new factory for Steel, Peech and Tozer was erected on the site of a Roman fort at Templeborough; construction had been delayed for several months for archaeological investigation.
104 Initial directors of the company came from John Brown and Company, Thomas Firth and Sons, Hadfields, Kayser Ellison and Company, the Newcastle Alloy Company, Samuel Osborn and Company, and Vickers.
105 See page 31 of *The Sheffield Gas Undertaking 1818-1949* by D. E. Roberts, published in Leicester by the East Midlands Gas Board in 1979.
106 From November 1917, the Ministry of Munitions' Sheffield office in Foster's Buildings administered a new transport scheme providing access to empty lorries which might be used (for a fee) to transport goods within the city and Rotherham. Initial advertisements suggested that this would shortly be extended to include horse-drawn vehicles.
107 The *Sheffield Daily Telegraph* of 25 September 1915 reported that '[m]ost of our soldiers carry in their kits a small mirror made of nickel-plated steel and supplied mainly by Sheffield houses. A local firm have received a letter from a wounded soldier stating that he owes his life to one of their mirrors which he was carrying in his pocket. A rifle bullet pierced a book and some papers, but the mirror prevented the missile from penetrating to his heart. The steel was shattered, but the bullet glanced off and merely injured one of the man's ribs.'
108 *The Record of Davy Bros. Ltd. in the World War 1914-1918* was published by the company and is available as PAMP 38 SQ in Sheffield Local Studies Library.
109 The term 'Great Victory' was initially used as a positive contrast to the recently ended 'Great War'. However, as disastrous consequences of the war became increasingly obvious, references to a great victory became less common. Later the 'Great Silence' became a popular term; see Chapter Seven.
110 Vickers separately employed several hundred Australian men from early in the war, before a general Commonwealth scheme was initiated in mid-1916. The British government then financed these workers' two-way travel, and married men received a family allowance paid through their own government. They were required to undertake munition work wherever directed, and at least 500 Australians were employed in Sheffield within an overall total of around 5,000 in the country. It is estimated that some ten per cent of all Australian war workers returned home early because of ill-health. Men also came from (neutral) Holland, but 1916 Sheffield reports suggest that many of these were unhappy with wages and conditions and soon returned home.

111 Most Belgian refugees in the city were instead provided with houses elsewhere in the city. See *Sheffield in the Great War* by Peter Warr, published by Pen and Sword Books in 2015.
112 A personal account of post-war childhood memories in a Tyler Street hut is provided by Betty Dickinson in *Shanty Town* (1985); see 942.74S in the city's Local Studies Library. A discussion and links to more photographs are at www.sheffield history.co.uk/forums/index.php?/topic/5349-tyler-street-huts-brightside, and details of the Tinsley settlement are on page 4 of the *Sheffield Daily Independent* of 2 June 1916 and on page 2 of that paper of 26 March 1919. Temporary accommodation was also financed by the Ministry in other parts of the country, and the *History of the Ministry of Munitions* (HMSO, 1922) sets the Sheffield huts into a national framework; see Volume 5, Part V, Chapters 2 and 3.
113 Disagreements with a workers-panel adviser were illustrated in February 1916 in Sheffield, when that person objected to the Chairman's opinion. In reply, he was told 'You may protest as long as you like. So long as I preside over this court I shall make certain rules. [. . .] You are here only to consult and nothing more.'
114 William Edwin Clegg (1852-1932) had played football for Sheffield Wednesday and was capped for England in 1873. He was also a noted cricketer and active golfer and tennis-player. He qualified as a solicitor in 1874 and was returned unopposed as a Liberal Councillor for Attercliffe in 1886. He became an Alderman in 1892, was Lord Mayor in 1898, and served as a magistrate and a Town Trustee. He was knighted in 1906. A strong advocate of both temperance and extended education, he served from 1897 as a Council member of the city's University College and later its University. During the war he was Chairman of the local Military Service Tribunal (see Chapter Six) as well as of the Munition Tribunal (this chapter); he was also Chairman of the Council's Education Committee and of the Licensing Magistrates, and a member of several other local committees. A photograph is included in Chapter Six.
115 Card-playing in a factory was sometimes justified by workers because their firm had left them without tasks to be done but required them to stay at their place of work.
116 At the end of the war Krupp was forbidden to produce any more armaments, its factories were partly demolished and much of its equipment destroyed; half the company's steel-making capacity was taken away. Krupp recovered by making non-military items ranging from lorries and railway engines to false teeth.
117 These and other aspects of the company's history have been detailed by Harold James in *Krupp: A History of the Legendary German Firm* (Princeton: Princeton University Press, 2012), William Manchester in *The Arms of Krupp 1587-1968* (London: Michael Joseph, 1968), and Bernhard Menne in *Krupp, or the Lords of Essen* (London: William Hodge, 1937).
118 A similar agreement was signed between Krupp and the Coventry Ordnance Works. That company, largely owned by Sheffield's John Brown and Cammell Laird, may have faced subsequent legal battles similar to those involving Vickers.

Chapter Five – The University and the Cutlers' Company
119 Accounts of the University in this and later periods have been provided by Arthur Chapman in *The Growth of a Modern University* (Oxford: Oxford University Press, 1955) and Helen Mathers in *Steel City Scholars* (London: James and James, 2005). In 1926, the University published a *History of the University of Sheffield at the Time of*

its Coming of Age, May 31st 1926. Although not indicated on the document, this was written by William Ripper, the long-time Professor of Engineering and Vice-Chancellor for part of the war.

120 In November 1915, the City Council granted £2,500 to the University in view of its reduced income due to war conditions.

121 A biographer notes that colleagues doubted the wisdom of moving to 'a provincial place so far from the metropolis' and also observes that 'eminence came to Fisher as a duty and a birthright'. See pages 49 and 16 in David Ogg's *Herbert Fisher: A Short Biography* (London: Edward Arnold, 1947).

122 Three of these addresses (31 August and September 1 and 2 1914) were quickly published by Longmans Green and Company as *The War: Its Causes and Issues*. For example, despite Herbert Fisher's expressed admiration for Germany's cultural and scientific achievements, 'we were in honour and duty bound to enter upon this war [. . .] and we must see it through to the bitter end' (p. 8). This book is available for online reading at https://archive.org/details/waritscausesissu00fish.

Mr Fisher was also one of the prominent people signing a letter to *The Times* of 30 September 1914, justifying and supporting the country's entry to the war. Other signatories included established authors J. M. Barrie, Arthur Conan Doyle, G. K. Chesterton, Rudyard Kipling and H. G. Wells.

123 In its 1916 issue, the *Yearbook* declared that the University's 'distinguished Vice-Chancellor, Mr H. A. L. Fisher, is stirring the imagination of a highly efficient but hitherto rather self-contained people. He has told them that there is no reason why in certain regions of applied science Sheffield should not be the intellectual capital of Europe in the next fifteen or twenty years.'

His wife, Lettice Fisher (1875-1956), was also influential in the city, with a special interest in improving the position of women. She chaired and spoke at meetings of the Women Workers' Organising and Interests Association (campaigning, for instance, for equal pay for women and men) and was President of the Sheffield branch of the National Union of Women's Suffrage Societies and of the local Federation of University Women. She was also active in the Sheffield Advisory Committee on Women's War Employment and the city's War Savings Committee, and was President of the Sheffield Alexandra Rose Day Committee. Local suffragettes were able to attend Mrs Fisher's garden parties at home in Ecclesall Grange, for instance in June 1916 listening to a talk by Mrs Bertrand Russell on the enfranchisement of women. Later in the war, in February 1918, Lettice Fisher founded the National Council for the Unmarried Mother and her Child.

124 For this government post, H. A. L. Fisher needed to be a Member of Parliament. The incumbent Member for the Sheffield Hallam constituency was raised to the House of Lords, and Mr Fisher was returned unopposed.

125 William Ripper (1853-1937) had for many years been associated with the University. From 1880 he had been a science teacher at the Central Higher School before moving on to the city's Technical School and then to Firth College; that became the University College and then part of the new University. William Ripper was appointed the University's Professor of Engineering and Dean of the Engineering Faculty, and he also served as a member of the University Council from 1905 to 1923. Nationally, he was appointed a Companion of Honour in 1917. In 1919 (aged 66) he resigned as Vice-Chancellor but continued to work as Professor of Engineering.

126 See page 346 of his autobiography *Men and Memories 1900-1922*, published by Faber and Faber in 1932. William Rothenstein had been born in Bradford, after his father had moved from Saxony in 1859. In reporting his University appointment, local newspapers emphasized that, despite his German-sounding name, he was a patriotic Englishman. His autobiography tells us that while in Sheffield 'I began two paintings in the steel works of a friend, Samuel Osborn, but the noise and heat defeated me, and they were left unfinished. However, I painted two buffer-girls'. (Those two worked for silver and electroplate manufacturers Walker and Hall. One version of the painting is held by Museums Sheffield. See http://www.bbc.co.uk/arts/yourpaintings/paintings/buffer-girls-72155.) For a period during the war William Rothenstein also served as an official war artist, and in 1920 his friend Herbert Fisher, now Minister for Education, was responsible for appointing him as Principal of the Royal College of Art (see page 365 of *Men and Memories*), a post he held until 1935. He resigned his part-time Sheffield appointment in 1926.

127 It appears that around a hundred and forty of these men were killed, but the University's Roll of Honour (on display in the main building) is unclear in that respect, since it also includes former students and non-University men who had joined its Officer Training Corps.

128 This concern was held by several prominent observers at the time, who feared that British society was losing too many of its future leaders and thinkers. See, for instance, J. M. Winter's account of 'Britain's "lost generation" of the First World War' in *Population Studies*, 1977, *31*, 449-466.

That article describes proportionately more casualties among middle-class (i.e., more educated) men than working-class men (p. 456), and identifies three reasons for the difference: middle-class men were more likely to volunteer for the services, working-class men were more likely to be rejected as medically unacceptable, and middle-class men were more likely to be appointed as junior officers – taking a very dangerous role in the battle-field.

129 Both the Vice-Chancellor and the Dean of Engineering were *ex officio* members of the Council of Sheffield's Chamber of Commerce.

130 Since 1899, Oliver Arnold had been Professor of Metallurgy, first at the Technical School and then at the University, and had developed wide-ranging and close links with Sheffield firms and with technical branches of the Admiralty and War Office. In the pre-war period he had devised new alloy steels and perfected new stress and other metal-testing procedures. A review of his work before the war has been provided by Michael Sanderson in *Economic History Review*, 1978, *31*, 585-600. Interestingly for the quality of air in Sheffield, Professor Arnold vigorously fought against the smoke abatement lobby, viewing attempts to reduce the emission of factory smoke as attacks on the steel industry and even on Sheffield itself (see page 594 of the cited article).

131 The government's *History of the Ministry of Munitions*, published by HMSO in 1922, records that 'a considerable amount of research into the methods of metallurgical analysis was carried on in one of the metallurgical laboratories of Sheffield University, and, in addition to the knowledge acquired for immediate purposes, very valuable information was placed at the disposal of industry generally (e.g., the use of improved annealing methods, especially salt bath annealing, the use of mechanical devices in the production of sound ingots, the influence of non-metallic impurities in copper

nickel and copper zinc alloys, and the use of electric furnaces for refining metals in the non-ferrous trades).' (Volume 7, Part 1, page 89).

132 The 1926 *History of the University of Sheffield* (see Note 119) reports (page 4) that 'the lectures were much appreciated in the city. They were given at a time of great national perplexity and anxiety, and they did much to steady the public mind and to point out clearly the issues at stake. Their effect was to stimulate and encourage the public to a confident and optimistic view, and at the same time to convey a great deal of information as to the steps which were being taken.'

133 Victoria Hall had been opened in 1908 on the site of Norfolk Street Wesleyan Chapel. It was intended (and served) as a 'neutral building' for both religious and community purposes.

134 Reserved seats were more expensive than others, but at each of the major meetings about a thousand unreserved seats were priced at three pence or six pence, and these were usually free for soldiers in uniform. Optional donations for an event's charitable recipient were also requested.

135 One beneficiary was ceramic artist Septimus Bennett, who is described in Display Box 4.3. Successful students received a certificate from the Department of Applied Science: 'This is to certify that *[name]* has received a preliminary course of training for a period of seven days in the Workshops of this Department in the general handling of the lathe and lathe tools as used for turning and boring. With the addition of a little instruction in the use of shell turning machines he should be able to render useful service.'

136 Students from the University were frequently involved in fund-raising for relief agencies, and some women students took temporary farming jobs to make up for the shortage of male agricultural workers.

137 The premises were then offered to the Workers' Educational Association for use as a study centre. By the autumn of 1917 the building provided a location for some of the city's Education Committee's courses for girls and women in commercial subjects.

138 Lieutenant-Colonel Arthur Connell, Commandant of Sheffield's Third Northern General Hospital, introduced a 1917 statement of support for the Depot with: 'My huge hospital would have been in a sorry plight had not your excellent organisation come to its rescue. I cannot speak too highly of the great value of the Depot.' (His wife was a principal member of the Depot's Executive Committee.) The hospital and its attached units received from the University Supply Depot around 120,000 articles in the course of the war, and in addition some 170,000 items were sent to the city's Wharncliffe War Hospital. Details of the city's many new military hospitals are in *Sheffield in the Great War* by Peter Warr (Barnsley: Pen and Sword Books, 2015).

139 The government at this time was determined to maintain trade union involvement, as part of wider negotiations to increase union flexibility in working practices; see Chapter Two.

140 Employer members of the delegation were from John Brown, Cammell Laird, Thomas Firth and Sons, Hadfields, Sheffield Chamber of Commerce, Steel Peech and Tozer, and Vickers. Union representatives were from the Amalgamated Society of Engineers, the Boilermakers Union, the Electrical Trades Union, the National Amalgamated Union of Labour, the Pattern Makers Association, and the United Machining Workers. The focus at this stage was thus on unionized workers in the city's large organizations, and the group was formally described in oppositional terms as having two 'sides'.

141 Herbert Hughes (1853-1917) was a prominent city solicitor with wide local interests. He had been a Conservative Councillor since 1886, became an Alderman in 1899 and served as Lord Mayor in 1905. In addition to being President of the Chamber of Commerce from 1914, he had been a Member of the University's Council since 1905 (and of the University College Council since 1898), and an active Law Clerk of the Cutlers' Company since 1902. He was University Treasurer from 1916, a director of several local companies, and his long involvement with military volunteers included regimental command in the York and Lancasters in the rank of Colonel and service as initial interim Commanding Officer of the Sheffield City Battalion created in 1914.

142 In addition to Herbert Hughes as Chairman and William Ripper as Vice-Chairman, initial members were Arthur Balfour, Albert Davidson (Secretary), Colonel A. W. Chapburn, Lennox Dixon, W. H. Ellis (the Master Cutler), David Flather, Albert Hobson (Treasurer), Robert Leader, the Lord Mayor, Fred Osborn, Walter Tyzack, and J. C. Ward. Almost all of these continued as members throughout the war, but Herbert Hughes died suddenly in January 1917. At that point Albert Hobson became Chairman, David Flather took over as Treasurer and Oliver Wilson joined as a member. Their services were unpaid.

Albert Hobson (1861-1923), the Committee's Treasurer and then Chairman, held many important positions in the city. He was the owner of Thomas Turton and Company and Chairman of William Jessop and its associated company J. J. Savile. He was a magistrate, and had been Master Cutler in 1902, President of the Chamber of Commerce in 1908, and Lord Mayor in 1911. In 1913, he became an Alderman and Chairman of the City Council's Finance Committee. He was a staunch supporter of the University of Sheffield, having been the initial Chairman of its Finance Committee and its Treasurer from 1911.

Albert Davidson, the Munitions Committee's Honorary Secretary, was an established consulting engineer with offices in Norfolk Street. He was on the Council of Sheffield Chamber of Commerce, and was well-suited to the many technical discussions that were initially required between the Committee and companies moving into munitions work. Another of his wartime contributions was in organizing volunteer car-drivers to convey newly-arrived military patients from the railway station to Wharncliffe War Hospital.

From early 1916, as the Munitions Committee's activities became primarily concerned with financial administration and the handling of contracts, William Gibbons, the University's Registrar, also served as a second Joint Secretary in addition to undertaking his university work. He became responsible for management of the office and internal procedures, while Albert Davidson handled the Committee's relations with the government and manufacturing firms. In May 1917, William Gibbons took over as sole Secretary and Albert Davidson returned full-time to his consulting activities but remained a member of the Committee.

143 Boards of Management had a variety of different names, such as 'Armaments Output Committee' or 'War Munitions Committee'. The Sheffield Committee (presumably like other groups) received an interest-free £5,000 start-up loan. Details of the national framework are in Chapter 7 of Part 2, Volume 2 of the *History of the Ministry of Munitions*, published by His Majesty's Stationery Office in 1922.

144 A memorial plaque is still present in the Committee's meeting room of that day –

now the John Carr Library in the University's Mappin Street building. A second plaque in that room commemorates the Committee's first Chairman, Herbert Hughes, who died suddenly in January 1917.

145 For example, 'Shell forgings will be supplied at 32/6 each and copper driving bands at 2/6, delivered to your works', 'Shell bars will be supplied to your works at £15 5 0 per ton', 'Blanks will be delivered free to your works', or 'Materials will be supplied to you according to the authorised schedule of prices and conditions of contract sent herewith'. Brass work sometimes required a firm to melt down empty fired rifle cartridges which were supplied. Later contracts included provision for government-determined price increases in line with specified national increases in wages or in component prices. In these and other ways, the Committee's administrative load and complexity became substantial.

146 Growing accommodation needs led the Committee to open offices in High Street as well as in St George's Terrace, an additional Metals Department in Eyre Street, a High-Speed Steel Department in Orchard Chambers, and a Steel Store in Canal Wharf. The Committee's operation was regularly inspected and assessed by officials from the Ministry of Munitions, as well as being annually audited by accountants from Sheffield.

147 This estimate is from page 263 of Arthur Chapman's *The Growth of a Modern University*, published in 1955 by Oxford University Press.

148 This list was produced by William Gibbons at the end of the Committee's life. The complete list, together with the Committee's Minutes and many contracts with individual firms, is available in the Special Collections Section of the University of Sheffield Library (Reference MS76).

149 The Committee delegated much of this work to members Lennox Dixon and Walter Tyzack.

150 As described in Chapter Two, women employed in relevant jobs were also entitled to wear a war-service brooch provided through their employer. These brooches were available for the Committee's female office staff.

151 For a similarly large number of telephone calls, the Committee had its own telephone exchange staffed by two full-time operators.

152 A 1924 accountants' report indicates a final positive balance of about £50,000.

153 For centuries the local area had been known as Hallamshire – the southernmost shire of Northumbria. Although definitions were not always clear, Hallamshire was often taken to include the parishes of Sheffield and Ecclesfield and the chapelry of Bradfield. It did not have political or administrative power.

154 Founded in 1624 as a craft guild to organize and control the cutlery trade in Sheffield and its region, the Company worked to arrange working practices, protect trademarks, and ensure that so-called 'Sheffield-made' products were indeed made in the city. Its scope was expanded to include steel-making in 1860. Detailed accounts have been written by R. E. Leader (*History of the Company of Cutlers in Hallamshire in the County of York*, two volumes published by Pawson and Brailsford in 1905 and 1906), and by L. du Garde Peache (*History of the Company of Cutlers in Hallamshire in the County of York, 1906-1956*, published in Sheffield by Pawson and Brailsford in 1960). A more recent volume is *Mesters to Masters*, edited by Clyde Binfield and David Hey (Oxford: Oxford University Press, 1997).

155 William H. Ellis was a Director of John Brown and Company. He was knighted in 1918 and became Managing Director of the Company in 1919. His brother Charles,

also a Director of John Brown, served during the war as Deputy Director of the Ministry of Munitions; see Chapter Two and Appendix Two.

156 The *Sheffield Daily Telegraph* reported in September 1915 that 'in a room at the Cutlers' Hall, a local hairdresser and several women are employed setting and packing the razors'. Those were dispatched in cases holding up to 1,000 items, which had been made by local companies such as Foulds and Howson (Eldon Case Works, 66-70 Eldon Street) and case manufacturer Alfred Rodgers of 41 Chester Street. Some of the razor-renovation work was undertaken by firms such as Joseph Elliott and Sons of Hollis Croft. For sharpening, hones were bought from James Rolley, grindstone merchant of 80 Howard Street.

157 A few items like table cutlery, fish hooks and buttons were excluded from the prohibition.

158 These were William Ellis (Master Cutler), J. Rossiter Hoyle, Arthur Balfour, W. F. Osborn, S. J. Robinson, Marmaduke Wardlow, W. Hobson, T. W. Ward, W. W. Wood, Herbert Barber, H. H. Bedford, M. J. Hunter, Herbert Hutton, James Neill, F. C. Wild, and S. J. Young.

159 After meeting all costs, the Cutlers' Company recorded a net profit of £6,800 from the scheme.

160 Only around a hundred and fifty planes were available to the services in August 1914, of which sixty-four accompanied the Expeditionary Force to France. See *Cavalry of the Clouds* by John Sweetman (Stroud: Spellmount, 2010).

161 'RE' stands for 'Reconnaissance Experimental'. The model was a biplane in service between 1916 and 1918, with a machine-gun in the rear cockpit and capacity for two bombs beneath its wings. Maximum speed was around 100 m.p.h.

162 Coal Aston airfield opened around the end of 1915, originally intended for the air defence of Sheffield. It was located at the south of Norton Lane, near Dyche Lane and what is now Bochum Parkway, and grew to cover a large area. In addition to a landing ground, it had hangars, workshops, stores, living quarters for men and for women, and a cinema, post office and church; the airfield also had its own light railway. It became mainly used for the Second Northern Aircraft Repair Depot, repairing or rebuilding over two hundred planes in the course of the war. Part of the airfield later housed German prisoners; see Chapter Six. Although discussions were initiated in 1918 to develop the airfield for civil aviation after the war, these came to nothing. A detailed account and map have been provided in the Norton History Group's *Norton in Wartime*, published by the Group in 1995.

163 A short film excerpt of the event (probably from the cameraman in the photograph shown here) is available at www.britishpathe.com/record.php?id=77770. Early in 1918 a commemorative flag was presented by the Imperial Air Fleet to the Cutlers' Company, with a replica to the City Council.

164 In addition to the Cutlers' Company donation which bore the name 'Sheffield', a senior Company member (Colonel Sir Albert Bingham, who became Master Cutler in 1918 and was Commanding Officer of the local Royal Engineers) himself financed an RE8. He named this 'Ranby', after the Nottinghamshire village in which he had a home. Ranby was also shot down, and was replaced by a second RE8 which was still on RAF charge in January 1919. A full list of presentation aircraft is in the magazine *Cross and Cockade*, 1983, *14*, number 2.

165 Several hundred of the more usable aircraft were given to countries in the Empire

through a post-war 'Imperial Gift'. However, decision-making and transportation were slow, and few transfers were made before the end of 1919. On arrival, many planes were rusty or otherwise in poor condition, and the shortage of airfields and mechanics with relevant knowledge meant that not all of them took to the air. Technological advances soon led to them becoming obsolete.

Chapter Six – 1917 and 1918: A troubled city

166 The British blockade also prevented supplies reaching German-occupied Belgium and northern France, both of which depended greatly on imports of food. Voluntary help to those countries included a very active Commission for the Relief of Belgium, led from London by American Herbert Hoover who later became president of his country. The Commission had seventy-five of its own clearly-labelled ships, of which more than a dozen were sunk by German submarines.

167 Underwater vessels had been tried for well over a hundred years before the First World War, but rapid developments in the immediately prior decade, especially in Germany, gave rise to longer-range diesel and electric engines (for surface and underwater travel respectively) and self-propelled torpedoes which provided great destructive power. Although Britain had a larger number of submarines than Germany in 1914, that country's activities (with more than 350 additional vessels) proved to be particularly punishing. Some estimates suggest that German U-boats sank over 4,000 ships.

168 Throughout the war, several retailers in Sheffield and elsewhere advertised their large stock of material for darkening windows.

169 On the positive side, the city's wartime introduction of motorized road-sweepers removed the need for nineteen horse machines.

170 The central position in many factories of skilled tradesmen in the Amalgamated Society of Engineers (ASE) gave them considerable power. The union now fought hard to protect its members from military call-up, causing disruption to the annoyance of many people in Sheffield. During an extended strike in May 1917 a music-hall song was turned into a parody of the ASE position in the city. Entitled 'A prayer to Lloyd George' and making reference to the union's privilege and power, this urged the Prime Minister: 'Don't send me in the army, George, I'm in the ASE' and told him 'You want me for a soldier? Well that can never be – a man of my ability, and in the ASE!'. See page 5 of the *Sheffield Daily Independent* of 18 May 1917, page 527 of Trevor Wilson's *The Myriad Faces of War* (Cambridge: Polity Press, 1986), or pages 209-210 of James Hinton's *The First Shop Stewards' Movement* (London: Allen and Unwin, 1973).

171 In July 1918 a question in parliament revealed that two families of disabled ex-soldiers were forced to live in disused wooden pigsties near Tinsley Park Road.

172 American pilots on the Western Front mainly used British and French planes, and prior familiarization with these was clearly important.

173 Conscription was not extended to Ireland, where conflicts about possible home rule were currently requiring major attention. However, about fifteen per cent of Irish men aged fifteen to forty-nine in the 1911 census volunteered to serve. In the rest of Britain, volunteers and conscripts together were equivalent to around fifty-eight per cent of that 1911 age-group.

174 A large number of men were found to have defective or decaying teeth, exposed nerves or septic roots. Qualified dentists were rare in this period, and the War Office

had to find or train several hundred more. These became commissioned in the Royal Army Medical Corps.
175 By the spring of 1918 the situation was so desperate that a 'clean cut' of all men aged below twenty-three was taken, almost irrespective of the importance of a man's job.
176 In some cases a man lodged a second claim against call-up at the end of his exemption period.
177 Several other employers applied to the Sheffield Military Tribunal to keep their few remaining men. For instance, in September 1916 the city's Grand Hotel obtained three months' extension for a porter on the grounds that it had lost almost all other male employees – fifty-three to the British army, two to the British navy, five to the French army, three to the Italian army, four to the Belgian army, two to the Serbian army and thirteen to munition firms. In April 1917 department store John Walsh informed the Tribunal that it had lost one hundred and sixty-eight of its original male staff; its remaining men were now granted a three-month extension. By January 1918 the Sheffield Lyceum and Theatre Royal Company had only two men of military age left, one of whom now received a three-month exemption.
178 In some cases, the jobs of temporarily-exempted men were identified by the Military Tribunal as suitable for substitution by a worker ineligible for call-up, and he or she would be sought during the period of deferment.
179 The Representation of the People Act of February 1918 disqualified conscientious objectors from voting for five years after the end of war unless they had convinced a subsequent tribunal that they had undertaken nationally important work.
180 From page 362 of *We Did Not Fight*, edited by Julian Bell (London: Cobden-Sanderson, 1935).
181 A primary source of Quakers' opposition to violence is the 'Peace Testimony' adopted in 1660, which includes 'All bloody principles and practices we [. . .] do utterly deny, [. . .] for any end, and under any pretence whatsoever'.
182 In addition to the Barbers, other prominent Quaker families in the city in this period included the Doncasters, Milners, Priestmans, Watsons and Yeomans; several of these were linked to others by marriage. Quaker John Doncaster served as a member and one of the court chairmen within the city's Military Service Tribunal.
183 These and other issues have been detailed by Peter Brock in *Twentieth-Century Pacifism* (New York: Van Nostrand Reinhold, 1970). See also John Rae's *Conscience and Politics* (Oxford University Press, 1970) and the general account at www.ppu.org.uk/coproject/coww1.html.
184 Imprisonment may often have followed arrest because of refusal to report for military service at the time of call-up, and such arrests would not have appeared in newspaper reports.
185 See Chapter Nine of *A History of the Sheffield Smelting Company Ltd. 1760-1960* by Ronald E. Wilson, published by Ernest Benn of London in 1960. Cecil Wilson (1862-1945) was a Labour councillor for the Darnall ward who later became chairman of the city's Labour Group (1919-1922) before being elected as a Labour member of parliament for Attercliffe (1922-1931 and 1935-1944). During the war he was an active member of Attercliffe's Zion Congregational Church and a major supporter of the Attercliffe Friends' Adult School.
186 In the winter of 1916-1917 a national petition organized by the 'Peace Negotiations

Committee' obtained more than 200,000 signatures in favour of peace discussions with Germany.

187 Meatless days provided commercial opportunities for other food producers. During December 1916 Sheffield newspapers carried advertisements of this kind: 'MEATLESS DAYS are no denial to those who eat St Ivel Cheese. Eat a diet of St Ivel Cheese two days a week'.

188 Published government advice included suggestions that crust cut from toast should be re-used in puddings or to thicken soup and even an invitation to save bread-crumbs from cut loaves. The public was also advised 'Eat slowly; you will eat less food', and the grandly-titled Director-General of Food Economy urged people, especially women, to 'look well on the loaf on your breakfast table and treat it as real gold, because the British loaf is going to beat the German'.

189 Some flower-beds in Buckingham Palace were re-planted with vegetables.

190 Local prices were based on a succession of nationwide Prices Orders from the Ministry of Food. Several Sheffield retailers were fined for exceeding the local committee's figure.

191 The government's Public Meals Order required that people eating in restaurants 'must provide their own sugar for sweetening beverages'. The national shortage of sugar also restricted the production of confectionery and jam.

192 Saturday was pay-day, when money was available for spending.

193 Administered through the Town Hall, these were in Gibraltar Street, Mowbray Street and Grimesthorpe Road, in Vestry Halls in Attercliffe, Burngreave and Cemetery Road, and in Kelvin Buildings. The 1919 *Sheffield Yearbook* refers also to one 'at Crookesmoor'. In November 1918, the city's Food Control Committee decided to supplement its kitchens (which provided only take-away food) with a restaurant, and after the war they became 'National Restaurants'.

194 Sheffield City Archives holds John Dyson's personal diary for 1918 (reference X548/1); he lived at 13 Moor Oaks Road.

On several days in February 1918 many pupils were reported as absent from Norton School because they were needed to replace their mothers in food queues. Some more expensive food items were still available to the public, but at prices beyond the reach of poorer families. Nationally, the Labour-supporting *Herald* newspaper published sarcastic reports about wealthy people's lavish dining under the heading 'How they starve at the Ritz'.

195 The Committee's work was co-ordinated by Edith Sorby, who was also active in the city's Personal Comforts Depot and in handicraft work for wounded soldiers.

196 One of Mrs Peel's talks was reserved for the city's domestic servants only, attracting more than 300 of these and exceeding the seats available.

197 Page 132 of the 1919 *Sheffield Yearbook* shows fourteen different categories of registered retailer. For example, the city in 1918 had 2,324 registered sugar retailers, 2,111 flour retailers, and ninety-two pork butchers. The total number of retail outlets in the Council's list was around 18,500, but some firms were included more than once, selling different controlled items. The Food Control Committee had to be in continuous contact with them all, and retailers were occasionally prosecuted for selling to unregistered customers or exceeding permitted prices. In addition to retailers, the city's wholesalers also had to be registered with the Committee, and their supplies had to be controlled and monitored. Considerable

bureaucratic complexity became unavoidable and increasingly part of everyday normal living.

198 Initial schemes used separate cards for particular commodities rather than the comprehensive books that came later. Administrative help with the new system came from the city's school-teachers. For example, in early March 1918 Norton School was closed for three days as staff were employed in the allocation and delivery of ration books.

199 In August 1918 the weekly individual allocation was four meat coupons valued at five pence each.

200 Special events had to obtain their own authorization for extra food. At Whitsuntide in 1918 Sheffield's Sunday Schools were specially allocated 'Whit treats' for their children; buns and tea could now be provided.

201 For example, in August 1917 the Sheffield Food Control Committee advertised for 'persons acting in a clerical capacity' to administer food distribution in the city. Permanent workers were all to be female, but some temporary positions were available for either men or women. Unpaid volunteers would be welcome as temporary workers.

202 The necessary bureaucracy gave rise to many official forms and cumbersome administrative routines. For example, a notice about coal allocations in Norton District indicated that 'Consumers who require Special Allowances other than those definitively mentioned under heading No. 2 in Form F. H. F. 2 should wait until they have received their Assessment Form (F.H. F. 3) and then apply for an additional allowance (Form F. H. F. 6)'.

203 As in many other respects the country had in 1914 no well-developed plans for captured troops, and new detention camps had to be found or constructed. Some army properties were quickly converted, but the number of men to be accommodated became very great and additional locations had to be found. Germany and Britain both separated captured officers from other ranks and provided more comfortable accommodation for officers. Camp conditions were generally good and subject to independent inspection, for example through the Geneva-based International Red Cross. See *The Prisoners, 1914-1918* by Robert Jackson (Routledge, 1989), John Yarnall's *Barbed Wire Disease* (History Press, 2011), and Chapter 11 by Heather Jones ('Prisoners of war') in volume 2 of *The Cambridge History of the First World War* edited by Jay Winter (Cambridge University Press, 2014).

204 As in other cases, the camp's internal operation was largely co-ordinated by prisoners themselves, and groups were allowed to take supervised walks in the countryside. Through an international agreement they were subject to British military law.

205 British prisoners of war had been released from Germany soon after the Armistice, but this country's policy was to delay post-war repatriation until after ratification of a peace treaty. Following signature on 28 June 1919 of the Treaty of Versailles, which included a requirement for early release, the continuing delay prompted Redmires prisoners on 5 August to write to both the King and the Prime Minister with separate requests for release. (This appears to have been part of a co-ordinated approach from many camps.) Across the country German prisoners were eventually repatriated during September and October 1919, but the Treaty was not fully ratified until January 1920. By the autumn of that year the city's Education Committee had arranged for Redmires Camp to be used by parties of school-children.

206 Some German prisoners were employed outside British camps from the summer of 1916, but farmers, factory owners and others were reluctant to take them on until labour shortages had become especially severe. Employers were required to pay a locally-agreed wage to military authorities for each German worker, and from that payment an allowance was passed to the individual. This could be spent in a camp canteen or saved on behalf of the person. Officers and senior N.C.O.s were exempt from labour duties under a 1907 Hague Convention.
207 This watercolour painting is held by Museums Sheffield and is displayed only infrequently to minimize its deterioration.
208 It became a national policy that gifts were acceptable subject to inspection by the camp authorities.
209 Cited numbers differ between published accounts. The country's flu deaths included around 10,000 of its troops.
210 See page 300 of *Septimus Bennett: Artist in Arms* by Martin Phillips and John Potter (Durham: Pentland Press, 2001).
211 Sheffield Archives have produced a helpful list of *Sources for the Study of the Influenza Pandemic of 1918*. This is available at https://www.sheffield.gov.uk/libraries/archives-and-local-studies/research-guides/influenza-pandemic.html.
212 Between the Armistice's signature at 5.10 a.m. and coming into force at 11.00 a.m. fighting continued in several locations, and it has been estimated that across all the armies around 2,500 more soldiers died. However, many of those were already suffering from life-threatening injuries.
213 The vicar of St John's at Ranmoor reported later that 'a flag was hoisted in the Church grounds by Lady Bingham *[who lived opposite]*, the National Anthem was sung, and a service of thanksgiving was immediately held. Church bells were rung, and the Church was decorated with flags for the next Sunday and the following few weeks'. Churches throughout the nation held their main thanksgiving service on the following Sunday – 17 November.
214 All the cheerful mingling may have added to the city's influenza problem, as germs passed from one person to another.
215 From page 381 of the book cited in Note 210.

Chapter Seven – Remembrance, riots and disability

216 Troops were still essential in certain roles, and there were continuing disputes about which groups to release early. Farm-workers usually received priority in order to boost food production. However, demobilization had become widespread by the spring of 1919.
217 Despite the Prime Minister's attempt to achieve a 'just peace' which was fair to both sides, influential politicians and newspapers (not only in UK) argued strongly for revenge: Germany should be severely punished for its aggression. Their campaign included an unsuccessful demand that the Kaiser should be hanged or at least imprisoned; he was by now living in neutral Holland.
218 The *Sheffield Daily Independent* subsequently noted the irony that the principal hymn at this service ('Now thank we all our God') came from Germany.
219 The published programme contained a Roll of Honour of company men killed in action, a list of all serving or demobilized troops, and the names of current employees and their years of service. The company's 705 workers included over sixty per cent

women and more than a quarter of employees had twenty or more years of service, up to one man with sixty-two years at the firm. The programme is available in Sheffield Local Studies Library.

220 Teas were held in twenty-four schools and public buildings around the city. Local volunteers and councillors made the arrangements, and catering was organized by the Corporation through the Master Bakers' Association and the Municipal Milk Supply Department.

221 St Dunstan's residential home in Regent's Park in London had been established in 1915 by newspaper proprietor Sir Arthur Pearson (1866-1921) to support blinded servicemen. Arthur had started work as a journalist before founding the *Daily Express* and other successful newspapers. Knighted in 1916, he was a prominent and effective fund-raiser for many causes who had himself been partially blind since 1908. The 1919 Pageant of Peace was financed by Sir Arthur to visit ten cities around the country, with income being passed to the charity.

222 The League of Nations came into being on 10 January 1920; Germany was admitted in 1926 but withdrew in 1936. Despite President Woodrow Wilson's earlier enthusiasm, the United States never became a member.

223 On 11 November 1919 Sheffield schools remembered the war and its end through special lessons and a religious service which also asked for God's blessing on the new League of Nations; they then closed at midday.

224 The government had considered it for the first time as late as the beginning of November, following a proposal from a previous High Commissioner to South Africa. He praised that country's regular 'Three Minute Pause' during the war, and recommended it to Britain for remembrance of those who had served their country.

225 See the *Sheffield Daily Independent* of Wednesday 12 November 1919.

226 UK burial was possible for the small number of servicemen who died in this country – during training, on homeland service, as hospital patients or after early invalidity discharge.

227 This appeared in *The Herald*, 'The National Labour Weekly' which had been established explicitly to promote trade unionism and a militant working-class movement. The paper was a strong opponent of the war and its harsh impact on workers and their families; in November 1919 it had condemned the conflict as a 'crime [. . .] in the murderous hands of a few cynical old men'. The 1920 account here may have reflected that critical outlook.

228 Despite many post-war battle-field searches, the bodies of well over 100,000 British men still remain unidentified or undiscovered. A minority of these were lost at sea.

229 Some descriptions of this event refer to six bodies. A 1939 account by the original officer-in-charge is reproduced in Chapter Seven of Max Arthur's *We Will Remember Them* (London: Weidenfeld and Nicholson, 2009). This refers to four bodies and makes no mention of the blindfold. Some events on the day can be viewed at www.britishpathe.com by searching for 'Armistice Day 1920'.

230 John McCrae himself died in France in January 1918, suffering from pneumonia.

231 In addition to USA, France and Britain, other countries adopting the poppy included Australia and Canada in 1921 and New Zealand in 1922.

232 In April 1922, founding President Earl Haig described the Legion's objectives: 'to bring about unity of the men who have served, in order to more surely perpetuate the

memories of the comrades who fell, and to look after the future welfare of ex-servicemen and their dependants'.
233 The organization became the 'Royal' British Legion in 1971. Author's royalties for this book will be sent directly by the publisher to the Legion for use in the Sheffield area.
234 Burial routines and clothing worn after a civilian death were often elaborate, so that, for example, Cole Brothers' department store had a special 'Mourning Department'. In January 1918 this advertised 'black dress materials in [a wide range of] fashionable fabrics'. The company could provide 'mourning millinery, coats, blouses, costumes and dresses, ready to wear'. 'Funerals furnished throughout. Shells, coffins, and caskets with exclusive fittings made in our own workshops.'
235 The Commonwealth War Graves Commission is funded by all the countries whose dead are cared for, in proportion to their numbers. Details are available at www.cwgc.org, which also provides information about individual persons' death and grave location. In addition to cemeteries for identified bodies, men assumed to be deceased in the Great War but whose graves are unknown are listed on special memorials, including the large Menin Gate at Ypres which has more than 55,000 names on 1,200 panels. See also illustrations at www.twgpp.org.

Considerable military and other information about the Great War is also held by the Imperial War Museum, which was established in 1917. The Museum now also covers subsequent wars; see www.iwm.org.uk.
236 The country had around 240,000 war widows and many more bereaved parents and other relatives. A large number of French and German families also visited the Western Front in this period.
237 Details of these overseas tours and also visits to memorials in Britain have been provided by David W. Lloyd in *Battlefield Tourism* (Oxford: Berg, 1998).
238 Another City Battalion memorial was dedicated in May 1923 in the village of Serre in northern France, where many local men had died on 1 July 1916; and in July 1923 a memorial to soldiers from the York and Lancaster Regiment as a whole was unveiled in the city's Weston Park.

Close to Serre is the village of Bapaume, which had also been devastated by years of continuous warfare. Linked to the League of Help for Devastated Areas of France which was formed nationally in the middle of 1920, Sheffield 'adopted' and sought to help Bapaume. Funds raised by the city's Lord Mayor through public subscription were allocated to several Bapaume projects including some ten 'Sheffield houses', and local razor manufacturer George Lawrence himself provided a village school. Further details are in *The Forgotten Philanthropist* by Brian Ward (Hucklow Publishing, 2010).
239 Details can be found in Neil Anderson's book *Sheffield City Hall 1932-2012*, published in Sheffield by ACM Retro in 2012.
240 Like others, the Barker's Pool memorial was funded by the public through donations and from collections in theatres, cinemas and house-to-house, a flag day and so on. The memorial's steel pole (which is set around six metres into the ground for stability) was made in Hull, and its length presented transportation problems through the city from the railway station.
241 From time to time city-wide 'intercession days' were held as part of a national period of prayer. For example, the *Sheffield Daily Independent* reported events on 2 January 1916: 'muffled peals were rung throughout the diocese' as 'a memorial of men

who have laid down their lives for their country in the past year'. On 1 July 1917 a special service was held in the cathedral to commemorate the bravery and losses of Sheffield men on the first day of the Battle of the Somme a year earlier; this became an annual event.

242 Names are not listed on this plaque, but it cites twenty-nine deaths rather than the elsewhere-mentioned twenty-eight. The discrepancy might be linked to a brief note in a subsequent *Sheffield Daily Independent*: 'a person died in hospital about three weeks later who was supposed to be indirectly a victim of the raid' (3 December 1918, page 3).

243 The Representation of the People Act of February 1918 granted the parliamentary vote to women aged over thirty who were householders or married to a householder as well to all men over twenty-one and younger men on active military service. (In 1928, all women over twenty-one became eligible.) As a result of the 1918 Act, almost 240,000 Sheffielders were able to vote in parliamentary elections compared to around 75,000 before the war; the new Sheffield total included more than 90,000 women – almost forty per cent of the list.

The constitutional position for *local* elections was slightly different, and in the autumn of 1918 Sheffield had around 180,000 listed municipal voters against around 100,000 in 1914. Forty-nine per cent of those now eligible were women, and two wards (Ecclesall and Sharrow) had slightly more women than men in their 1918 lists. In practice many people did not vote; in the parliamentary elections of December 1918, only forty-eight per cent of eligible Sheffield people took part, and in the 1919 municipal election turnout was a mere thirty-five per cent.

244 Advertisements in Sheffield newspapers were enthusiastic about the way in which a 'Victory Loan' would reduce the need for the government to borrow from the banks: 'It will set free the resources of the Banks to come to the aid of commerce and industry. [...] Production will be stimulated; new avenues of employment will be opened; the stream of liberated money that will be poured into the mills and factories and commercial houses will pour forth again as a stream of goods, and that is the one real remedy for the high cost of living.'

245 Female workers were by now becoming acceptable in offices and shops, but jobs there were mainly offered to middle-class, usually unmarried, women. And of course many women, especially those with children and an adequate family income, preferred to leave the labour market at this stage.

246 Already by the middle of 1919 German cutlery and scissors were – entirely legally – available in the city.

247 Payments were made at the rate of fifteen shillings (£0.75) a week for men and twelve shillings (£0.60) for women. Individuals without all the requisite contributions could make special application and might be allowed a proportionate sum. Domestic servants and farm labourers were excluded from the scheme.

248 Men received more than women and supplements were paid for dependent children. In practice, only a small number of women had served as troops and very few received this 'donation' – nationally around 1,800 in May 1920 compared to some 207,000 ex-servicemen.

249 Rates levied to pay for the Guardians' work were collected jointly with city rates through the Town Hall, and the City Council appointed the Boards' Overseers. Further details of local welfare provisions at this time are in *Sheffield in the Great War* by Peter Warr (Barnsley: Pen and Sword Books, 2015).

250 In June 1921, as well as those funded by the City Council more than 13,000 men were undertaking relief work through the city's two Boards of Guardians. Work funded by the Council or the Guardians in this period included the construction of Prince of Wales Road, Whirlowdale Road through Ecclesall Woods, Herries Road and Ridgway Road, road work in Pitsmoor and Twentywell, widening Abbey Lane, Abbeydale Road South, Middlewood Road and Worksop Road, relaying tram tracks, constructing Wadsley Service Reservoir, setting out recreation grounds, levelling slopes at Wincobank, garden-building at Firvale, and contributing to sewage and other improvements. Wages paid to relief workers necessarily added to the city's (rate-financed) expenditure, although a proportion of the cost was paid to the Council by the government – around fifty per cent for road-making and less for other work. Relief workers were employed for up to four days a week, often on alternate days, and received tram tokens for travel to and from their place of work.
251 See also Note 193. During 1921 Sheffield's national kitchens served around 30,000 meals in every month. By then, they were in Burngreave Vestry Hall, Gibraltar Street, Hoyle Street, Neepsend and Nursery Street.
252 A site in West Bar became a customary 'speakers' corner' for meetings of unemployed men. One prominent speech-maker in this period was Tom Pickering, who wore the clerical collar of a clergyman. He loudly advocated forceful actions of protest and was himself arrested in the city on 17 August 1921. He was also part of the unemployed demonstration which attempted to enter the Cathedral on 30 April 1922 (see the text) and was present at the funeral on 29 June 1922 described in Note 254. During 1923, and possibly at other times, he was active in unemployed men's marches in London; in March of that year he was housed in the workhouse in London's Poplar.
253 The authorities were concerned that revolutionary ideas of Russian Bolsheviks were being transferred to Britain as part of a world-wide attempt to overturn established governments; several countries' royal family had already been deposed. Sheffield engineering worker J. T. Murphy actively promoted the working-class seizure of control. He visited Communist officials in Moscow in 1920 and 1921 and became a prominent organizer for the Party; see, for instance, Chapter Ten of David Price's *Sheffield Trouble-makers* (Stroud: Phillimore, 2008). The city's Communist Party was at this time very active in the many demonstrations by unemployed men.
254 One of the protesters died three weeks later, possibly because of injuries received at Walkley although that was disputed by the medical profession and rebutted at a public inquest. His burial on 29 June 1922 was attended by around 5,000 people, some 3,000 of whom had marched in front of the hearse from his home. Labour councillors and prominent members of the Communist Party took part, some wearing a Soviet emblem. One label on a wreath indicated that 'He died for liberty', and the committal service was taken by the Reverend T. E. Pickering – an ardent and very public supporter of radical protest (Note 252, above). The crowd was orderly and respectful, and sang 'The Red Flag' before leaving the graveside.

The Walkley incident and later events were described in 1983 by John Baxter, in a publication by the Holberry Society for the Study of Sheffield Labour History: *The Battle of Walkley*. This also contains reminiscences from some individuals who were present. See reference 331.8SQ in the city's Local Studies Library.
255 As described earlier, Poor Law provisions were funded by local rates; these figures

do not concern claims on the government's own schemes. Populations in the city's two Poor Law areas in 1922 were around 267,000 for Sheffield Union and 205,000 for Ecclesall Union. In 1925 the two were combined into a single Sheffield Union, and Boards of Guardians continued until 1929 when a Local Government Act abolished all Poor Law Unions in England and Wales and passed their powers to local authorities. A local study guide has been published by Sheffield City Archives; see www.sheffield.gov.uk/libraries/archives-and-local-studies/research-guides/poor-law.html.

256 In addition to the many already lost, servicemen continued to die from wounds or war-induced illness – around two hundred more Sheffielders after the Armistice.

257 It was no longer defined as a 'War Hospital' but had been operated by the Ministry of Pensions since August 1920.

258 The Scheme was administered in Sheffield through the King's Roll Committee based in the Ministry of Labour office in West Street. James Dixon and Sons were members into at least the 1930s, indicating membership though an official symbol on their letterhead.

259 The Ministry of Pensions also made available aids and physical supports, such as artificial legs and arms, crutches, invalid chairs, stump socks and artificial eyes (ordinarily up to two in any one year). In the early 1920s the city was home to around 22,000 men in receipt of a disability pension.

260 The first Sheffield registration under the War Charities Act of 1916 was by 'Arts and Crafts' at Wharncliffe War Hospital, established in October 1915. The address then was the Comforts Depot in Leopold Street, and Edith Sorby was listed as Chairman and Annie Carter as a member of the Committee. On 4 June 1918, 'Painted Fabrics' Disabled Sailors' and Soldiers' Mutual Association was separately registered (number 166) at Sasma Works, Meadowhead. This certificate was later overwritten to cite 'Painted Fabrics Ltd.', with Mrs Carter as Secretary and her home (49 Kingfield Road) as the office address. Committee members included the Bishop of Sheffield and manufacturer John Doncaster. Two objectives were listed: '(a) to teach disabled sailors and soldiers to paint fabrics so that they may earn their own living; (b) to apply any profits made from the sale of fabrics towards helping and assisting disabled sailors and soldiers'.

261 The wartime exhibitions received widely-reported visits from the Countess of Wharncliffe, the Countess of Lanesborough, the Duchess of Sutherland, Lady Fitzwilliam and her daughter, Lady Bingham, Lady Stuart of Wortley, as well as from the Master and Mistress Cutler, the Lord Mayor and many other socially-prominent people.

262 For example, a scheme co-ordinated by Mrs Edith Finch at the Third Northern General Hospital assisted convalescent soldiers with leather-work, needle-work, wood-carving, mat-making and water-colour painting. Profits from sales were added to Colonel Connell's fund which financed hospital visits by needy families of patients.

263 A blue memorial plaque is located in Little Norton Drive.

264 A gallery of the company's designs is at www.bbc.co.uk/southyorkshire/content/image_galleries/painted_fabrics_gallery.shtml, and many photographs are at www.picturesheffield.com. Painted Fabrics continued in operation until 1959, later also employing some disabled men from the Second World War. Until his death in 1940 Annie Carter's husband Geoffrey was an Honorary Director of the company; he

was a successful manufacturing chemist in the city who had served in the army during the Great War.

265 Arthur Fisher and several others had been hit by an exploding shell. His survival was aided by a large blood transfusion from another man, and he later underwent six operations during ten months in the Fourth Northern General Hospital at Lincoln before being discharged in mid-1919. Sheffield Archives hold much original material about Arthur in their Painted Fabrics collection (reference X210). They have kindly granted permission for the reproduction of letter content here (X210/2/3 and X210/2/5).

Index

PEOPLE

SUBJECT